D1436091

# NESTING BIRDS, EGGS AND FLEDGLINGS

# NESTING BIRDS

## Eggs and Fledglings

*by*
### WINWOOD READE
*and*
### ERIC HOSKING

*With plates of Eggs by*
PORTMAN ARTISTS

*and drawings by*
ROBERT GILLMOR

LONDON
BLANDFORD PRESS

© 1967 Blandford Press Ltd
167 High Holborn, London  WC1V 6PH
Revised edition 1968
Third edition 1971
Reprinted 1972

ISBN 0 7137 0444 6

*Printed and bound in Great Britain
by Jarrold & Sons Ltd, Norwich
Type set in Imprint*

# CONTENTS

# ACKNOWLEDGEMENTS

In preparing this book a number of colleagues have given me valuable advice and assistance. It is not possible to mention them all by name but I am particularly grateful to Dr Bruce Campbell whose generous help to naturalists of all kinds is widely recognised, even though it is given so unobtrusively.

It has given me special pleasure to work with Robert Gillmor. His many fine monochrome illustrations, especially his habitat profiles, are examples of the way in which he continues to add to our knowledge and appreciation of birds.

The author of a book of this nature works in isolation in the preliminary stages, but due to the constant encouragement and skilled advice of the publishers the final product becomes an expression of teamwork. As a BBC television producer I became aware of my indebtedness to people whose names were never known to the public. The production of this book has provided me with a similar experience.

Mr Hosking and I would also like to acknowledge the contributions which have been made in the photographic section by the following:

Colonel R. H. Palmer, Pl. No. 175
John Markham, Pl. No. 189
M. D. England, Pl. Nos. 38, 118, 186
Photo Researchers for Pl. Nos. 36 and 75 by S. C. Porter
John Palm, Pl. No. 206
George Nystrand, Pl. Nos. 121, 203
Svante Lundgren, Pl. No. 132
Göran Hansson, Pl. No. 137

Acknowledgement is also due for the assistance given in the drawing of the egg plates by the British Museum (Natural History), South Kensington, and the Zoological Museum, Tring.

WINWOOD READE

# AN INTRODUCTION TO BIRDS
## IN THE BREEDING SEASON

*Selecting the nest-site*

The nest of a bird is virtually its home during the breeding season, a place where the family can be reared in comparative safety. The site of the nest is selected with as much apparent eye for detail as a young couple going house-hunting. Once you know the habits of different kinds of birds, it is relatively easy to predict where they are likely to nest. Although there is a wide variety of sites available, all birds tend to select nesting places that are typical of their species. Finding nests is largely a matter of knowing the habits of different species. A number of species share the same habitat but each one occupies its own niche. This is well illustrated by Robert Gillmor's diagrammatic representations of some of the main habitats with typical nesting species. (See pages 12–19.)

When you think of a nest as a family home it is obvious that it needs to be in a safe place where it will be as free as possible from the attention of predators. It must also be in surroundings which provide an abundant supply of the right kind of food. Different species have different ways of meeting these basic essentials of security and food. Terns and gulls, for instance, need plenty of company of their own kind when nesting; this lessens the risk from predators as many pairs of eyes provide an efficient look-out system and warning calls are easily heard by the whole colony. Birds of prey, on the other hand, need comparative isolation from their own species in order to avoid close competition for food.

Some species prefer to nest on the ground, some under the ground and others at varying heights above the ground. Rooks and herons are the equivalent of top storey flat residents, waders take over the ground floor and puffins occupy basement tenements. There are unsociable as well as sociable types in the bird world. Golden plover and ring ouzel are the cottage-on-the-moor types but sparrows and swifts show a preference for built-up areas. Pied wagtails and swallows also nest near houses, making use of ledges unwittingly provided by man. Some kinds of birds adapt themselves readily to man-made sites: a robin nesting in a discarded kettle or a wren in the pocket of an old coat hanging in the garden shed are familiar examples, but artificial sites may also be used well away from human activity. At Dungeness, for instance, stock doves have been found nesting in derelict army tanks and wheatears occupying empty ammunition tins. Other species seem to require perfectly natural sites. Woodcock, for example, rely on leaf litter and rough ground to blend with their plumage and thus avoid detection by predators.

Sometimes the same site is occupied year after year. Herons and dippers both favour traditional sites but the majority of species select a new site each year and in most cases it is the male which chooses the site. Generalisations about birds, however, are as risky as sweeping statements about humans. In ducks and geese, for instance, the choice of site is left almost entirely to the female. In some species, such as the great tit, the male does the house-hunting, inspecting likely holes and then waiting for the female to accept one of them. The male wren shows even more initiative and actually builds a number of nests, one of which is selected by the female who then adds a lining of feathers. To find the nest of a species it is a great help to know whether to watch the male or female when nest-building is due to start.

*Building the nest*

Birds flying to and fro, carrying nest material, tend to catch the eye, and nest-building is often the easiest stage in the breeding cycle at which to locate nests. (Another opportunity comes later when the adults pay constant visits to their nests with food for the nestlings.) Not all species, however, use nest material. We usually think of a nest as a bowl-like structure made of natural materials, gathered by the birds and shaped into a receptacle. In fact a bird's 'home' may be no more than a shallow depression in the ground, scraped out by the bird, or even just a natural ledge of rock with no nesting material of any kind. A goldcrest's nest, a miniature cradle of moss and cobwebs lined with soft feathers, slung under the branch of a conifer, seems to us to be a work of art; by comparison, the sprawling heap of seaweed in which a young gannet emerges from the egg looks like a rubbish dump. A gypsy encampment may not appeal to a Mayfair resident but the gypsy would not relish the artificial atmosphere of sophisticated city surroundings. Each site is appropriate to the needs of the home-maker.

Not every species builds its own nest. The cuckoo is well known for its parasitic habits, waiting for the owner of a nest to leave the premises before laying its egg and abandoning it to its foster-parents. The equivalent of a tenant-occupier is also to be found in the bird world. One remarkable example of this is the green sandpiper, a wader which often takes over the nest of a song thrush. Some birds of prey tend to take possession of nests of other species; the hobby, for example, often flattens a nest built originally by the crow.

**Nest-building:** *Top left* **Lapwing** (ground-nester)
*Right* **Lesser Spotted Woodpecker** (hole-nester)
*Middle* **Chaffinch** (bowl-like structure)
*Bottom* **Puffin** (burrow-nester)

## The role of the male and female

Just as there are a great many varieties of nest and nest-site, there is also a wide variation in the roles played by the male and female, not only in house-hunting but at all stages in the breeding cycle. Spotted flycatchers provide an example of what some people might describe as the happily married couple, both sexes sharing the parental duties at every stage. The male long-tailed tit, however, apparently draws the line at feeding the young; he takes his share in building the nest and incubating the eggs but although he brings food to the nest, it is the female which puts the food into the gaping mouths of the nestlings. In some species the male will gather nest material but leave the actual building and construction to the female; this is typical of the male song thrush which also leaves the major share of incubating the eggs to the female but helps to feed the young. The male red-necked phalarope not only waits for the female to court him but also incubates the eggs and looks after the young birds when they have hatched.

Natural selection determines the role played by each sex under normal circumstances. One obvious example of how this works to the advantage of the species is in the incubation of eggs by drab-coloured ducks while the more colourful drakes remain in the neighbourhood, diverting attention of possible predators from the nest. By contrast, both sexes of nightjar have much the same plumage and both share in incubating the eggs. Natural selection, however, is a complex process and it is not safe to assume, for example, that incubation is shared in all cases where the sexes look alike. The male and female nightingale look very similar but it is the female which incubates.

## The start of the breeding cycle

Physiological changes in birds take place with the start of the breeding season. Changes in the bird's environment, such as temperature and light, favour the survival of the species and stimulate these changes in physiology and behaviour. The breeding cycle starts with the business of finding a mate and a suitable place in which to lay eggs and rear young. The detailed method by which this is done varies according to the species. A bird does not usually breed until it has acquired the plumage which is characteristic of that species in the breeding season. The plumage of many adults varies with the time of year. In winter, for instance, the ptarmigan's plumage is white, concealing it from enemies against a background of snow; in the breeding season, its upper-parts are mottled grey, blending remarkably well with the background of lichens and scree amongst which it nests. Adult males of many species acquire a more colourful plumage as the breeding season approaches and they make use of any bold patch of contrasting

*Left* **Skylark**
*Right* **Chaffinch**

colour in their plumage, showing it off in various forms of display. Some species even develop special adornments for this purpose, such as crests and ruffs.

These displays often look weird and wonderful to us, even grotesque in that the birds appear to adopt unnatural postures. Each form of display is a means of drawing attention to the bird and advertising itself. Males show off not only to attract a mate but also to frighten other males. A show of strength is often an effective way of dealing with a rival and is far less dangerous to life than indulging in a fight. The process of attracting a partner and holding territory against rivals is achieved in many species by both vocal and visual methods. A skylark towering in the sky, singing as though fit to burst, is virtually signalling to others that a particular open space is already occupied. Species which nest in dense cover, such as warblers, rely almost entirely on distinctive songs, some of which have remarkable carrying power. Others, like the corncrake, have monotonous calls which continue long after dark.

Song is a means of establishing territory. A chaffinch will sing from various perches, using them as song-posts, staking out the boundary of its territory as effectively as a man putting in fence posts to enclose his property. With a breeding territory established and a partner successfully attracted to it, mating has still to be achieved and various forms of display help to strengthen the bond and synchronise the emotional pitch of the partners. The breeding season is comparatively short in most species and no useful purpose would be served by the equivalent of a long engagement.

**Displays:**
*Top* **Great Crested Grebe** (courtship display)
*Middle* **Robin** (territorial aggressive display)
*Bottom* **Little Ringed Plover** (distraction display) **and chick**

Each species has its own instinctive form of display. Birds make signals to each other and incidentally make themselves conspicuous to humans. Once you know the characteristic postures adopted by various species, you can not only locate a breeding pair but also interpret what they are doing, even to the extent of knowing which stage they have reached in the breeding cycle. Specialists can distinguish between threat postures and submissive postures, greeting ceremonies and mutual displays, all of which help to evoke a suitable response and establish the appropriate level of excitement in a partner. It takes time and practice to interpret what you see, and some of the scientific jargon used by specialists tends to make it all sound very confusing, but it is no more complicated than interpreting conventional human behaviour. A man who pulls his hand out of his pocket might be going to shake hands or raise his fist to you; normally you would have no difficulty in deciding which form of greeting ceremony he was displaying because you would be familiar with the signs. Birds also have ways of signalling which can easily be recognised if you study them in sufficient detail.

Some bird signals are so obvious that they cannot be missed. For instance the clamour of small birds mobbing an owl or a bird of prey serves to warn other birds in the neighbourhood of the presence of an enemy. Birds which adopt unnatural positions, such as trailing their wings or running along the ground, looking more like a small mammal than a bird, obviously draw attention to themselves, thus diverting a predator from their eggs or young. A specialist, however, might well be able to say from this distraction display whether the bird was trying to protect eggs or young; a ringed plover is likely to behave in this way when it has eggs whereas a little ringed plover tends to do it when the eggs have actually hatched.

*Eggs and their incubation*

Species lay their eggs in different months of the year. For successful rearing of the family, it is essential that the chicks hatch at a time when sufficient food is available, readily accessible to the parents. Great tits, for instance, prefer to feed their young on caterpillars and it has been found that the first set of eggs laid in the season tend to hatch at a time when caterpillars are plentiful, a period which is relatively short and subject to slight variation according to the season. We do not yet know how tits manage this synchronisation but the fact that they do so, varying the date of laying the first clutch according to the 'caterpillar season', has been well established. Birds which feed their young on adult insects, such as swallows which catch insects on the wing, naturally hatch their young a little later in the season. Once you know the typical food of each species, it is easy to understand why eggs are laid on different dates.

Identifying eggs which have been removed from a nest may be difficult because the eggs of some birds vary within quite a wide range of colour and marking as between individual members of the same species. Eggs laid in a typical nest, in a characteristic site, are much easier to identify than a single egg in a person's hand.

Eggs of passerines, birds that sing and perch, are usually laid early in the morning at 24-hour intervals. The average size of the clutch, a complete set of eggs, varies according to the species but there may also be some variation within the limits that are typical of the species. Some lay more than one clutch per season and even where a single clutch is characteristic of the species, a replacement set of eggs is usually laid if the first is lost.

There is also a big variation between species in the time from the laying of eggs to their hatching, known as the incubation period. During incubation, heat is applied to the eggs by the body of one or other of the parents in order to develop the embryo. Many birds have brood patches or areas of bare skin which are brought into direct contact with the egg as the bird sits on the nest. The duration of the incubation period is typical of the species. A chiffchaff, for instance, incubates for nearly a fortnight whereas a swan incubates its eggs for about five weeks. Most species start incubating after the last egg of the clutch has been laid. A blackbird does this but a tawny owl starts incubating after the first egg in the clutch has been laid.

### Development of the chick

One of the factors which accounts for these differences in the incubation period of different species is the stage of development the chick has reached when hatching takes place. A blackbird nestling is born naked and blind, able to make only small movements; it will remain in the nest for a further period of development. A mallard duckling, on the other hand, is born with its eyes open, a covering of down, and is able to move around freely, leaving the nest very soon after hatching.

Young birds which remain in the nest after hatching are known as 'nidicolous', those that leave the nest soon after hatching are known as 'nidifugous'. Parents of nidicolous species still have to keep their nestlings warm and, of course, bring food to them. The nest has to be kept very clean or the generation of heat is not effective. In many cases the parents remove bits of eggshell and droppings (the latter are enclosed in a white 'envelope'), either by swallowing them or carrying them some distance from the nest; this avoids attracting the attention of predators to the nestlings.

*Left* **Nidicolous young—Blackbird**
*Right* **Nidifugous young—Mallard**

You might think that parents of nidifugous species, which leave the nest shortly after hatching, have a much easier time but they also continue to exercise parental care, varying in degree with the species. The young show a tendency to follow the parent which leads them away from the nest. Some species, such as lapwing, are capable of feeding themselves whilst others, such as young great crested grebes, are not only fed for a time but even rest on their parent's backs. Parental care may also include sheltering the young from hot sun or heavy rain, as well as warning them of danger. Special call-notes are often given at the approach of a predator. These calls, together with the more obvious distraction displays of some species, give away the fact that young birds are somewhere near you when you are searching an area for a likely nest.

To many people the hatching of an egg is still a miraculous process. It is sometimes possible for the human ear to detect a chirping sound, coming from inside the egg, two or three days before it hatches. At about this time the embryo starts to take in air from a space at the blunt end of the egg; this space has been formed between two membranes of the shell by the evaporation of water from the eggshell, resulting from the heat applied during incubation by the parent bird. The majority of embryos develop a little 'tooth' on the upper part of the bill; this is a horny excrescence which enters the air space between the two membranes of the eggshell and is virtually used as a miniature pick for prising open the eggshell from within. Having cracked the shell with this 'egg-tooth', the baby bird extends its head and legs, thus pressing against the shell and bursting it still further.

Hatching is usually achieved without the aid of the parent although some species have been seen giving minor assistance by pecking at the shell. A gannet, for instance, has been observed prising half an eggshell off a hatching chick. When a parent goes to pick up the shell, it may tip the chick out but it is the chick which makes the first move to break out.

## The role of the bird-watcher

When you think of all the difficulties which birds have to overcome in rearing their young and the remarkable diversity of development which ensures survival of the species, you will doubtless think twice before disturbing birds in the breeding season. The removal of eggs is such an obvious act of robbery and violence that the evils of egg-collecting need not be laboured, quite apart from the fact that it is illegal to take eggs of most species. Through ignorance, however, you can make a bird's chance of rearing its young much less certain of success. Upsetting the normal routine of the parent's behaviour at various stages in the breeding cycle may result in a failure to rear young. Some species are very sensitive at the nest-building stage and you may cause them to desert and take valuable time in finding another site, so delaying the whole process of rearing young and possibly missing the best food supply. Others are more sensitive at the incubation stage. Even if the parents do not desert the nest, you may keep them off so long that the eggs become cold. Birds know instinctively how long it is safe to leave their eggs but if you sit down near the nest, however unintentionally, you may prevent nervous parents from returning to incubate. This also applies to the stage when young are being fed; if you notice a bird carrying food in its bill and hanging about in rather a diffident manner, the chances are that you are much too close to the nest. Shift your position and you may see the bird go right to the nest.

Some birds approach their nests by a regular series of landing-places; remove one of these and you may have taken away a familiar landmark, leaving a gap in what was previously a routine approach to the nest. Even if you only pull back the cover surrounding a nest, perhaps to take a photograph, you are marking the site by altering its appearance and making it easy for the next predator to find it. Imagine how you would feel if you returned home one evening and found that someone had altered the entrance to your house. Getting in at the front door is a routine process, your hand goes automatically to the right place to put the key in the lock; if someone alters the position of the lock, you waste time and energy trying to get in, not to mention the mounting temper which results from your frustration. It may not be scientific to apply human standards to judging birds' reactions but it can be helpful on occasions to put yourself, in imagination, in the bird's place.

No scientist, for instance, would say that a bird disliked rude behaviour. Rudeness is a human concept, usually involving making others feel uncomfortable. We regard it as rude to stare at a person and, although a bird is unaware of rudeness, it looks uncomfortable and often shows positive alarm if you stare straight at it. A bird sitting on eggs will often remain on the nest even if you continue to garden just below it but if you stop and look up at it, the bird usually flies off. Saunter nonchalantly past a known nest-site, look at it out of the corner of your eye in passing, and you can see if the bird is there without disturbing it. Birds may frequently deceive gullible and anthropomorphic humans by their own behaviour but it is possible, with a little guile, to deceive them.

Human reactions, however, are not always a safe guide and many people out of mistaken kindness will pick up a fledgling which seems to be deserted as it calls for food. They do not realise that the parent birds are probably lurking in cover, waiting for the human to depart before carrying on with their parental duties. The old adage of 'Leave it to Mother Nature' is not as foolishly sentimental as it may sound. Natural selection, which is one aspect of 'Mother Nature', is a powerful force producing evolutionary changes which work towards the eventual survival of the species. Even if we do not fully understand how it works, we can at least try to ensure that we do not make survival more difficult.

A wonderful variety of birds nest in Britain and western Europe. In this book species are described in a way that aims at enabling people to enjoy them during the breeding season. Some species which do not breed in Britain have been included mainly for the benefit of Continental readers, but they may also be of interest to British readers who take their holidays abroad. Scientific names, whenever possible, are those given by Charles Vaurie in *The Birds of the Palearctic Fauna* (1959–1965. London. Witherby).

Some of the rarer species can be seen at the reserves of the Royal Society for the Protection of Birds (R.S.P.B.) and at other reserves. These sanctuaries have been established primarily to conserve something of interest to naturalists. Even if you are not particularly interested in plants and insects or other forms of wild life, remember that they are all part of the world in which birds live. Wardens of reserves do everything they can to conserve nature, including shepherding and advising members of the public on how to behave in the reserve; they may not have time to explain everything in detail but unless you listen to what they say you may cause disturbance through lack of knowledge.

A vast amount of information about birds has been gained in patient field work by a great many people, amateurs contributing observations as well as professionals. No single volume can include all this knowledge and a short list of books, all of which have been used for reference purposes in compiling this 'pocket encyclopaedia', is to be found on page 269, together with names and addresses of some of the societies and periodicals which enable enthusiasts to keep in touch with current events about birds.

Birds are part of the world in which we live and, whether we study them scientifically or simply enjoy them for their own sake, they can provide us with constant pleasure and interest.

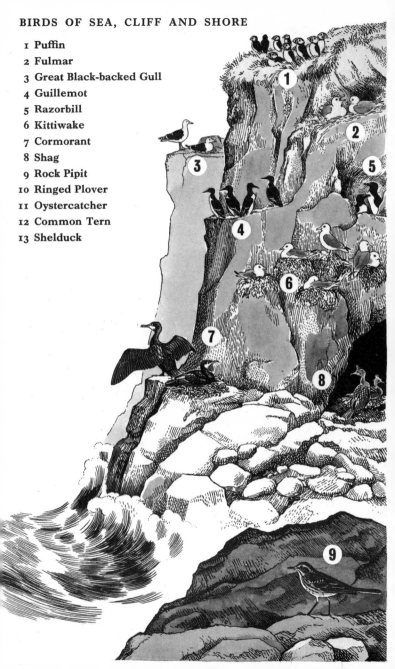

BIRDS OF SEA, CLIFF AND SHORE

1 Puffin
2 Fulmar
3 Great Black-backed Gull
4 Guillemot
5 Razorbill
6 Kittiwake
7 Cormorant
8 Shag
9 Rock Pipit
10 Ringed Plover
11 Oystercatcher
12 Common Tern
13 Shelduck

# BIRDS OF WOODLAND AND FARMLAND

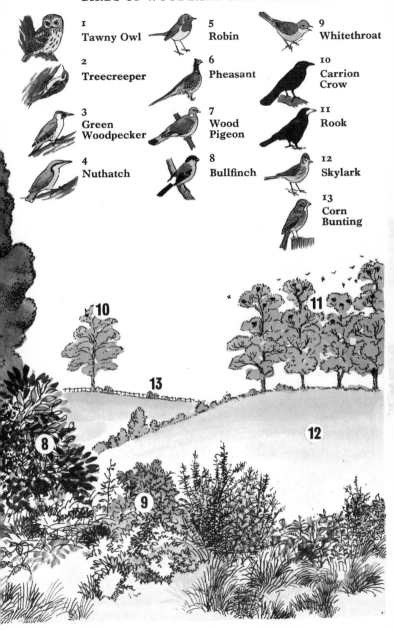

1 Tawny Owl

2 Treecreeper

3 Green Woodpecker

4 Nuthatch

5 Robin

6 Pheasant

7 Wood Pigeon

8 Bullfinch

9 Whitethroat

10 Carrion Crow

11 Rook

12 Skylark

13 Corn Bunting

# BIRDS OF GARDEN AND TOWN

1 Chaffinch

2 Blue Tit

3 Hedge Sparrow

4 Blackbird

5 Spotted Flycatcher

6 Starling

7 Swift

8 Jackdaw

9 House Martin

10 House Sparrow

11 Song Thrush

# BIRDS OF FRESHWATER

1 Heron
2 Kingfisher
3 Great Crested Grebe
4 Coot
5 Reed Bunting
6 Moorhen

7 Mallard
8 Sedge Warbler
9 Reed Warbler
10 Mute Swan
11 Little Grebe
12 Lapwing

# PREFACE TO PHOTOGRAPH SECTION

We have aimed to present an aspect of ornithology which has not been attempted before so comprehensively in a pocket-sized book—namely to show by photographs as far as possible the principal breeding birds of Northern Europe. Among my own collection of photographs, gathered over some forty years, I have more than 7,000 in colour and over 32,000 in black-and-white. These have been taken in many European countries as far north as Finnish Lapland and as far south as Southern Spain. This has provided the main part of the photograph section, but it has been necessary in a few cases to enlist the help of photographic colleagues to provide particular shots of those species which have so far eluded my colour camera. Specific acknowledgement for these is made earlier and I am grateful that by this cooperation it has been possible to make the book more complete.

This leads to a further point concerning the policy of the photographs. Our main concern has been to provide reliable ornithological references, and so in some cases a black-and-white photograph has been selected rather than a colour one because it is a more representative or interesting result.

Bird photography is a fascinating hobby but it does require a great deal of time to do properly and should not be undertaken lightly. It must always be remembered that the interests of the bird must come first. If photography is being done at the nest great care should be taken to see that the eggs do not become chilled or the young exposed to extremes of heat or cold. Every effort should be made to ensure that the parents are not prevented from feeding or brooding their young. Real success will never be achieved if these points are not always kept in mind.

Behind many of the photographs which appear in this book lie stories of excitement. The Golden Eagle's eyrie on page 39 was on a sheer cliff edge and could only be approached with the aid of ropes—dangling in mid-air is always thrilling. Incidentally, this photograph was one of the first ever taken in colour with Kodachrome film when the colour balance was not nearly as good as it is at present. The photograph of the Hobby (Photo: 43) was the outcome of ten days waiting and planning, in which half an hour each day was spent in erecting a tubular steel scaffolding 64 feet high which weighed more than 5 tons. It was built gradually so as to give the adult Hobbies plenty of time to become accustomed to the tower which was growing so near to their nest. But so successful was this plan that the falcon used to sit on her nest watching our activities. Once the hide was completed it was occupied from dawn till dusk almost every day by a team of ornithologists and photographers, ranging in age from a schoolboy of thirteen to a Field-Marshal of nearly sixty-five, until the young flew.

ERIC HOSKING

1   **Red-throated Diver**

2   **Black-throated Diver**

3 **Little Grebe**

4 **Slavonian Grebe**

5 **Great Crested Grebe**

6 **Fulmar**

7 **Manx Shearwater**

8 **Storm Petrel**

9 **Gannet**

10  **Cormorant**

11  **Shag**

12  Bittern

13  Bittern feeding young

14   **Little Bittern**

Spoonbill

15   **White Stork**

18   **Canada Goose**

19  Mute Swan

20  Grey Lag Goose

16  Heron

21 Shelduck eggs (covered)

22 Shelduck eggs (revealed)

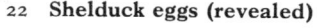

23 Shelduck

24　**Teal**

25　**Mallard**

26  **Pintail**

27  **Gadwall**

28  **Tufted Duck**

29 **Shoveler**

30 **Wigeon**

31 **Scaup**

32 **Eider**

33  **Red-breasted Merganser**

34  **Goosander**

35  **Red Kite**

36  **Osprey**

37  **Sparrowhawk**

38  **Buzzard**

39  **Golden Eagle**

40  **Peregrine**

41 **Hen Harrier**

42 **Marsh Harrier**

43 **Hobby**

44 **Merlin**

45 **Kestrel**

46 **Willow Grouse**

47 **Ptarmigan**

48 **Black Grouse**

49 **Red Grouse**

50   **Capercaillie**

51   **Red-legged Partridge**

52 **Partridge**

53 **Pheasant**

54 **Crane**

55 **Water Rail**

56 **Corncrake**

57 **Moorhen**

58 **Coot**

59 **Oystercatcher**

60 **Ringed Plover**

61   **Little Ringed Plover**      62   **Lapwing**

63   **Dotterel**

64 **Golden Plover**

65 **Turnstone**

66   Temminck's Stint

67   Reeve (female Ruff)

68  **Redshank**

69  **Greenshank**

70    Wood Sandpiper

71    Common Sandpiper

72  **Black-tailed Godwit**

73  **Curlew**

74 **Black-winged Stilt**

75 **Woodcock**

76 **Snipe**

77 **Avocet**

78 **Avocet nest**

79  **Red-necked Phalarope**

80  **Stone Curlew**

81 **Kittiwake**

82 **Great Skua (Bonxie)**

83 **Arctic Skua**

84　**Black-headed Gull**

85　**Lesser Black-backed Gull**

86  **Herring Gull**

87  **Common Gull**

88  **Great Black-backed Gull**

89 **Black Tern**

90 **Sandwich Tern**

91    Common Tern

92    Arctic Tern

93 **Roseate Tern**

94 **Little Tern**

95 **Razorbill**

96 **Guillemot**

97  **Black Guillemot**

98  **Puffin**

99 **Wood Pigeon nestling**

100 **Stock Dove**

101 **Stock Dove eggs**

102 **Collared Dove**

103 **Turtle Dove**

104 **Nightjar**

105 **Kingfisher**

106 Young Cuckoo tipping eggs out of nest

107 Marsh Warbler and Cuckoo nestling

108 **Young Cuckoo being fed by Reed Warbler**

109 **Young Cuckoo**

110 **Barn Owl**

111 **Long-eared Owl**

112 **Short-eared Owl**

113 **Little Owl**

114  **Tawny Owl**

115  **Wryneck leaving nest**

116  **Wryneck**

117 **Bee-eater**

118 **Roller**

119 **Hoopoe**

120 **Green Woodpecker**     121 **Black Woodpecker**

122  Great Spotted Woodpecker

123  Lesser Spotted Woodpecker

124 **Woodlark**

125 **Skylark**

126 **Sand Martin**

127  **Swallow**

128  **House Martin**

129  **House Martin**

130   **Tree Pipit**

131   **Meadow Pipit**

132   **Rock Pipit**

133    **Yellow Wagtail**

134    **Grey Wagtail**

135    **Pied Wagtail**

**136 Red-backed Shrike**

**137 Waxwing**

138 **Dipper**

139 **Wren**

140 **Dunnock**

141 **Dunnock eggs**

142 **Grasshopper Warbler**

143 **Wood Warbler**

144 **Sedge Warbler**

145 **Marsh Warbler**

146 **Reed Warbler**

147　**Icterine Warbler**

148  **Garden Warbler**

149  **Blackcap**

150 **Whitethroat**

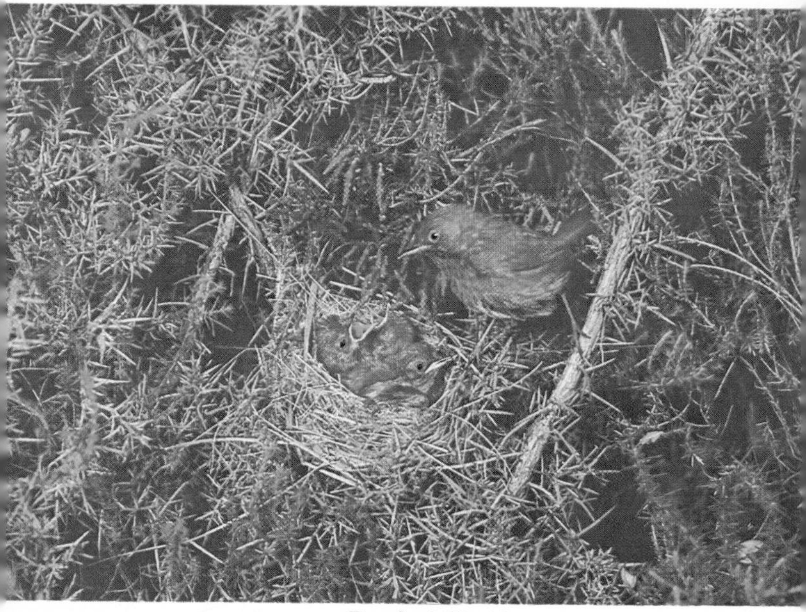

151 **Dartford Warbler**

152 **Willow Warbler**

153 **Chiffchaff**

154 **Goldcrest**

155 **Spotted Flycatcher**

156 **Pied Flycatcher**

157 **Whinchat**

158 **Stonechat**

159 **Wheatear**

160 **Black Redstart**

161 **Redstart**

162 **Robin**

163 **Nightingale**

164 **Red-spotted Bluethroat**

165 **Fieldfare**

166 **Ring Ouzel**

167 **Blackbird**

168 **Redwing**

169 **Song Thrush**

170  **Mistle Thrush**

171  **Bearded Tit**

172 **Long-tailed Tit**

173 **Marsh Tit**

174 **Willow Tit**

175 Crested Tit

176 Blue Tit

177 Coal Tit

178 **Great Tit**

179 **Nuthatch**

180 **Tree-creeper**

181 **Corn Bunting**

182 **Yellowhammer**

183 **Ortolan Bunting**

184 **Cirl Bunting**

185 **Reed Bunting**

186 **Rock Bunting**

187 **Chaffinch**

188 **Brambling**

189 **Greenfinch**

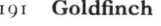

190 **Siskin**

191 **Goldfinch**

192  **Lesser Redpoll**

193  **Twite**

194  **Scarlet Grosbeak**

195  **Linnet**

196 **Crossbill**

197 **Bullfinch**

198 **Hawfinch**

199 **Starling**

200 **Tree Sparrow**

201  **Golden Oriole**

202 **Jay**

203 **Siberian Jay**

204 Carrion Crow

205 Jackdaw

206  **Hooded Crow**

207  **Magpie**

208 **Rook**

209 **Raven**

216      217      218      219      220      221

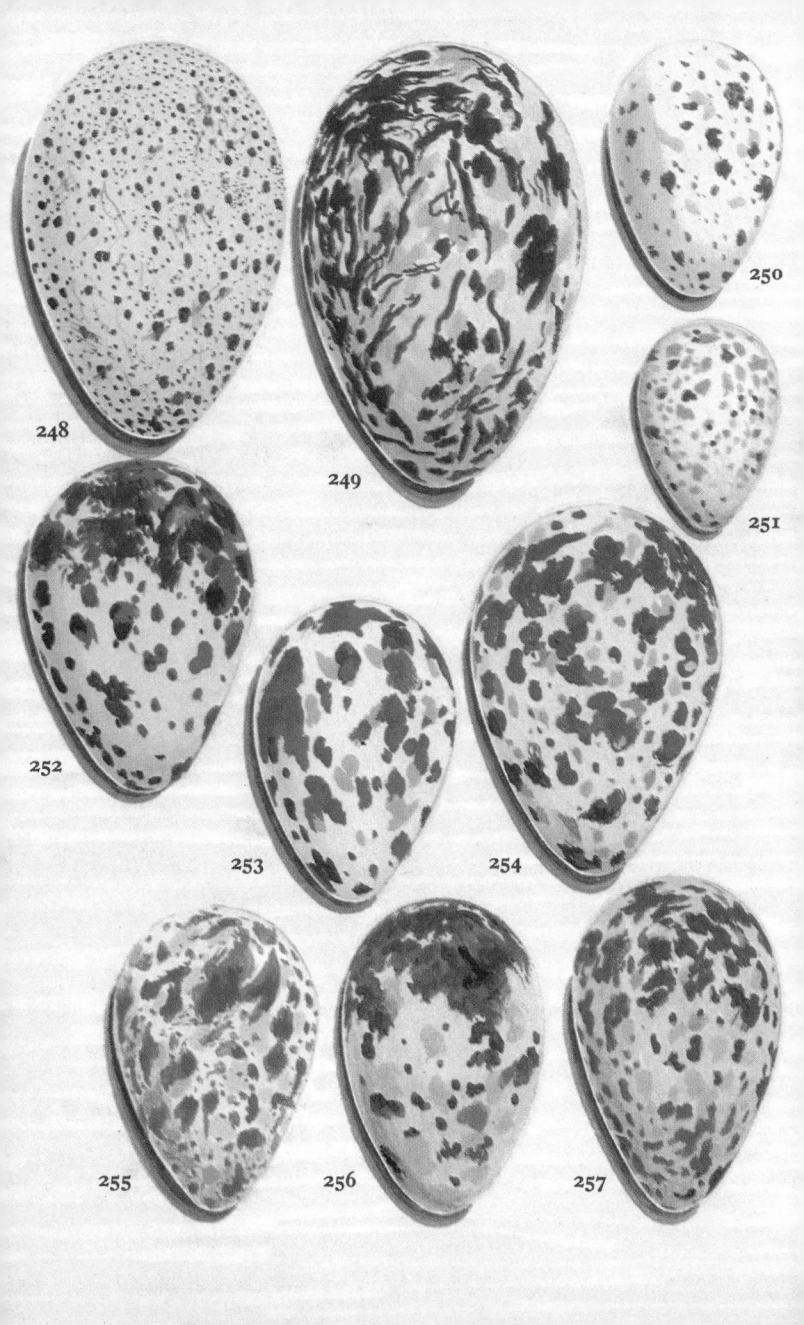

273     274     275     276

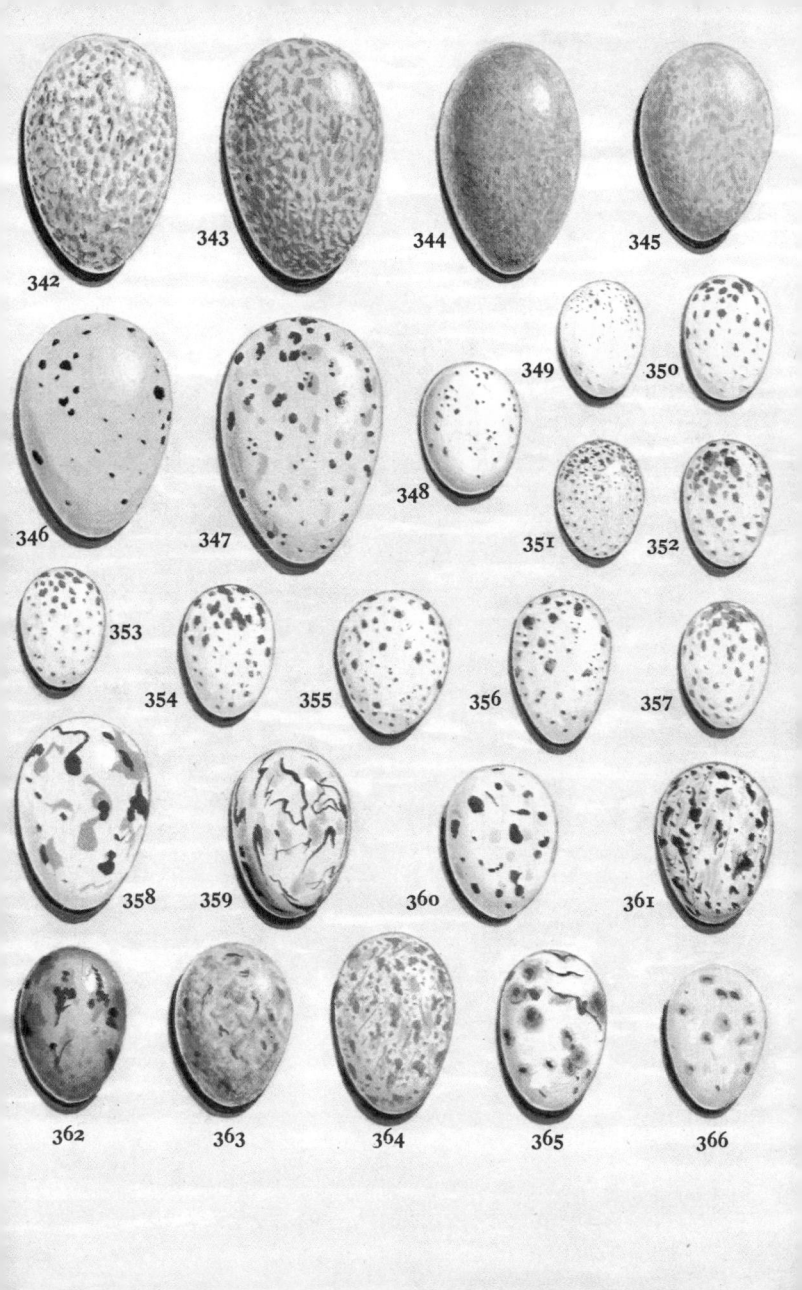

389

387

388

396

397

398

399

400

# KEY TO EGG PLATES

# DESCRIPTIONS OF
# THE BIRDS

Descriptions include the time of year at which nesting takes place, the kind of habitat where the pairs are usually found, the nest-site and construction of the nest. The number of eggs and their typical colour are also mentioned, but it should be appreciated that these are very variable. The incubation period is given, together with information about the role of the sexes during incubation and after the young are born. Adults, nestlings and fledglings are described, the latter being regarded as young birds able to fly but which are not fully mature.

Breeding distribution is given in a condensed form, which should be interpreted as follows:

'British Isles' includes England, Ireland, Scotland and Wales.

'Britain' includes England, Scotland and Wales.

'Scandinavia' refers to Finland, Norway and Sweden and is used where species breed in all these countries.

'In Europe' indicates that the species breeds in Belgium, Denmark, France, Germany, Holland, Italy, Spain and Switzerland. (Portugal is not separated from Spain.)

'Local' implies that the species is not a widespread breeder.

'Has bred' indicates that the species does not normally breed in the country mentioned but has done so on one or a few occasions.

The plate number in bold refers to the photograph section; that in italics to the egg plates.

---

**Red-throated Diver** *Gavia stellata.*
Pl. **1**, *211*
*Breeds* late May–July, by comparatively small but deep lochs and pools in desolate spots. (In N. Scotland, NW. Ireland and Scandinavia.)
*Nest* varies from a scrape or flattened vegetation near water to a mound of damp vegetation on the bank or built-up in shallow water.
*Eggs* 2, olive-green or brown, with dark markings. Incubated by both sexes for about 4 weeks.
*Nestlings* dark brown and grey down, whitish round eyes. Leave the nest shortly after hatching, tended by

both parents. Fly after about 8 weeks. *Adults* slightly smaller than Black-throated Diver, larger than grebes; sexes similar, slender bill tilted up (not straight) is usually visible even at a distance; soft grey head, greyish-brown upper-parts have no patterning; red patch at throat may look black at long range. Can take off from water in confined space, agile on the wing; clumsy on land but occasionally take off from the ground. *Fledglings* brown rather than grey on upper-parts.

*Hints* quacking calls are heard in flight above the breeding areas. Weird wails and growls accompany elaborate display which includes several divers swimming after each other with their bodies half submerged and bills pointing obliquely up; they also rush along the surface, threshing the water with their wings. The nest may be some distance from the water's edge, but there is usually a well-defined runway down to the water, worn down by the diver as it leaves the nest, heaving itself along and flapping its wings, making a kind of slide to the water. In some areas a number of pairs nest close together, only a few yards apart, but in Scotland there is usually only one pair on a loch.

**Black-throated Diver** *Gavia arctica*. Pl. **2**, *211*

*Breeds* May–June, on islands or shores of comparatively deep lochs, usually near an extensive sheet of water, but occasionally by a smaller, shallower pool. (In Scotland, N. Germany and Scandinavia.)

*Nest* usually a scrape near water, but built-up nests of reeds and grass have been recorded in shallow water.

*Eggs* 2, olive-green or brown, with dark markings. Incubated by both sexes for about 4 weeks.

*Nestlings* dark brown and grey down, whitish round eyes. Leave nest shortly after hatching, tended by both parents, often transported on the backs of adults in water. Fly after about 9 weeks.

*Adults* slightly larger than Red-throated Diver; sexes similar, soft grey head and back of neck, sides of neck patterned black and white, throat black, straight slender bill; upper-parts boldly marked with black and white pattern. Often flies, instead of diving, when disturbed.

*Fledglings* look rather 'scaly' and are difficult to distinguish from young Great Northern Diver.

*Hints* they fly some distance in search of food and a diver seen on a loch is not necessarily nesting there. A barking call is often given in flight and a wild wailing is heard as they call to each other. Assemblies have been seen on calm evenings in May, the divers splashing and skating along the surface, giving weird cries and then flying off in pairs. A female has been seen swimming along in front of a male, turning on her side and even somersaulting. During incubation, the off-duty parent usually remains near the nest. Look along the verges of lochs for any sign of a 'slipway' leading to the water. Distraction display has been observed when young are present, the adult flapping helplessly over the water.

**Little Grebe** *Podiceps ruficollis*. Pl. **3**, *212*

*Breeds* usually April–July (occasionally February–September), on all kinds of fresh water with some kind of cover, including lakes in town parks. (In British Isles and Europe. Has bred in Norway.)

*Nest* a floating mound of aquatic plants and dead leaves, anchored to submerged spit or to vegetation, built by both sexes, usually in thick cover.

*Eggs* usually 4–6, white, but soon become stained. Incubated by both sexes for about 3½ weeks.

*Nestlings* blackish-brown with reddish stripes. Fed by both parents for about 6 weeks but male takes over if a second clutch is started. Swim shortly after hatching but are often transported on the backs of adults.

*Adults* the smallest of the grebes, sexes similar; comparatively short neck, very round and dumpy in appearance; dark brown above, dusky but paler below, reddish tone on cheeks and throat, no head adornments, yellowish-green near the bill, which is relatively stout and straight. Faint wing-bar shows in flight.

*Fledglings* striped head similar to other young grebes; sides of head and neck look more streaked than adult in winter.

*Hints* high-pitched whinnying call is often the first indication of their presence. They dive as soon as they are aware of an intruder. The display is less elaborate than in other grebes, but the pair will face each other with their necks stretched upwards. Trilling duets take place and there are noisy chases from late March. The nest is usually near the water's edge in thick cover and there may be more than one nest in the same area.

## Black-necked Grebe *Podiceps nigricollis*

*Breeds* mid May–July, on lochs and lakes with reed-beds in shallow water, pools and quiet stretches of rivers with plenty of aquatic vegetation. (Irregularly in British Isles; regularly in Europe. Local in S. Sweden.)

*Nest* a floating mound of freshly rotting vegetation in shallow water, usually in dense cover, built by both sexes.

*Eggs* usually 3–5, white, but soon become stained. Incubated by both sexes for about 3 weeks.

*Nestlings* blackish upper-parts, striped head and neck, some white on under-parts. Fed by both parents for about 4 weeks, transported on the backs of adults, after which they become independent.

**Black-necked Grebe**

*Adults* looks same size as Slavonian Grebe; sexes similar, black neck, golden tuft of feathers fans out on either side of black forehead and crown; slender bill is tilted up, unlike Slavonian Grebe's, which is straight, and the head looks more rounded. Both species show white wing-bar in flight.

*Fledglings* down may be present on head in November; bill less clearly tilted up and may be confused with young Slavonian Grebe.

*Hints* sites tend to be abandoned after a few years but colonies have been found in a number of counties in the British Isles, in lowland areas rather than in highland districts. Shy and comparatively silent even when aware of intruders, they are not easy to find in the breeding season. Trilling note has been described as 'bidder - vidder - vidder - vidder', uttered during the display which includes head-shaking and 'Penguin-dance'. Vigorous fights between males have also been seen, water splashing about and making a commotion. There is usually more than one pair nesting in the same area and dense colonies are found in regular breeding areas.

## Slavonian Grebe *Podiceps auritus*. Pl. 4, *213*

*Breeds* late May–July, in shallow bays of lochs with aquatic vegetation in Scotland; also on slow-running rivers, lakes and pools in flooded areas in Scandinavia.

*Nest* a floating mound of aquatic plants anchored in shallow water, built by both sexes.

*Eggs* usually 3–5, white, but soon become stained. Incubated by both sexes for about 3 weeks.

*Nestlings* resemble Great Crested Grebe but have darker upper-parts. Tended and fed by both parents for over 4 weeks, often transported on the adult's back on the water.

*Adults* smaller than Great Crested Grebe; sexes similar, chestnut neck and breast, dark upper-parts, pure white under-parts; black cheeks and ear-tufts, golden horned appearance, straight bill (not tilted). They look like Black-necked Grebe in the distance and both species show white wing-bar in flight.

*Fledglings* striped down on head lingers; they become more like adult in winter.

*Hints* your best chance of locating them early in the season is to use binoculars on bays in lochs of Sutherland and Inverness-shire from mid March. Lochs with sedges and marestails growing in shallow water seem to be favoured. Rippling trills and gurgling calls may be heard during the display which includes spreading the ear-tufts, head-shaking and bowing, and a 'Penguin-dance'. Nesting material is added during

incubation, as in other grebes. The change-over at the nest takes place at intervals of 4–5 hours. There may be several nests in the same area, and these grebes are said to be comparatively easy to approach when nesting.

## Great Crested Grebe *Podiceps cristatus*. Pl. 5, *214*

*Breeds* April–August, on sheets of fresh water, including gravel-pits, reservoirs, lakes, pools and slow-running rivers. (In British Isles, Europe and S. Scandinavia.)

*Nest* a floating mound of decaying aquatic vegetation, anchored on submerged spit or to surrounding plants, built by both sexes; also recorded on artificial raft.

*Eggs* usually 3–4, white, but soon become stained. Incubated by both sexes for about 4 weeks.

*Nestlings* blackish-brown, yellow and white, with striped effect and bare patches of reddish skin on head. They nestle under the parents' wings, transported on the water; they dive after about 6 weeks and are independent after about 9 weeks.

*Adults* the largest British grebe, roughly half the size of Red-breasted Merganser; sexes similar, slender white neck with dark ear-tufts and chestnut 'frill' at sides of head, greyish back which is rounded at the stern, pure white under-parts. Dive frequently, swim rather low in the water.

*Fledglings* striped down on head may still be present in November; they become more like adult in winter.

*Hints* it is worth keeping a watch on any shallow water of about 4 acres or more from late February onwards. Various rattling, raucous notes may be heard during an elaborate display. This includes fast chases over the water and ceremonial displays in which the pair face each other, frequently shaking their heads, presenting weed to each other and performing a 'Penguin-dance'. Locating the nest is comparatively easy during incubation as the off-duty parent patrols the water in the area of the nest and there is a change-over roughly every 3 hours.

**Fulmar** *Fulmarus glacialis*. Pl. **6,** *215*

*Breeds* May–September, usually on precipitous sea cliffs but also on inland crags and on flat ground, exceptionally on buildings. (In British Isles and N. Europe. Local in Scandinavia.)

*Nest* usually on bare rock or in turf; no nesting material carried.

*Egg* 1, white. Incubated by both sexes for 6–8 weeks.

*Nestling* white down on head and under-parts, pale grey on upper-parts. Fed by both parents for 6–8 weeks after which it leaves the nest.

*Adults* size in between Lesser Black-backed and Black-headed Gull, sexes similar; bull-necked appearance, tubular nostril, dark grey back, wings and tail, white head and under-parts. (Dark variety has smoky grey plumage and dark wing-tips.) Distinguishable from gulls in flight by rigid appearance of wings which are held stiffly in long glides; wheels about the cliffs, balancing on wind currents, using the tail as a rudder.

*Fledgling* similar to adult.

*Hints* Fulmars wheeling above a cliff during the breeding season are not necessarily breeding; they prospect new sites for several years without laying, although they sit on ledges as though incubating. Nests are usually difficult to reach and as you approach, an oily fluid is often ejected from their mouth, leaving a smell which lingers indefinitely if it lands on your clothes. Pairs often face each other when displaying, jerking their heads from side to side, making a cackling noise with their bills wide open. When watching a possible site for a new colony, remember that they leave the cliffs for about a fortnight before egg-laying, and it is worth returning to check the site later.

**Manx Shearwater** *Puffinus puffinus*. Pl. **7,** *216*

*Breeds* late April–August, usually on islands with rocks and turf, occasionally on mainland promontories. (Off N. and W. coasts of British Isles and in the Mediterranean area.)

*Nest* both sexes excavate a burrow in grassy slope or in loose soil under rocks, frequently in rabbit burrows; nesting chamber usually contains a few bits of dry bracken or local material and may be several feet in from the entrance.

*Egg* 1, white. Incubated by both sexes for about 7 weeks.

*Nestling* greyish-brown down above, greyish-white below. Both parents take turns in feeding the young, flying in after dark at irregular intervals for 8–9 weeks. Chick remains in the burrow for another 2 weeks and then makes its own way to sea.

*Adults* smaller than Fulmar, roughly pigeon-size; sexes similar, black above, pure white below, long narrow wings, longish bill with hooked tip. In flight, tilts first to one side and then the other, showing dark and light alternately in long glides between fast wing-beats; shuffles awkwardly along the ground.

*Fledgling* similar to adult.

*Hints* nocturnal calls of a colony, half-strangled 'crowing' notes as they fly in after dark, create an atmosphere of wild excitement. Softer crooning notes can be heard from burrows. If you shine a torch on a shearwater that has just alighted, keeping the beam just behind the eye, it is often possible to catch one, but you should wear thick gloves as both the bill and claws can draw blood. About 35,000 pairs nest on the island of Skokholm, which has a bird observatory where visitors can stay. (Inquiries to The Warden, Dale Fort Field Centre, Haverfordwest, Pembs.) After a winter at sea, the birds return to the island in February and spend an increasing amount of time in their burrows. After the egg is laid, the male often takes the first spell of incubation while the female goes to sea to feed. A male has been known to incubate for 26 days at a stretch. Chicks are fed every 1–2 days at first. It is possible to find birds in the burrows during the day, but after handling them push them well down the burrow before leaving them.

**Storm Petrel** *Hydrobates pelagicus.* Pl. 8, *218*

*Breeds* June–September, on islands with turf and boulders. (Off W. coast of British Isles, NW. France and in the Mediterranean area.)

*Nest* both sexes excavate a burrow in turf or loose soil with rocks, also in stone walls and in rabbit burrows; the soil is loosened with the bill and kicked backwards; a few bits of dry vegetation may be present in the nesting chamber, but do not appear to be carried there.

*Egg* 1, white, often with brownish spots at one end. Incubated by both sexes for nearly 6 weeks.

*Nestling* silvery-grey down, paler on under-parts. Both parents take turns in feeding the young, flying in at night at irregular intervals for about 9 weeks. After this the chick makes its own way to sea.

*Adults* roughly Swift-size, smaller than Leach's Petrel; sexes similar, sooty brown, white rump patch is 'squared off' and not V-shaped as in Leach's Petrel (visible in the hand). Erratic flight course, bat-like motion, unforked tail, faint white wing-bar.

*Fledgling* similar to adult, white wing-bar is more conspicuous.

*Hints* over a thousand birds are usually present in the breeding season on Skokholm Island. (Visitors' inquiries to The Warden, Dale Fort Field Centre, Haverfordwest, Pembs.) Many non-breeders also occupy burrows. The petrels arrive in late April. Purring song reaches its peak in May–June when the display flight can also be seen, several birds circling and doing figures-of-eight above the burrows. Sit down among the boulders after dark, preferably in a gully so that you can get the dark silhouette of the birds in flight against a light patch of sky. Purring sounds, interrupted by an occasional 'hiccup', can be heard from burrows and there is a rather weak 'chittering' in flight. By day it is worth sniffing at any likely holes for a characteristic musky scent. Purring is also heard occasionally by day.

**Leach's Petrel** *Oceanodroma leucorrhoa*

*Breeds* late May–August, on remote islands with rocks and turf. (Off N. Scotland. Has bred off Ireland.)

*Nest* male excavates a burrow, usually in peaty soil, sometimes right under boulders and also in stone walls. Nesting chamber may have an accumulation of a few bits of dry vegetation.

*Egg* 1, white, often with dark spots at one end, larger than Storm Petrel's egg. Incubated by both sexes for about 7 weeks.

*Nestling* greyish-brown down, paler

on under-parts. Both parents take turns in feeding the young, flying in at night at irregular intervals for about 7 weeks. After this the chick makes its own way to sea.

*Adults* slightly larger than Storm Petrel; sexes similar, longer wings than Storm Petrel, forked tail; dark V-shaped patch in white rump (not 'square' as in Storm Petrel) and pale grey patch on wing, visible in the hand. More powerful flight than Storm Petrel but similar erratic course.

**Leach's Petrel**

*Fledgling* similar to adult.
*Hints* colonies are generally very difficult to reach, even if landing on remote islands is possible. Loud calls are heard at night as they fly in, aptly described as maniacal laughs. Churring song from burrow is also audible. Access to the St Kilda colony is possible for anyone with a head for heights, descending a steep grass gully near Mullach Bi to the boulder-strewn slopes of Carn Mor, if necessary 'bumping' down on your backside and digging your heels into the turf. By getting into position by 10.30 p.m. you witness a fly-past of Puffins, Storm Petrels, Leach's Petrels and Manx Shearwaters; it is worth remaining till dawn to hear the Wrens singing. Sniffing at burrows by day for typically musky

scent sometimes enables you to bring out a petrel and have a good look at it in the hand before returning it to the burrow.

**Gannet** *Sula bassana.* Pl. 9, 217
*Breeds* April–August, usually on precipitous cliffs but also on flat ground, chiefly on rocky islands. (Off N. and W. coasts of British Isles and off Alesund in Norway.)
*Nest* a mound of seaweed and local vegetation, about 2 ft high; material is gathered by both sexes but only by male before the eggs are laid.
*Egg* 1, chalky-white, soon becomes stained. Incubated by both sexes for about 6 weeks.
*Nestling* black skin shows through white down at first, down becomes thicker but bare patches remain on face and chin. Fed by both parents for about 8 weeks and then makes its own way to sea.
*Adults* goose-size, white plumage with black wing-tips, some yellow on head and neck, pointed tail, dagger-like bluish bill; sexes similar. Spectacular dives from 100 ft or more when fishing.
*Fledgling* speckled greyish-brown upper-parts, greyish-white under-parts; body becomes whiter during second year but wings and back still speckled, very spotted in third year and some spotting in fourth year.
*Hints* if you want to see the largest gannetry in the world, join one of the cruises organised by the National Trust for Scotland, 5 Charlotte Square, Edinburgh 2, which visits St Kilda. The only mainland colony in Britain is at Bempton in Yorkshire. It is sometimes possible to land on the island of Grassholm, off the Pembrokeshire coast. (Inquiries to The Warden, Dale Fort Field Centre, Haverfordwest, Pembs.) A characteristic stench greets you and the

Gannets fly up, looking like a snow-storm. The nests in a colony are close together and care has to be taken to avoid stabbing bills as you pass. Display includes Pelican-like postures, bowing and fencing with bills, accompanied by loud grunts. The single egg is incubated under the webbed feet and when it starts to hatch the egg is transferred to the top of the web.

## Cormorant *Phalacrocorax carbo*. Pl. 10, *219*

*Breeds* April–August (occasionally extended season), on rocky coasts with ledges and sloping slabs, occasionally on inland cliffs near water and regularly in trees in Ireland and on the Continent. (In British Isles, N. Europe and Scandinavia.)

*Nest* a mound of seaweed, sticks and local vegetation, gathered by both sexes; old nests of other species are sometimes used in trees.

*Eggs* 3–5, pale blue with chalky markings. Incubated by both sexes for about 4 weeks.

*Nestlings* naked at first, then dark brown down. Fed by both parents. Leave nest after about 4 weeks. Fly after about 8 weeks.

*Adults* sexes similar, head and neck look snake-like when swimming, heavier built than Shag which has a crest; white patches on chin, cheeks and thighs, rest of plumage looks black. Often stand with wings half-open, as though hanging them out to dry. (White feathers show at sides of head and neck of *Phalacrocorax carbo sinensis* during breeding season, in various parts of Europe.)

*Fledglings* upper-parts look brown rather than black, pale under-parts look mottled.

*Hints* binoculars are a help in working out possible routes down the cliffs to nesting colonies where the nests are often close together. When young are present these areas can look distinctly whitened. Female appears to entice male by standing with head and neck drawn in, tail raised, flapping her wings slowly; as male approaches, her tail is almost vertical and she thrusts her head and neck backwards and forwards, half opening her bill; he may respond by raising some of his feathers and distending his throat. Growling notes are heard. If you approach an adult on the nest, it will probably hiss at you.

## Shag *Phalacrocorax aristotelis*. Pl. 11, *220*

*Breeds* April–July (from mid January in Mediterranean), on rocky coasts with ledges and crevices, often in sea caves. (In British Isles, France, Spain and N. Scandinavia.)

*Nest* a mound of seaweed, sticks and local plants, chiefly gathered by male and arranged by female.

*Eggs* usually 3, pale blue with chalky markings, smaller than Cormorant's. Incubated by both sexes for about 4 weeks.

*Nestlings* naked at first, then light brown down. Fed by both parents. Leave nest after about 6 weeks but remain near it. Fly after about 7 weeks.

*Adults* sexes similar, smaller than Cormorant and more lightly built with no white in plumage, tuft of feathers on forehead shows in breeding season. Often jumps clear of the water when going into a dive; similar habit to Cormorant of hanging wings out when standing.

*Fledglings* easily confused with Cormorant but bill is more slender.

*Hints* colonies tend to be lower down the cliffs than Cormorant's and the nests are usually more scattered, often in the shelter of an overhang or in a cave, making access difficult.

Shags often pull at each other's tails in the early stages of courtship; the display of the female is very like that of the female Cormorant. As you approach a colony there is usually a lot of grunting and hissing. Young Shags are said to be inquisitive and any object near the nest is often picked up and passed from one bird to another.

**Bittern** *Botaurus stellaris*. Pl. **12, 13, 221**

*Breeds* late March–May, in reed-beds of fens and marshes, on swampy ground along banks of rivers and lakes. (Mainly confined to East Anglia in England. Throughout Europe. Has bred Finland.)
*Nest* on the ground or in aquatic vegetation; female builds wide, loose platform of reeds, sedge, etc.
*Eggs* 4–6, olive-brown, sometimes with dark markings. Incubated by female for about 3½ weeks.
*Nestlings* reddish and white down, bare patches on head, neck and sides of body. Fed by female. Leave nest after about 2 weeks, can fly after about 8 weeks.
*Adults* smaller than Heron, twice the size of Short-eared Owl; sexes similar, richly mottled and barred black and brown plumage. Heron-like posture, skulks in reeds, flies short distances looking rather 'hump-backed' with rounded wings.
*Fledglings* similar to adult but less distinctly marked.
*Hints* the boom of a Bittern sounds rather like a muffled fog-horn and may be audible at a mile or more. Skulking behaviour makes it difficult to track down, but aerial displays have been seen in which they soar and circle above the reeds, sometimes climbing rapidly and floating down. A Bittern has also been seen resting along the back of another in flight. If disturbed on the ground, it usually adopts a protective attitude, neck elongated so that the bill points vertically, the streaked patterning on the underside blending with the reeds, standing motionless in an elongated posture. The feathers on the neck are expanded like a fan when it is aggressive. The female sometimes crawls off the nest, flying at a range of about 12 yds. A visit in July to the R.S.P.B. reserve at Leighton Moss in Lancashire may well provide a sight of young Bitterns on the wing.

**Little Bittern** *Ixobrychus minutus*. Pl. **14**

*Breeds* May–June (occasionally later), usually in reed-beds or swampy ground, often on banks of river or lake, but also recorded in trees. (Throughout Europe, except Denmark. Absent British Isles and Scandinavia.)
*Nest* usually on the ground amongst matted reeds or just above level of water, but sometimes 10–12 ft up in a tree; reeds, twigs and dead leaves are loosely built, probably by female only, into a rough but compact platform.
*Eggs* usually 5–6, white. Incubated by both sexes for about 2½ weeks.
*Nestlings* reddish-buff and white down, bare patches on head and neck. Fed by both parents. Leave nest after about 1 week, can fly after about 4 weeks.
*Adults* roughly Coot-size, half the size of Bittern; both sexes have dark crown, plumage of male looks definitely black and buff, female much browner. Skulking habits, flies low above reeds with rapid wing-beats alternating with glides, neck retracted, legs extended.
*Fledglings* mottled and streaked version of adult female.

*Hints* it is possible that they bred in East Anglia towards the end of the last century, but they are now seen irregularly on passage, mainly in SE. England. Male's call-note is described as a repetitive croak or cough, approximately 25 calls to the minute, by day and night. When approached at the nest-site, it extends neck and head vertically and stands motionless facing the intruder, the streaking on the breast closely matching the background of reeds; it appears to 'freeze' in this posture and has even been picked up.

### Heron *Ardea cinerea*. Pl. 16, 222

*Breeds* February–June (occasionally July–August), usually in trees near water (S. England), but also on cliffs, in reed-beds and on marshes. (In British Isles and most of Europe. Local in Spain and on coasts of Norway and Sweden.)

*Nest* from ground-level up to about 80 ft; branches, sticks, sometimes reeds, are built into a platform several feet wide and lined with twigs, bracken and grass. Nests are added to each year, the male bringing most of the material for the female to arrange.

*Eggs* 3–5, greenish-blue. Incubated by both sexes for about 3½ weeks.

*Nestlings* brownish down on crown has white tips, giving crested appearance. Fed by both parents. Leave nest after about 8 weeks.

*Adults* large Stork-like birds, grey and white with drooping black crest and yellowish dagger-like bill; sexes similar. Often seen standing near water, head sunk into 'shoulders'. Rounded wings in flight, dark on underside, slow flapping motion, neck retracted, feet extended.

*Fledglings* brownish-grey, shorter crest than adult.

*Hints* heronries are usually occupied for many years and nests are conspicuous in the winter, the bulky pile of sticks showing up well in the crown of the trees. In February the birds gather either at the heronry or on the ground near by; 'dancing' with wings half-open may be seen and there are zigzagging dives on to the heronry. Various displays include stretching the head and neck vertically, flexing the legs, bill-clapping, mutual preening and caressing, accompanied by various calls. Pellets on the ground below trees are a useful sign that a heronry is occupied.

### White Stork *Ciconia ciconia*. Pl. 15, 223

*Breeds* late March–May, on buildings, telegraph-poles, haystacks, trees, usually near houses. (In most parts of Europe. Has bred France, Italy and S. Sweden.)

*Nest* both sexes build a bulky structure of dead sticks, branches, twigs and lumps of earth, lined with grass, moss, rags, paper, etc.

*Eggs* 3–5, chalky-white. Incubated by both sexes for about 4½ weeks.

*Nestlings* white down, sparse at first. Fed by both sexes. Flap wings after 3 weeks, fly after about 8 weeks.

*Adults* larger than Heron, slightly larger than Black Stork; sexes similar, white plumage except for black wing-feathers; long red bill and legs. Often perches on one leg, bill tucked into neck when at rest. Extends neck in flight, legs and neck tend to hang down slightly.

*Fledglings* wings are brownish-black, legs brownish-red.

*Hints* the only breeding record for Britain of wild stock dates back to 1416 when a pair nested on St Giles's Cathedral in Edinburgh. They are now seen infrequently on passage in E. and S. England. In Holland and France they are becoming scarcer, but pairs can still be seen giving their typical bill-clapping display in which the neck is curved right back, so that the crown rests on the back and the bill points over the tail. There are usually several nests in the same area.

## Black Stork *Ciconia nigra*

*Breeds* late March–April (S. Spain), mid April–May (N. Germany and eastwards), in mature trees in dense forests with some secluded expanses of marsh and meadow, also in dry areas with scrub and on cliffs. (Has bred in recent years in Denmark and Sweden.)

*Nest* a solid structure, built by both sexes, usually in a tree in secluded part of forest; nest of previous year is often occupied and old nests of other species are repaired with sticks and earth, lined with moss and grass.

*Eggs* 3–5, white. Incubated by both sexes for about 5 weeks.

*Nestlings* scanty down at first, similar to White Stork, but yellow bill is larger. Fed by both parents. Fly after about 10 weeks.

*Adults* slightly smaller than White Stork; glossy black above, white below, red legs and long red bill; male's bill is slightly stouter, female's wings look less glossy at close range. Solitary and wary.

*Fledglings* browner than adult, greenish bill and legs.

*Hints* owing to its preference for privacy, nests are usually in sites which are inaccessible. Nests have been found from 12 ft to 40 ft, rarely in the tops of trees. Two occupied nests have been recorded in one tree, but usually nests are well scattered. Bill-clapping is much less frequent than in White Stork and there are various notes, some of them described as like a saw being sharpened and others more musical. Courtship display includes the pair circling round each other on the ground, spreading white under tail-coverts and pressing bills against their necks. Fresh material may be added to the nest during incubation. This species is seen occasionally in Britain, chiefly in E. and S. England, on passage.

## Spoonbill *Platalea leucorodia*. Pl. **17**, *224*

*Breeds* in extensive reed-beds and low shrubs on marshes, also on bare islets. (In Holland and S. Spain. Has bred Denmark.)

*Nest* a substantial structure of reeds, usually 1–1½ ft high, built by both sexes on trodden-down reeds; dead twigs are used in bush nests.

*Eggs* 3–5, whitish with dark markings. Incubated by both sexes for about 3 weeks.

*Nestlings* silky tipped whitish down. Fed by both parents. Leave nest after about 4 weeks but return to it. Fly after about 6 weeks.

*Adults* roughly Heron-size, sexes similar; snow-white plumage and long spatulate bill are distinctive; at close range white crest, yellowish patch at base of neck, orange patch on throat, are all visible; corrugations on the spoon-shaped bill may also be seen. Looks like a Heron on the ground, but in flight the neck is extended, making a straight line with the legs which project behind.

*Fledglings* black wing-tips, pinkish bill becomes dark by the winter, plumage entirely white by third year.

*Hints* Spoonbills bred in Norfolk and Suffolk in the seventeenth century, but they are now usually seen during the winter, mainly along the coast or up estuaries in East Anglia, the West Country and Wales. Colonies breed in three places in Holland: the island of Texel, the Naardermeer bird sanctuary and the Zwanenwater reserve.

(Full particulars regarding visitors' access to Dutch nature reserves can be obtained from Vereeniging tot Behoud van Natuurmonumenten in Nederland, Herengracht 540, Amsterdam-C.) Spoonbills usually return to their Dutch breeding sites during March. Courtship display includes mutual preening, the pair standing face to face, one bird nibbling the other's neck-band while its partner caresses its throat. Nests are often built close together.

## Canada Goose *Branta canadensis*. Pl. **18**, *225*

*Breeds* late March–May, in the neighbourhood of ornamental lakes and gravel-pits, often in parkland and on islets. (Regularly in Britain and Sweden.)

*Nest* on the ground, sometimes under bushes; a depression is lined with leaves, grass and down by female. Has been recorded on rocky ledges, in old nests of birds of prey and on artificial rafts.

*Eggs* 4–6, whitish. Incubated by female for about 4 weeks.

*Nestlings* greenish-brown down on upper-parts, greenish-yellow on under-parts, narrow eye-stripe. Leave nest shortly after hatching, both parents in attendance. Fly after about 6 weeks.

*Adults* sexes similar, large greyish-brown goose with black head and neck, except for oblique white patch on face which looks like a chin-strap; black bill and legs. They spend a lot of time swimming and have been seen somersaulting when bathing.

*Fledglings* resemble adult.

*Hints* originally introduced from N. America as 'ornamental', many now live wild, mainly in the Midlands and East Anglia. In flight, they give a double honk. the second syllable pitched higher, but they do not move about much except during the winter. Islets in lakes are worth searching for nests, the gander standing guard while the goose sits on the eggs and he may give a warning honk as you approach. Display and typical nervous posture are similar to Grey Lag's. The goslings often dive when danger threatens.

## Grey Lag Goose *Anser anser*. Pl. **20**, *387*

*Breeds* late April–June, on Scottish moorland amongst heather and on islands in lochs and off the coast; some 'escapes' from ornamental collections also breed locally, mainly in Norfolk. In Central Europe they also breed in extensive reed-beds, sometimes in March. (In Britain, Denmark, E. Germany and on coasts of Scandinavia. Has bred Holland.)

*Nest* near water, on the ground amongst heather or rushes, sometimes floating platforms in reeds; twigs, grass and moss, lined with down by female.

*Eggs* usually 4–6, whitish but often stained. Incubated by female for about 4 weeks.

*Nestlings* olive-brown and greenish-yellow down. Leave nest shortly after hatching, tended by both parents. Fly after about 8 weeks.

*Adults* sexes similar, easily confused with other grey geese; pink legs, orange bill with white tip, greyish-brown plumage with some white around the tail; pale grey forewing in flight. (Ancestor of typical farm-yard goose.)

*Fledglings* resemble adult but legs are greyish, not pink.

*Hints* they are said to pair for life and a male (gander) is sometimes seen running at an intruder with head lowered, hissing loudly, then hurrying back to his mate. Communal ceremonies have been seen in which the ganders form a rough circle, one of them in the centre with head held low, apparently hissing. They are very wary, but you may catch sight of the gander standing in the neighbourhood of the nest; if you surprise the goose on the nest, she usually adopts a typical nervous attitude, lying with her neck stretched forward along the ground.

## Mute Swan *Cygnus olor.* Pl. **19**, *389*

*Breeds* April–June, near fresh water in countryside and built-up areas, less frequently by sea-lochs and estuaries. (In British Isles, Denmark, Germany, Holland and S. Sweden.)
*Nest* huge pile of sticks, reeds and local vegetation built on the ground into an open nest in which feathers accumulate; male brings material for female to arrange, always near water.
*Eggs* usually 5–7, greyish-green. Incubated by both sexes for about 5 weeks.
*Nestlings* known as cygnets, greyish-brown down on upper-parts, white on under-parts. Tended by both parents. Leave nest after a day or so, take to water, often riding on adult's back. Fully fledged after about 4 months.
*Adults* familiar large white bird with long neck and orange bill with black knob which is smaller in the female. In flight their wing-beats make a 'singing' sound.
*Fledglings* greyish-brown plumage, becoming whiter over several years.
*Hints* typical display consists of swimming along with wings arched over the back and neck drawn back, looking thoroughly aggressive. Pairs face each other, turning their heads from side to side and dipping their bills in the water. 'False preening' also takes place in which they rub their heads along the closed wings. Various hissing notes can be heard and a rattling sound is often heard after an intruder has been driven off. A visit to Abbotsbury Swannery, in Dorset, during the breeding season is well worth while. Two other species of swan are seen in the British Isles, mainly during the winter: Bewick's Swan (*Cygnus bewickii*) which breeds in Russia and Whooper Swan (*Cygnus cygnus*) which breeds regularly in N. Scandinavia and has bred in Scotland.

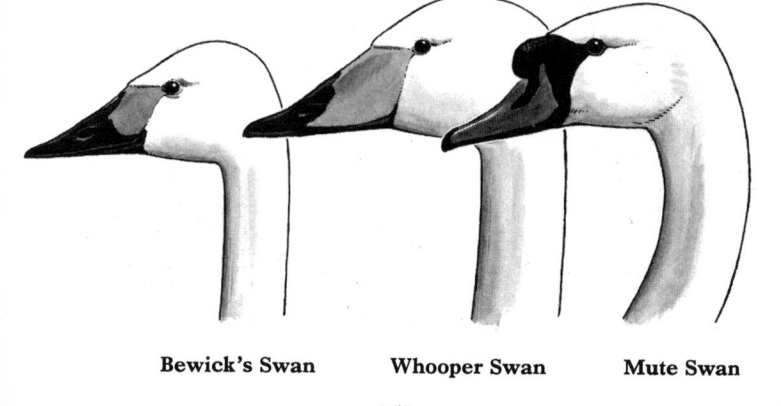

**Bewick's Swan**          **Whooper Swan**          **Mute Swan**

**Shelduck** *Tadorna tadorna.* Pl. **21, 22, 23,** *390*

*Breeds* May–June, on dunes and rough ground along estuaries, occasionally inland on farmland or in woodland within reach of water. (In British Isles, most of Europe and Scandinavia.)

*Nest* usually in a rabbit burrow or under brambles or bushes, sometimes in heather or rushes, also in hollow trees; burrow or hollow is lined with down by female.

*Eggs* 8–16, whitish. Incubated by female for about 4 weeks.

*Nestlings* marbled dark brown and white above, yellowish-white below. Leave nest shortly after hatching, tended by female, male sometimes in attendance. Fly after about 8 weeks.

*Adults* sexes very similar; in the distance they look like small black-and-white geese, at close range the chest-band is seen to be chestnut, the head and neck greenish-black; pink legs, red bill which has a definite knob in the male.

*Fledglings* greyish-brown upperparts, white face and throat, white breast without band; plumage more like adult during first winter.

*Hints* listen for cackling and whistling during March when nest-sites are being chosen. There are aerial chases and various postures adopted by courting males which swing their heads up and down, both on land and when swimming. Duck foot-prints leading down a burrow are a useful clue and sometimes bits of down get caught at the sides of the entrance. The male stands guard near the nest and calls the female off the eggs twice a day. Distraction display has been recorded. The duck calls the ducklings with a repeated 'sissy sissy' note.

**Mallard** *Anas platyrhynchos.* Pl. **25,** *388*

*Breeds* chiefly mid March–May but recorded from February to November, almost anywhere within reach of fresh water, including built-up areas. (In British Isles, Europe and Scandinavia.)

*Nest* from ground-level up to about 30 ft, usually on the ground in thick cover, also in hollow trees, old nests of other species and on buildings in towns; made of leaves, stems and grass, lined with down and feathers by female.

*Eggs* usually 8–10, greenish. Incubated by female for about 4 weeks.

*Nestlings* marbled yellowish and dark brown. Leave nest shortly after hatching, tended by female, male sometimes in attendance. Fly after about 8 weeks.

*Adults* familiar 'wild duck'; male has dark green head, white collar, purplish-brown above with four black feathers curling up from tail; female mottled brown. In flight, purplish-blue patch on wing, edged with white,

**Mallard and young**

152

usually shows up. (Ancestor of many domestic ducks; hybrids are often seen.)

*Fledglings* resemble adult female; adult plumage shows about August.

*Hints* pairs are formed in the autumn and they move to breeding grounds early in the year. Courtship display includes several males (drakes) chasing a female in flight and swimming round her, heads sunk into 'shoulders', bills frequently dipped into the water and then jerked up as the males rear up in the water; sometimes they swim round the duck with their necks stretched along the surface. The duck does not usually flush until the last minute, although the drake may break from cover in the vicinity of the nest in the early stages. Distraction display, the duck floundering about, has been seen from eggs and when ducklings are near.

**Teal** *Anas crecca*. Pl. **24**, *391*

*Breeds* mid April–June, on moors and heaths, in woods and hedge bottoms, within reach of fresh water. (In British Isles, most of Europe and Scandinavia. Has bred Spain. Absent most of Italy.)

*Nest* on the ground in shelter of vegetation; a hollow lined with dead leaves, bracken, etc., and down by female.

*Eggs* 8–10, creamy-buff. Incubated by female for about 3 weeks.

*Nestlings* more rufous on upper-parts than Mallard. Leave nest shortly after hatching, tended by female, male often in attendance. Fly after about 3½ weeks.

*Adults* noticeably smaller than Mallard; male has green band, outlined in yellow, running from eye to nape, which contrasts with reddish-brown head, white streaks along sides of body and yellowish-buff 'triangles' on either side of black stern; female

is speckled brown and buff. Both sexes have green and black patch on wing which shows well in fast, wheeling flight.

*Fledglings* resemble adult female; adult plumage acquired by November.

*Hints* small ducks flying fast, twisting and diving in fast manœuvres, usually turn out to be Teal. Pairs are formed in the autumn. Double call-note of male, described as 'krit krit', carries a long way. Display is somewhat similar to Mallard's, the male raising and lowering his head, swimming round the female, sometimes elevating the tail. Nests are not easy to find as they are usually well hidden in cover and may be almost anywhere on the ground. Distraction display by both sexes has been recorded.

**Gadwall** *Anas strepera*. Pl. **27**, *393*

*Breeds* May–June, near quiet stretches of water with plenty of natural cover, on banks of lakes, pools and slow-running rivers. (In British Isles, Germany and Holland. Local in S. France and Sweden. Has bred Spain.)

*Nest* usually near water on dry ground, hidden in vegetation; a hollow lined with bits of local plants and down by female.

*Eggs* 8–12, creamy-buff. Incubated by female for about 4 weeks.

*Nestlings* rather similar to Mallard. Leave nest shortly after hatching, tended by female. Fly after about 7 weeks.

*Adults* slightly smaller than Mallard and less heavily built; male looks drab brownish-grey in distance, with black stern, but at close range beautiful pattern of speckles and vermiculations is visible; female looks more mottled than female Mallard and has orange line along sides of bill. Both sexes have white patch, bordered with black and chestnut, on hind edge of wing which shows well in flight.

*Fledglings* rather similar to adult female; adult plumage acquired by March.

*Hints* drab colouring and wary behaviour make them unobtrusive, but croaking and whistling calls during display help to locate them. Male bows to female and pursues female in the air, much as in Mallard. Distraction display has been observed at the incubation stage. They nest in several counties, including the London area, and in the R.S.P.B. reserve at Minsmere, in Suffolk, they are the commonest breeding duck.

## Wigeon *Anas penelope*. Pl. **30**, *396*

*Breeds* May–June, on moors, marshes and rough ground near fresh water, often on islands in lochs. (In N. England, Scotland, Denmark, E. Germany and most of Scandinavia. Has bred Holland and Ireland.)

*Nest* usually in heather or bracken near water; made out of local vegetation lined with grass and down by female.

*Eggs* 6–10, cream or buff. Incubated by female for about 3½ weeks.

*Nestlings* dark brown, buff and rufous down. Leave nest shortly after hatching, tended by female, usually joined later by male. Fly after about 6 weeks.

*Adults* smaller than Mallard, roughly Gadwall-size; male has chestnut and buff head, yellowish streak on crown may look white in certain lights, white streak along sides of body becomes broad white patch along front edge of wing when flying; female is rufous-brown, small bill helps to identify from other female ducks.

*Fledglings* resemble adult female except for front edge of wing which is greyish rather than white; adult plumage may still be incomplete by March.

*Hints* whistling 'whee-oo' calls of males are often heard during display as they crowd round a female, raising their crests, before moving to breeding grounds. Several nests may be in the same area and the male stands guard near the female during incubation and rejoins the family when they leave the nest and take to the water. Scottish Highlands are the main breeding grounds in Britain.

## Pintail *Anas acuta*. Pl. **26**, *394*

*Breeds* May–June, inland on moors and marshes near fresh water, often on islands in lochs; locally along the coast on dunes and marshes. (In E. England, Scotland, NW. Ireland, Denmark, Germany, Holland and N. Scandinavia. Has bred Belgium, France and S. Spain.)

*Nest* on the ground, often in open site; a hollow lined with grass, leaves and down by female.

*Eggs* usually 7–9, creamy or yellowish-green. Incubated by female for about 3½ weeks.

*Nestlings* brownish down above, with white spots and white eye-stripe, greyish-white below. Leave nest shortly after hatching, tended by female, male often in attendance. Fly after about 6 weeks.

*Adults* roughly Mallard-size but much more elegant; male has elongated pointed tail and a conspicuous white streak running up each side of neck which contrasts with chocolate-brown head and neck; female is like an elegant female Mallard with a pointed tail. In flight both sexes have a white border to hind edge of wings.

*Fledglings* resemble adult female but upper-parts are darker and there is no white border to wings.

*Hints* secretive and wary, their courtship display which takes place in January and February is not often seen in Britain. It is somewhat similar to Mallard's with the bill depressed and the tail cocked up. There are not many breeding colonies, the best known being at Loch Leven in Kinross. The male stands guard in the vicinity of the nest during incubation. Distraction display includes running along the ground with wings drooping and flying just above the ground with legs dangling, as though flying with great difficulty.

## Garganey *Anas querquedula*

*Breeds* late April–June, on marshes and fens near shallow water, also in rank vegetation and in meadows near rivers. (Local in England. In most of Europe and S. Sweden. Has bred Ireland and Spain.)
*Nest* in tussock of rushes or in long grass; a hollow lined with grass and down by female.
*Eggs* 7–12, creamy-buff. Incubated by female for about 4 weeks.
*Nestlings* similar to Mallard but with dark line through eye and across cheek to bill. Leave nest shortly after hatching, tended by female. Fly after about 4 weeks.

**Garganey**

*Adults* slightly larger than Teal but paler; wings look a lighter colour than rest of body; male has white stripe which sweeps back from over the eye to the nape, mottled brown breast and grey flanks; female is easily confused with female Teal. In flight, fore-wing is pale bluish-grey with white on either side of green patch, the pattern only showing faintly. Fast and agile on the wing.
*Fledglings* similar to adult female; adult plumage may still be incomplete in March.
*Hints* croaking calls of males are heard in March as they fly after a female. Males dip their bills in the water as they swim round the females. During the early stages of incubation, the male is often on guard near the nest, but moves away before the eggs hatch. Small numbers breed in southern counties and East Anglia; a few pairs nest in the R.S.P.B. reserve at Minsmere in Suffolk.

## Shoveler *Anas clypeata.* Pl. 29, 395

*Breeds* April–June, on marshes and meadows near water, also some distance from water on bushy ground such as heaths and commons. (In British Isles, most of Europe and S. Scandinavia. Has bred Spain and Switzerland. Absent Italy.)
*Nest* usually on dry ground in low vegetation or in open site; a deepish hollow lined with grass, feathers and down by female. Some nests are tent-like, surrounding vegetation forming a 'roof', and haystack site has been recorded.
*Eggs* usually 8–12, greenish-buff. Incubated by female for about 3½ weeks.
*Nestlings* resemble Mallard, broad bill develops slowly. Leave nest shortly after hatching, tended by female, male sometimes in attendance. Fly after about 6 weeks.
*Adults* smaller than Mallard, roughly Gadwall-size; both sexes have broad spatulate bill which hangs down, giving characteristic silhouette to head; male has dark green head,

white breast, dark brown flanks and belly; female is drab brown. Pale blue forewing and green patch show up well when male flies; wings appear to be set back in flight, making both sexes look rather heavy in the air.

*Fledglings* rather similar to adult female; full adult plumage may still be incomplete in April.

*Hints* display is comparatively unobtrusive but spectacular flights over the nesting area have been seen in which a number of males swoop and dive in figures-of-eight. Several males will also pursue a female in the air. When searching likely marshes or meadows, keep a watch for the male as he stands in the vicinity of the nest during incubation. Distraction display has only been seen occasionally.

**Red-crested Pochard**

### Red-crested Pochard *Netta rufina*

*Breeds* May–June, in reeds in shallow water of extensive lagoons, also in cover surrounding secluded pools. (In most of Europe. Has bred England and Belgium.)

*Nest* on the ground or built-up in shallow water, in some kind of dense cover, including under a bush; deep cup of roots and local stems, lined with feathers and down by female.

*Eggs* usually 6–12, creamy-yellow. Incubated by female for about 4 weeks.

*Nestlings* olive-brown with white spots on upper-parts, yellowish-white under-parts. Leave nest shortly after hatching, tended by female.

*Adults* roughly Mallard-size, larger and plumper than Pochard; male has chestnut head with orange crest, finely tapering red bill, black neck and breast, broad white bar on the wing shows in flight; female has faint wing-bar, greyish cheeks and dark brown crown, altogether rather drab.

*Fledglings* resemble adult female, no crest.

*Hints* Lincolnshire and Essex are two counties where pairs have bred, probably 'escapes' from ornamental collections, but it is possible that the breeding range of wild stock is extending and any pairs seen together from April onwards should not be disturbed. A three-syllable croak has been recorded in breeding areas and the male has been heard giving a whistling note, ending in a grunt while lowering himself into the water after 'standing up' during display. During incubation the male stands guard in the vicinity of the nest, flying off when disturbed, warning the female who tends to slip into the water before flying away. Nests with more than 12 eggs are usually the result of more than one duck sharing the nest; eggs of Gadwall and Pochard have been found in the nests of Red-crested Pochard.

### Pochard *Aythya ferina*

*Breeds* late April–June, on shores of lakes and pools with plenty of surrounding cover, also on banks of slow-running rivers, often on islands

**Pochard**

in lakes. (In British Isles, most of Europe and S. Scandinavia. Has bred Belgium, Spain and Switzerland. Absent Italy.)

*Nest* usually in reeds close to water or in tussocks in shallow water; a pile of local aquatic plants, lined with down by female.

*Eggs* usually 6–12, greenish-grey. Incubated by female for about 3½ weeks.

*Nestlings* yellowish-grey down with marbled effect of blackish-brown. Leave nest shortly after hatching, tended by female. Swim and dive after a few hours, fly after about 8 weeks.

*Adults* smaller than Mallard, Wigeon-size; male has finely patterned grey back and flanks, which look white in distance, and a red eye is visible at close range; female is drab brown with pale shading at throat. No wing-bar in flight.

*Fledglings* resemble adult female but look mottled on under-parts.

*Hints* courtship display takes place from March onwards. The males stretch their necks, puffing out their feathers and throwing their heads up and down, giving a soft whistle. The

females have a much more raucous note and frequently dip their bills in the water. The nest is usually in thick cover, close to the water, at the end of a dark 'tunnel' and a runway sometimes gives it away. The male stands guard during incubation, flying off at the approach of an intruder and warning the female, who slips off the nest into the water. Breeding pairs are mostly found in the eastern part of Britain.

**Tufted Duck** *Aythya fuligula*. Pl. **28,** *392*

*Breeds* mid May–July, close to fresh water lakes and pools with some cover available on the banks, mainly in the country, but also in built-up areas with suitable park lakes. (In British Isles, Denmark, Germany, Holland, and most of Scandinavia. Has bred France and Switzerland.)

*Nest* on the ground near the edge of the water in a tussock of reeds; female uses grass and reeds as a foundation, sometimes forming a 'tent', lined with down. Wall site has also been recorded.

*Eggs* 6–14, greenish-grey. Incubated by female for about 3½ weeks.

*Nestlings* brownish and yellowish-white down. Leave nest shortly after hatching, tended by female. Swim and dive within a few hours, fly after about 6 weeks.

*Adults* roughly Pochard-size, slightly smaller than Scaup with which confusion occurs; both sexes have rounded body and a drooping crest from the crown, less obvious in female; purplish-black plumage of male contrasts with white flanks; female is dark brown with greyish flanks and sometimes has a pale area near the base of the bill. (Female Scaup has bold white area round the bill.) Both sexes show broad white wing-bar in flight.

*Fledglings* resemble adult female; full plumage may show in November but is not complete until March.

*Hints* courtship display starts in March and soft whistling notes can be heard from the males as they throw their heads back; females frequently dip their bills in the water and give a more raucous call. Islands in lakes are worth searching. There may be several pairs nesting in the same area. In Sweden they often breed in colonies of terns and gulls.

**Scaup** *Aythya marila.* Pl. **31**

*Breeds* late May–June, on islands in lakes and on open ground near water, such as moors and tundra. (In N. Scandinavia. Has bred Scotland and Holland.)

*Nest* on the ground, sometimes in some cover from heather or rough grass, sedge, etc.; a hollow lined with bits of local material, feathers and down, making a deep bowl.

*Eggs* from 6 to 13 recorded, greenish-grey. Incubated by female for about 4 weeks.

**Scaup**

*Nestlings* dark brown and greenish-yellow down. Leave nest shortly after hatching, tended by female, male sometimes in attendance.

*Adults* slightly larger than Tufted Duck; in the distance male looks

black at both ends, white in the middle, but at close range, back is pale grey; female is dark brown with a well-defined white area round the base of the bill. Broad white wingbar, as in Tufted Duck, shows in flight.

*Fledglings* may be confused with young Tufted Duck as area of 'white' round the bill tends to be grey in young females and grey vermiculations of back in young males are not very clear.

*Hints* breeding pairs have been reported from the Outer Hebrides, Caithness, Ross, Sutherland and Orkney, and possibly from Lincolnshire. In regular breeding areas there are several nests quite close together. The male has a 'cooing' note as he displays, throwing his head up into the air. The female dips her bill into the water and gives a 'chup chup' call. In Britain they are normally seen off-shore in the winter.

**Eider** *Somateria mollissima.* Pl. **32**, **397**

*Breeds* May–July, usually near the sea along rocky and sandy coasts, locally inland by lakes or on islands. (In N. British Isles, N. Europe and Scandinavia.)

*Nest* on the ground in heather or rough grass, sometimes in shelter of boulder; a hollow lined with grass, feathers and down by female.

*Eggs* 4–6, greenish-grey. Incubated by female for about 4 weeks.

*Nestlings* dark brown and brownish-white down, pale eye-stripe. Leave nest shortly after hatching, tended by female. Fly after about 8 weeks.

*Adults* Mallard-size, heavily built with 'straight line' profile from forehead to tip of bill; male has distinctive black belly and white back, black crown contrasts with white head with some green at nape; female is mottled brown. Wings of male look black and white in flight, female has buffish wing-bar.

*Fledglings* resemble adult female at first, young males go through 'patchy' stage, acquiring most of adult plumage by second winter.

*Hints* crooning calls are part of an unobtrusive display, the head being jerked back as the male gives an 'appreciative cooing' note, described as 'ah-oo'. Isolated nests are more frequent in Britain, but on the Farne Islands and abroad there are often many nests close together. The female sits so closely that you have to be careful not to tread on her; if she flushes, remember to cover the eggs with down. A female shepherding her brood to the water is a delightful sight, and broods often join up into large groups with several females in attendance.

## Common Scoter *Melanitta nigra*

*Breeds* June–July, on high-lying moors and tundra, associated with small lochs, heather and dwarf scrub. (Local in N. Scotland and Ireland. In N. Scandinavia.)

*Nest* on the ground amongst heather, dwarf willow or birch, in tussocks of grass; a hollow lined with grass, moss, lichen and down by female.

*Eggs* 5–7, creamy-buff. Incubated by female for about 4 weeks.

*Nestlings* dark brown and greyish-white down. Leave the nest shortly after hatching, tended by female. Fly after about 7 weeks.

*Adults* Scaup-size; male is completely black except for orange area on bill; female is sooty brown with whitish cheeks and throat and paler, mottled under-parts. No wing-bar; pointed tail sometimes shows up when swimming.

*Fledglings* resemble adult female; male's black plumage develops gradually from December.

**Common Scoter**

*Hints* small numbers breed on the mainland north from Inverness and on the Inner Hebrides; many are seen in the winter all round the coasts of Britain. Displaying males skate along the surface of the water with neck extended low and also 'stand up' in the water with the head held high. There are rattling and whistling notes. The male deserts the female when she starts to incubate.

## Long-tailed Duck *Clangula hyemalis*

*Breeds* late May–July beyond the tree-line on rocky barren ground with stunted heather or dwarf birch, along rivers and lakes, often on islands in lakes. (In N. Scandinavia.)

*Nest* in sphagnum, dead leaves, stunted vegetation or under rocks, a hollow lined with grass, twigs and down by female.

*Eggs* 5–11, yellowish-buff. Incubated by female for about 3½ weeks.

*Nestlings* blackish-brown and greyish-white down. Leave nest shortly after hatching, tended by female. Fly after about 5 weeks.

*Adults* smaller than Eider with pointed tail, very elongated in male, and small round head. Plumage of both sexes can be confusing at different seasons, but it is a mixture of brown and white, 'patchy' in

**Long-tailed Duck**

appearance, the wings being uniformly dark. Small neat head is a good guide to identification.

*Fledglings* resemble adult to some extent; elongated tail in male develops in 3 years.

*Hints* breeding has been suspected in Orkney, although they are usually seen only as winter visitors along Scottish coast and islands. Anyone finding a possible nest is advised to keep some of the down for identification. In regular breeding areas there may be a number of nests in the same area. Noisy, goose-like calls attract attention and skirmishes often take place. The males display by jerking their heads back, opening their bills and calling frequently, then bowing; both sexes extend their necks along the water. The male remains in the vicinity of the nest during incubation, but departs before the eggs hatch. Broods sometimes join up and are cared for by more than one female.

### Goldeneye *Bucephala clangula*

*Breeds* mid April–May (Germany), May–June (Scandinavia), in forests with lakes and rivers. (Has bred England and Switzerland. Absent most of Europe.)

*Nest* usually in a hole in a tree up to about 50 ft, but uses nest-boxes frequently in Scandinavia and is said to have nested in a rabbit burrow in England; chips of wood mixed with feathers and down by female.

*Eggs* 6–15, bluish-green. Incubated by female for about 4 weeks.

*Nestlings* dark brown and white down. Leave nest after about 24 hours, probably scrambling out unaided and dropping to the ground, where the female tends them. Fly after about 8 weeks.

*Adults* slightly larger than Tufted Duck, slightly smaller than Scaup; male has black 'triangular' head with distinctive round white patch near base of bill, black back, white underparts and neck; female has brown head with narrow white collar and mottled grey upper-parts. Both sexes have big white 'squares' on the wing.

*Fledglings* brown on head, white face patch of young male may show from October.

*Hints* the pair reported to have nested in 1931–2 were in rabbit burrows in Cheshire. Display and mating has been seen fairly often on lochs in Inverness-shire, but so far there is no confirmation that they have bred in Scotland. Displaying male swims round a female, jerking its head up and lifting its tail, sometimes kicking

**Goldeneye**

up a spray of water and has been seen shooting backwards. Male gives a hoarse double-note; female is said to utter 'cuk cuk cuk' when searching for likely nest-site. Spruce and pine forests in Scandinavia often have suitably decaying trees and old Black Woodpecker holes are also taken over.

## Red-breasted Merganser *Mergus serrator*. Pl. **33**, *398*

*Breeds* late May–July, on islands and shores of both fresh water and salt water, in heather or rocks and on tundra. (In N. England, N. Wales, Scotland, Ireland, Denmark, N. Germany and Scandinavia. Has bred Holland.)
*Nest* on the ground in a hollow, nearly always close to water and in shelter of some kind such as under tree roots; depression is lined with grass, leaves and down by female.
*Eggs* 7–13, yellowish-grey, sometimes greenish. Incubated by female for about 4 weeks.
*Nestlings* dark brown with patches of white and tawny down, cheeks yellower than in Goosander. Leave nest shortly after hatching, tended by female. Fly after about 5 weeks.
*Adults* slightly smaller and slimmer than Goosander; male has ragged double crest (greenish-black) and white collar, chestnut breast and grey flanks; female also has ragged crest (chestnut), no collar but pale chin and throat merges into whitish neck. Double white wing-bar in flight.
*Fledglings* resemble female with short crest; adult plumage acquired by second winter.
*Hints* a lively display which starts well before the mating season includes convulsive movements of the head and neck, showing off the red interior, raising the crest, bowing and bobbing, arching the wings and skating along the water creating a lot of spray. Loud purring notes may be heard. Islands on lochs are worth searching for nests and there may be more than one in the same area. The female sits close when incubating and if you flush her, see that the eggs are covered with down before you leave. Shallow burrows and recesses are worth investigating.

## Goosander *Mergus merganser*. Pl. **34**, *399*

*Breeds* mid April–June, usually in wooded country near fresh water, but also beyond tree-line. (In N. England, Scotland, Germany, Switzerland and Scandinavia.)
*Nest* in hollow tree up to about 25 ft, on the ground under bank or boulder; often in nest-boxes abroad and has been recorded in cliff and on buildings; cavity is lined with leaves, feathers and down by female.
*Eggs* 7–13, yellow to creamy-white. Incubated by female for about 5 weeks.
*Nestlings* dark brown with patches of white and tawny down. Leave nest after a few days, apparently tumbling down from nests in trees. Fly after about 5 weeks. Both parents have been seen in attendance on young, but female usually tends them.
*Adults* slightly larger than Mallard and Red-breasted Merganser; male has no crest or collar, head looks black at a distance, contrasting with pinkish-white under-parts, thin red bill; female has chestnut head with shaggy crest, grey above and white below. In flight, male has white wings with black tips and female has white square patch on grey wings; flight silhouette is attenuated.
*Fledglings* resemble adult female with small crest; adult plumage acquired by second winter.

*Hints* display includes the male tossing up his head, 'standing up' in the water, sinking down again and raising the crest. There is a certain amount of splashing and low, croaking notes may be heard. The pair are frequently on the wing in the early hours of the morning, prospecting the area for nest-sites. One reasonably close to water is usually chosen. Later, there may be signs of down at the entrance hole.

**Osprey** *Pandion haliaetus*. Pl. **36**, *230*

*Breeds* mid April–May (Scotland), March–May (S. Spain), June–July (Scandinavia), in pine forests near water in Scotland, in wide variety of sites abroad, including trees, cliffs, bushes, pylons and on the ground in shingle, sand or rocks. (In E. Germany, Sicily, S. Spain and Scandinavia. Local in Scotland.)

*Nest* bulky platform of sticks mixed with heather or local material, lined with turf, moss and bark, built by both sexes.

*Eggs* 2–3, white with dark markings. Incubated mainly by female for about 5 weeks.

*Nestlings* nearly naked at first, then thick sandy and greyish-brown down, giving speckled appearance as they grow. Fed by female with food brought by male in feet, often passed to the female in the air. Fly after about 7½ weeks.

*Adults* roughly Buzzard-size but more heavily built; female usually larger than male; both sexes have dark brown upper-parts and white under-parts, dark brown band across breast, white head with dark streak through eye. Plunges feet first into water when fishing.

*Fledglings* resemble adult but more steaked appearance on head.

*Hints* the easiest way of seeing Ospreys in Britain is to take advantage of the excellent facilities provided by the R.S.P.B. in Speyside. The birds can be seen through powerful binoculars at the observation post without any risk of disturbance, providing you follow the official route which is well signposted to Loch Garten. They arrive late in March or early April, the male frequently making wide circles above the eyrie, calling in a high-pitched whistle, and diving down with wings half-closed. When building the nest, they both gather material but the female appears to do most of the building. Sticks are collected from the ground or broken off trees as they fly past. The nest is usually in a tall tree in the bare part of the top canopy. Nesting material is added during incubation and fledging periods.

**Honey Buzzard** *Pernis apivorus*

*Breeds* late May–June, in open mature woods and copses. (In most of Europe and S. Scandinavia. Local in England. Absent Holland.)

*Nest* in tall tree, favouring deciduous, usually on foundation of old nest of other species; decorated and lined with fresh greenery by both sexes.

*Eggs* 2, white, heavily marked with reddish-brown. Incubated by both sexes for about 4½ weeks.

*Nestlings* cream, grey and white down. Fed by both parents. Leave nest after about 6 weeks.

*Adults* Buzzard-size, sexes similar; longer wings, tail and neck than Buzzard, head looks small; tail has dark broad band towards end and two narrower bands above; dark brown upper-parts, under-parts white and boldly marked with brown, sometimes suffused with brown. Soars less frequently than Buzzard, wings droop slightly when gliding, tips curved upwards.

*Fledglings* very variable in plumage, often showing a lot of white on head. *Hints* they nest irregularly in England, chiefly in the New Forest. Usually more silent than Buzzard, notes are described as more squeaky and grating. Similar display above nest-site, rising and hovering briefly while tips of wings practically touch over the body, then diving down again. Towards evening, keep a watch for the pair carrying boughs to the nest. When feeding they spend quite a lot of time walking about on the ground and wasps' nests are particularly attractive to them.

**Red Kite** *Milvus milvus.* Pl. **35, 400**
*Breeds* mid April–July, in wooded valleys of hilly country in Wales; in open country with scattered trees as well as woodlands abroad. (In most of Europe. Local in Sweden and Wales. Has bred Denmark and Norway.)
*Nest* usually in a fork high up in a tree; flat-topped and untidy looking nest, built by both sexes of sticks and earth, lined with all kinds of rubbish, wool and moss; also recorded on old nest of crow.
*Eggs* 2–3, white with dark markings. Incubated by both sexes for about 4 weeks.
*Nestlings* white and buff down. Male brings food for female to feed them in early stages, then both parents feed them. Leave nest after about 7 weeks.
*Adults* Buzzard-size, sexes similar; long deeply forked tail, narrow wings with dark tips and white patch on underside, distinctly angled in flight; white streaks on head, dark brown upper-parts, reddish-brown under-parts with dark streaks. Soars like a Buzzard but forked tail silhouette is usually clearly visible.
*Fledglings* darker head than adult, generally more drab in appearance.
*Hints* Kites in Britain are now so rare that people are asked not to visit the one area in central Wales where small numbers breed as they desert readily at all stages. They use their forked tails like rudders in a circling, soaring display flight and have also been seen hovering. Their mewing note is more shrill than Buzzard's and sometimes merges into a whinnying note. In Spain they are relatively numerous in woodlands south of Seville and nests may contain eggs in March.

**Goshawk** *Accipiter gentilis*
*Breeds* late March–June or April–June (according to latitude), in conifer forests and mixed woodlands. (In Europe and Scandinavia. Has bred England.)

**Goshawk**

*Nest* usually in stout forks of trees rather than in canopy, height varying from 15 ft to 75 ft, but also recorded on the ground; foundation of old nest is often used, fresh branches and twigs being added with greenery by both sexes.
*Eggs* 3–4, whitish, soon become stained. Incubated chiefly by female for about 5 weeks.

*Nestlings* scanty greyish down at first, becoming 'woolly'. Male brings food to nest at first for the female to feed them, later both sexes hunt. Leave nest after about 6 weeks.
*Adults* roughly Buzzard-size, female larger than male but plumage is similar and both sexes resemble large female Sparrowhawk. Dashing flight, dodging between trees; heavily barred under-parts with white patch under barred tail; also soars like Buzzard.
*Fledglings* upper-parts look brighter brown than adult and under-parts are streaked (not barred).
*Hints* the same nest-site is used year after year and the pair can be seen circling and soaring above the trees before breeding starts. Display includes flying with markedly deliberate wing-beats, reminiscent of a Harrier, and sweeping upwards on stiff wings, reminiscent of Wood Pigeon's display. Normally rather silent, a harsh 'gek gek gek' may be heard as you approach the nest. Goshawks recently bred in SE. England but it is thought that they may have been escaped falconry birds. In Holland they are regarded as a threatened species.

**Sparrowhawk** *Accipiter nisus.* Pl. **37**, *226*
*Breeds* May–July, in wooded countryside and on outskirts of towns where there are copses. (In British Isles, Europe and Scandinavia.)
*Nest* normally fairly high in a tree, but also recorded in low bushes; bulky and untidy but shallow structure of dead sticks, bits of bark and dead leaves, often on foundation of old nest of other species; both sexes bring material but female does most of the building. White down acts as a lining when incubation is under way.

*Eggs* 4–6, whitish, often with dark markings. Incubated chiefly by female for about 5 weeks.
*Nestlings* scanty whitish down at first, becoming 'woolly'. Fed by female with food brought by male. Leave nest after 3–4 weeks.
*Adults* roughly Kestrel-size, female larger than male, with rounded (not pointed) wings, barred under-parts and long tail; male is bluish-grey above, brown on wings and tail which has dark bands; female is darkish brown above. Rapid flight with a lot of gliding, beating from side to side along a hedge or dodging between trees.
*Fledglings* browner than adult and irregular barring on under-parts.
*Hints* display includes the pair soaring in wide circles above the nesting area and flying with deliberate wing-beats; the male also shoots down into a tree where the female is perching. The nest is built several months before the eggs are laid. The male brings food to the nest or to a plucking place near by; food is also transferred in the air. There may be several nests in the same area, but during incubation an occupied nest usually shows a white rim of feathers.

**Buzzard** *Buteo buteo*. Pl. **38**, *227*
*Breeds* April–July, on moors and mountains, in wooded valleys and along coastal cliffs. (In Britain, N. Ireland, Europe and most of Scandinavia.)
*Nest* from ground-level up to 50 ft or more in a tree and on high rock ledges overlooking the sea; flat but bulky structure of sticks, heather, bracken, moss and bark, decorated from time to time by female with fresh greenery. Old nests, including those of other species, are often freshly lined.
*Eggs* 2–4 eggs, white and dark mark-

ings. Incubated chiefly by female for about 4 weeks.

*Nestlings* greyish and white down. Male brings food at first for female to feed them, later both parents hunt and feed nestlings. Leave nest after about 6 weeks.

*Adults* smaller than Golden Eagle, female usually larger than male but similar in plumage; dark brown upper-parts, mottled brown and white under-parts, unfeathered yellow legs; often seen soaring, broad rounded wings with 'finger-tips' spread, tail looks rounded, sometimes losing height rapidly with wings half-closed.

*Fledglings* similar to adult.

*Hints* mewing cries, heard on the wing and when perching, often attract attention. Pairs soar in spirals, apparently floating on air currents, in wide circles over the nest-site. There is also an aerobatic display, rolling and tumbling, sometimes looping the loop. Several nests may be freshly lined by one pair in the same season. During incubation they usually flush easily. Trees covered with ivy are promising sites.

## Golden Eagle *Aquila chrysaetos.* Pl. **39**, *231*

*Breeds* mid March–July, mainly confined to remote mountain areas in Scotland, including some islands; also in the Alps, Italy, Spain and N. Scandinavia. (Has bred Ireland.)

*Nest* on ledge of rock or in tree, often in Scots fir, occasionally on the ground; both sexes build bulky structure of dead branches, heather, bracken, fresh greenery added during the season, lining it with dead grass, ferns and often with woodrush. *Eggs* usually 2, white; often one of the two eggs has reddish markings. Incubated chiefly by female for about 6 weeks.

*Nestlings* whitish down. Male brings most of food in early stages, then both parents share in feeding the nestlings. Leave nest after about 12 weeks.

*Adults* larger than Buzzard, female usually larger than male but plumage is similar; huge wing span (6–7 ft), 'finger-tips' spread as in Buzzard, long square tail; flight silhouette shows longer tail and head projecting farther beyond wings than in Buzzard; dark brown or chestnut plumage, with a golden area on the head.

*Fledglings* white patch on tail which ends in black band.

*Hints* a pair may have more than one traditional site in its territory; the eyrie becomes fouled by the end of the season and one of the other sites is usually occupied in the following season. The nest is built several months before the eggs are laid. Early in the breeding season, the male soars above the territory, and there are aerial displays in which the pair soar in spirals, then plunge down with half-closed wings, sometimes rolling over so that their talons appear to touch. They can also fly very fast; one record claims a speed in level flight, clocked from an aeroplane, of more than 90 m.p.h. Mewing and barking sounds may be heard but they are comparatively silent. They readily desert the nest if disturbed.

## Hen Harrier *Circus cyaneus.* Pl. **41**, *229*

*Breeds* mid May–July, on moorland and damp ground with rushes, also in reed-beds and young conifer plantations. (In Scotland, N. Wales and Ireland, most of Europe and Scandinavia.)

*Nest* on the ground, often in heather; surrounding vegetation trampled down and lined with grass, bracken, heather, etc., built chiefly by female. Material is usually added during incubation.

*Eggs* 3–6, whitish, soon become stained. Incubated by female for about 4 weeks.

*Nestlings* similar to Montagu's Harrier. Fed by female who receives food in the air from male. Leave nest after about 6 weeks, tended by both parents.

*Adults* very similar to Montagu's Harrier, slightly larger, male smaller than female; male has bold white patch on rump, no dark band across wings and no streaks on flanks; female has larger white patch on rump (pure white, not greyish-white) than female Montagu's Harrier but otherwise very similar. Flight silhouette same as Marsh Harrier but more graceful action.

*Fledglings* streaked under-parts, otherwise similar to young Montagu's Harrier.

*Hints* from about March, aerobatic displays can be seen above nesting area, the pair circling and soaring, stooping at each other, the male sometimes buffeting the female as she turns over. The male has a spectacular dive, hurtling down as though out of control in a spin, pulling out at the last minute. Watch where the female goes when they break off as she often lands on the nest-site. In Britain their main breeding areas are in Scotland. Orkney, where they are more numerous, there may be more than one nest in the same area, spaced roughly 200 yds apart; they favour the lower spurs of hills amongst heather and rushes.

**Montagu's Harrier** *Circus pygargus*

*Breeds* late May–July, in reed-beds and on marshes, like Marsh Harrier,

but also in conifer plantations and on rough ground of moors, heaths and dunes. (Local in Britain and S. Sweden. In N. Italy and throughout rest of Europe.)

*Nest* on the ground in cover, surrounding vegetation trampled down; both sexes gather material, female does most of the building of nest which varies in size and is made of sedge, reed and grass.

*Eggs* 3–6, whitish, soon become stained. Incubated chiefly by female for about 4 weeks.

*Nestlings* whitish down with buff areas, brown ring round eye. Fed by female, who receives food from male in the air. They can fly after about 5 weeks but may leave the nest before this, scattering and being fed separately, both parents hunting.

*Adults* smaller than Buzzard, closely resemble Hen Harrier but greyish-white patch on rump is less extensive; sexes same size, male has dark band across grey wing which also shows on the underside and brown streaks on flanks; female has dark brown upper-parts and streaked buffish under-parts (same as female Hen Harrier). Flight silhouette same as Marsh Harrier but particularly elegant and more slenderly built than Hen or Marsh Harrier.

**Montagu's Harrier**

*Fledglings* dark brown upper-parts like adult female but no streaks on under-parts.

*Hints* towards the end of April they soar and circle above nest-sites, the display flight being similar to that of

Marsh Harrier but the calls are less harsh and higher pitched. Small numbers breed fairly regularly in East Anglia, locally in other parts of England and Wales and occasionally in Scotland. On the Continent, where they are more numerous, there are often several nests in the same area.

## Marsh Harrier *Circus aeruginosus.* Pl. **42**, *228*

*Breeds* late April–July, on marshes and fens with extensive reed-beds. (Local in England; has bred Wales. Throughout Europe and in S. Scandinavia.)

*Nest* on the ground amongst reeds or other aquatic vegetation, often surrounded by water; larger than other harriers' nests, female builds a bulky pile of reeds, sedge, etc., sometimes adding a few branches of alder, etc., lined with finer grass. Male builds a supplementary nest and may add material to occupied nest during incubation.

*Eggs* 4–5, bluish-white, soon become stained. Incubated chiefly by female for about 5 weeks.

*Nestlings* whitish down with areas of buff. Fed by female who usually catches food in the air from the male, who calls her off the nest. They remain in or near the nest for about 5 weeks, leaving it after about 8 weeks.

*Adults* roughly Buzzard-size with longer wings and tail, more heavily built than other harriers, sexes same size; male has grey tail and grey band across upper part of wing, black wing-tips contrast with grey area and rest of plumage which is mainly dark brown; female and young male have buffish 'shoulders' and head. Flight silhouette is typical of harrier with long wings held at high angle and long tail projecting, a few wing-beats followed by a long glide, quartering the ground at low level and pouncing on prey.

*Fledglings* darker wings and tail; head usually has some buff.

*Hints* watch for diving display in which the male soars high and then plunges down in a series of swoops, wings half-closed, twisting and turning, sometimes looping the loop. A loud shrill call is often heard during this display. Transfer of food from male to female in aerial pass above the nesting area may also be seen. The female has been heard calling loudly for food when incubating. These harriers now nest in such few numbers in Britain that they should be left completely undisturbed. At the R.S.P.B.'s reserve at Minsmere, Suffolk, suspected breeding is not investigated until the young are safely on the wing. About 500 pairs breed in Holland.

## Peregrine *Falco peregrinus.* Pl. **40**, *232*

*Breeds* April–July, now mainly in remote parts of Scottish Highlands and Ireland, on sea-cliffs and crags; also in forests abroad. (In British Isles, Europe and Scandinavia.)

*Nest* a scrape is made in some kind of soft layer, usually on an inaccessible rock ledge or on old nest of other species when the debris is flattened; nests on tall buildings and on flat ground have also been recorded. No nesting material is carried to the site which is known as an eyrie.

*Eggs* 3–4, reddish-brown, some white may show through. Incubated chiefly by female for about 4 weeks.

*Nestlings* creamy-white down at first, bare patches round eyes and on sides of neck. At first male brings food for female to feed them, later he also feeds them. Leave nest after about 5 weeks.

*Adults* noticeably larger than Hobby; female larger and darker than male; bluish-grey upper-parts, pale under-parts with dark barring which is not always apparent at long range, very dark moustachial stripe ends in a lobe. Long pointed wings, flight silhouette reminiscent of Pigeon except for tapering tail; fast wing-beats alternate with glides, headlong stoop at prey with wings closed.

*Fledglings* dark brown upper-parts (not grey) and streaked (not barred) under-parts.

*Hints* very shrill, repetitive 'kek kek' is often heard before you catch sight of the Peregrine as you approach nest-site and are still some distance from it. During early stages of incubation the male (tiercel) passes food to the female (falcon), the male calling the female off the nest and dropping the prey as she turns on her back to catch it; prey is also brought to a ledge near the eyrie, where it is plucked. When the young (eyasses) are about 2 weeks old, the male feeds them at the eyrie when the female is absent but the male does most of the hunting. Traditional sites are used year after year, but in Britain there has been a serious decline in numbers in recent years.

**Hobby** *Falco subbuteo.* Pl. **43**, *233*

*Breeds* late May–July, in open country such as commons, downs and heaths with scattered trees or shelter belts, also in open woodlands. (In S. England, throughout Europe and in S. Scandinavia.)

*Nest* old nests of other species are used, Carrion Crow's often appropriated and squirrel's drey also recorded, height usually from 30 ft to 50 ft; no nesting material is gathered, debris is often flattened.

*Eggs* usually 3, reddish-brown, some

white may show through. Incubated chiefly by female for about 4 weeks.

*Nestlings* creamy-buff down at first, bare patches round eyes and on sides of neck. Male brings food for female to feed them in early stages, but he also feeds them later. Leave nest after about 4½ weeks.

*Adults* smaller than Peregrine, roughly Kestrel-size, female usually larger than male; plumage is somewhat similar to Peregrine's except for reddish thighs, pointed (not lobed) end of dark moustachial stripe and streaked (not barred) under-parts. Flight silhouette suggests a large Swift without the forked tail. Fast wing-beats alternate with glides; remarkably agile on the wing.

*Fledglings* dark brown upper-parts with light edgings to feathers, buff under-parts heavily streaked but no red near tail.

*Hints* watch for soaring aerobatic displays of pairs and fast flight, dodging between trees. There are aerial passes and the male also presents food to the female on a branch, flying into the tree with a continuous whickering call. A soft 'wer wer wee wee' is heard as he presents the food to her. This call is also heard very loud when disturbed at the nest. Look for crows' nests, which are in groups of trees rather than in isolated trees.

**Merlin** *Falco columbarius.* Pl. **44**, *234*

*Breeds* May–July, mainly on heather moors and rough ground in hilly country, also on sea-cliffs and dunes. (In British Isles and most of Scandinavia. Absent Europe.)

*Nest* usually on the ground in heather, also in marram and bents on dunes, and many recorded in old nests of other species, including Buzzard and Carrion Crow; no real nest made, bits of vegetation or debris scraped together or flattened. *Eggs* usually 4, reddish-brown, pale ground sometimes shows through. Incubated by both sexes for about 4 weeks.

*Nestlings* whitish down at first. Male brings food but female usually feeds them. Leave nest after about 4 weeks.

*Adults* smaller than Kestrel, male roughly Mistle Thrush-size, female larger; no moustachial stripe, heavily streaked under-parts, greyish tail with dark bars; male has bluish-grey upper-parts, female is darkish brown. Dashing swerving flight, low over the ground, when hunting in open country; pointed wings, fast wing-beats, occasional glides.

*Fledglings* similar to adult female.

*Hints* pairs circle above the nest-site, but there are no elaborate aerobatics. The male presents food to the female at the nest-site and does most of the hunting throughout the breeding season, usually carrying it to a plucking place near the nest; occasionally the female receives food in the air. Loud chattering note 'quik ik ik' is usually heard as the nest is approached. Many nests have been found in old heather on hill-sides, giving an extensive view over a valley. Regular perching places, such as boulders become whitened and serve as a guide, the nest usually being somewhere below them. In Britain Merlins breed mainly in the north and west.

**Kestrel** *Falco tinnunculus*. Pl. **45**, **235**

*Breeds* mid April–July, from large towns to remote sea-cliffs, in all kinds of country, including moorland, agricultural land and open woodland. (In British Isles, Europe and Scandinavia.)

*Nest* from ground-level (often in heather) up to various heights,

**Kestrel**

including ledges on tall buildings, cliffs and in tree-nests of other species; a scrape of debris, no real nesting material. Open type of nest-box used.

*Eggs* usually 4–5, white with reddish markings. Incubated chiefly by female for about 4 weeks.

*Nestlings* scanty white down at first. Male brings food to female in early stages, later they both hunt and feed nestlings. Leave nest after about 4 weeks.

*Adults* roughly Pigeon-size, long pointed wings, typical hovering action with tail fanned; male has bluish-grey head, rump and tail, the latter has a broad black band near the white tip and upper-parts are spotted chestnut; female has brown head, brownish upper-parts and tail, both of which are barred black.

*Fledglings* similar to adult female.

*Hints* shrill 'kee kee kee' call is often heard near the nest-site. Circling and stooping above the female have been recorded, but spectacular aerial displays seem to be infrequent. They often occupy the same site as in previous year and there may be more than one pair nesting in the same area; on the cliffs, they may nest close to other birds of prey. Ground nests are frequent on the mainland of Orkney, mainly in tall heather, but a few nest in burrows or under banks. Some sit so close during incubation that they can be lifted off the nest.

**Willow Grouse** *Lagopus lagopus*. Pl. **46**, *236*

*Breeds* May–June, on moors and heaths with birch and willow scrub in Scandinavia. (Absent S. Sweden.)
*Nest* a scrape lined by female with dry grass and leaves.
*Eggs* variable, usually 6–16, greyish-yellow with dark markings. Incubated by female for about 3 weeks.
*Nestlings* no description available; leave nest shortly after hatching, tended by both parents. Fly after about 2 weeks.
*Adults* easily confused with Ptarmigan as both have white wings, but rest of Willow Grouse's plumage is darker (reddish-brown) than Ptarmigan's and at close range a stouter bill is visible. Whirring flight as in Red Grouse.
*Fledglings* no description available.
*Hints* the male has a solitary display. Rapid 'crowing' is reminiscent of Red Grouse. The nest is often hidden under a bush and the male stands guard in the vicinity of the nest. This species has not been recorded in Britain.

**Red Grouse** *Lagopus lagopus scoticus*. Pl. **49**, *239*

*Breeds* April–June (occasionally earlier), on moors, peat-bogs and rough ground with heather, crowberry and cranberry. (In N. England, Scotland, Wales and Ireland.)
*Nest* female makes a scrape, usually in cover of heather, and frequently adds a scanty lining of bits of local vegetation.
*Eggs* variable, usually 6–10, creamy-white with dark markings. Incubated by female for 3–4 weeks.
*Nestlings* marbled effect of buff and black with reddish down on crown;

down covers toes. Leave nest soon after hatching, tended by both parents for about 6 weeks. Fly when about 2 weeks old.
*Adults* stout game birds, female slightly smaller than male and noticeably paler; plumage is dark reddish-brown, wings and tail look darker than rest of body, unforked tail; low flight over the ground, whirring quick wing-beats alternating with glides in which wings are held in a downward curve. (Irish Grouse is yellower.)
*Fledglings* similar to adult female at first, become darker in winter like adults.
*Hints* familiar 'go-back go-back' notes are heard as males challenge each other from their territories, flying up about 15 ft into the air, then descending at a steep angle, neck and feet extended and tail fanned. During incubation, the cock is usually near the nest and as you walk across the moor, it is worth trying to remember where you first see the male as the female may flush from this site. When the eggs have hatched, the female often gives a distraction display, also recorded in male, running along with wings beating the ground and tail depressed. Another form of diverting attention is by walking round you in circles.

**Ptarmigan** *Lagopus mutus*. Pl. **47**, *237*

*Breeds* May-June or June–July, according to latitude, on desolate mountain-tops of Scottish Highlands amongst scree where vegetation is sparse; in similar habitat in the Alps, Pyrenees and in Scandinavia.
*Nest* female makes a scrape amongst low-growing plants or in shelter of a rock, adding a scanty lining of grass and feathers.
*Eggs* usually 5–9, creamy-white with

dark markings, smaller than Red Grouse. Incubated by female for nearly 4 weeks.

*Nestlings* marbled effect of black and buff down, paler under-parts than in Red Grouse; down covers toes. Leave nest shortly after hatching, tended by both parents. Fly after 10 days.

*Adults* roughly same size as Red Grouse; both sexes have blackish-brown patterning on upper-parts, female looks tawnier than male, white on wings and belly and white-feathered feet. Red wattle over eye is larger in the male. (Plumage varies with the seasons.) Flight is reminiscent of Red Grouse.

*Fledglings* similar to adults' summer plumage, but has blackish flight feathers.

*Hints* the mottled plumage provides remarkably good camouflage against the background of moss and lichen in the screes; they crouch when nervous, and although some can be approached without difficulty they are easily overlooked. Males occupy territory from late March and croak while displaying, leaping into the air and descending with wings extended. They chase females in flight and on the ground, drooping their wings and spreading their tails. When walking up a stony summit, look out for the male perched on a boulder, usually near the nest while the female is incubating. The croaking call has a ventriloquial effect, apparently coming from some distance away; look carefully at any lichen-covered rock close to you. Distraction display, feigning injury, is often seen when chicks are present.

## Hazel Hen *Tetrastes bonasia*

*Breeds* May–June, in forests of mixed species and age groups, often with birch and alder, chiefly in hills but locally in plains. (In France, Germany, N. Italy, Switzerland and Scandinavia.)

*Nest* a scrape on the ground, usually hidden under a bush or fallen tree, scantily lined by female with grass.

*Eggs* 7–12, brownish-yellow with dark markings. Incubated by female for about 3 weeks.

*Nestlings* no description available; leave nest shortly after hatching, tended by both parents. Fly after about 2 weeks.

**Hazel Hen**

*Adults* slightly smaller than Willow Grouse; upper-parts grey to reddish-brown mottled with black, broad white streaks run down sides of neck across the back, under-parts whitish mottled with brown, longish grey tail with black band. Male has black patch on throat outlined in white, female's throat is whitish. Perches in trees.

*Fledglings* no description available.

*Hints* essentially a woodland species, nesting in the most inaccessible part of the forest so that the nest is said to be remarkably difficult to find. When flushed, it has a weak flight, showing the black band on the grey tail, perching in a tree only a short distance from where it was disturbed. The male is said to display on his own rather than in a formal assembly. High-pitched whistling notes are heard. This species has not been recorded in Britain.

## Black Grouse *Lyrurus tetrix*. Pl. **48**, *238*

*Breeds* late April–June, on rough damp ground with scattered trees, young plantations and felled clearings, sometimes in woods, and on open moorland. (In Britain, parts of Europe and most of Scandinavia. Absent most of France, Italy and Spain.)

*Nest* usually a scrape, made by female, on damp ground in cover of heather, grass, whortleberry, etc.; exceptionally in old nest of other species in a tree up to about 20 ft.

*Eggs* usually 6–10, buff with speckled appearance. Incubated by female for about 4 weeks.

*Nestlings* similar to Red Grouse, but there is no down on toes. Leave nest shortly after hatching, tended by female. Fly after about 2 weeks.

*Adults* larger than Red Grouse; both sexes have white wing-bar; male has glossy black plumage with white under tail which is lyre-shaped; female (known as Greyhen) is mottled brown and black, less rufous than female Red Grouse or Capercaillie, forked tail seen at close range. Walks rather slowly, perches in trees, flushes comparatively silently.

*Fledglings* similar to adult female.

*Hints* males crowing from trees may be heard from early February before

**Black Grouse**

the 'lek', as the formal display is called, builds up to its main peak; the lek continues even after the eggs have hatched and usually takes place at dawn and dusk in open ground with low vegetation. The display ground is not a clue to the nest-site but is well worth finding. The males assemble and their 'rookooing' calls can be heard some distance away. The Blackcocks threaten each other with tails fanned, showing white 'bottoms-up', the wings are held loosely and they jump into the air and make dashes at each other; the Greyhens arrive and mating takes place. Some females flush easily and fly off without any form of demonstration; others sit close and distraction display may take place.

**Capercaillie**

## Capercaillie *Tetrao urogallus*. Pl. **50**, **240**

*Breeds* mid April–June, typically in conifers in hilly regions, also in mixed conifer and deciduous woods and in scrub on high ground. (In Scotland, France, Germany, Italy, Spain, Switzerland and Scandinavia.)

*Nest* usually a scrape on the ground by a tree, lined by female with bits of local vegetation and feathers; sometimes amongst heather and occasionally in a tree 10–15 ft above ground.

*Eggs* usually 5–8, yellowish with dark markings. Incubated by female for about 4 weeks.

*Nestlings* striped effect of sandy, chestnut and black down. Leave nest shortly after hatching, tended by female. Fly after about 2 weeks.

*Adults* look like small turkeys with very dark plumage, rounded fan-like tail and whitish hooked bill; dark grey and brown, female more richly barred and mottled than male with rufous patch on her breast. Often seen walking about in forest; also perches in trees and has powerful, dodging flight between trees.

*Fledglings* similar to adult female.

*Hints* a sound like corks popping out of bottles may guide you to a display ground. Males strut around with 'swollen' necks, fanning their tails almost vertically and drooping their wings, which they 'rattle', while the females stand near by. In Abernethy Forest, in Inverness-shire, 25 males have been seen at a communal display ground but there are also individual displays given from a prominent perch in the nesting area. Walking through forests where Capercaillies may be nesting can be hazardous as the males are often very aggressive; they may rush up to you, peck hard and whack you with their wings, and it is not worth trying to stand your ground. Eggs may be hidden under pine needles. Distraction display is more likely to be seen when the eggs have hatched.

## Red-legged Partridge *Alectoris rufa*. Pl. **51**, *241*

*Breeds* April–June, in similar habitat to Common Partridge, favouring dry ground, chiefly in SE. and E. England; also in Spain, parts of France, Italy and Switzerland, in woods, orchards, vineyards, on sandy and stony ground, boulder-strewn hill-sides and in scrub.

*Nest* male makes scrapes, usually in low cover but also recorded in haystack, tree and on roof, lining the nest with leaves and grass.

*Eggs* usually 10–15, pale buff or yellowish-brown with dark markings. Male and female both recorded as incubating, period about 3½ weeks, male probably incubating second clutch.

*Nestlings* marbled effect of chestnut and buff down, whitish at throat. Leave nest shortly after hatching, tended by both parents. Fly after about 2 weeks.

*Adults* slightly larger and looks taller than Common Partridge; sexes similar; white throat usually shows up at long range, but at short range there is a white streak above the eye and the white patch on the throat has a narrow black border; greyish flanks richly barred with chestnut, black and white, red bill and red legs. Alleged to perch more freely in trees and on posts than Common Partridge.

*Fledglings* very similar to young Common Partridge.

*Hints* much the same as for Common Partridge. The alarm-note is 'chuck chuck'. A harsh 'creaking' note is used during display, described as suggesting a laboured steam-engine, 'teuk-teuk-teuk-err'. Distraction display has been observed.

**Partridge** *Perdix perdix*. Pl. **52**, *242*

*Breeds* April–June, on arable land with rough grass on verges, in hedge-bottoms, on downs, heaths, moors, dunes and marshes. (In British Isles, Europe and S. Scandinavia.)

*Nest* a scrape made by female, usually in long grass, lined with leaves and grass; usually in open country but occasionally in wood, also recorded on haystacks.

*Eggs* 8–20, olive-brown. Incubated by female for about 3½ weeks.

*Nestlings* marbled effect of yellowish-buff, black and rufous down. Leave nest shortly after hatching, tended by both parents. Fly after about 2 weeks.

*Adults* comparatively small, plump game birds which look brown in the distance; chestnut barring on flanks, dark horseshoe mark on breast, male more boldly marked than female. Runs fast with head well up, whirring and gliding flight, skimming low, showing rounded wings and short rufous tail.

*Fledglings* more streaked appearance than adult.

*Hints* the presence of coveys in winter is usually obvious from 'creaking' calls, particularly noticeable at dusk, and the Partridges often run very fast after each other. The coveys split up into pairs by February. Pairs can be seen standing breast to breast, bills pointing up, rubbing their necks and bills together. The male stands guard in the vicinity of the nest during incubation. A runway leading to the nest is often visible but the nest is hidden in rough grass or vegetation and because of its value as a game bird, searching for partridges in the breeding season is likely to be unpopular with landowners and farmers.

**Quail** *Coturnix coturnix*

*Breeds* mid May–July (sometimes August–September), in crops and rough grassland. (In British Isles and Europe; local in S. Scandinavia.)

*Nest* female makes a scrape, lining it with a few bits of grass or local vegetation, often in corn, clover and bean crops.

*Eggs* usually 7–12, yellowish-white with dark markings. Incubated by female for about 3 weeks.

*Nestlings* marbled effect of orange-buff and black down. Leave nest shortly after hatching, tended by female. Fly after about 1½ weeks.

*Adults* look like tiny Partridges; sandy-brown above with pale buff and black streaks, paler below with light streaks on flanks; male has faint 'collared' effect, black and cream feathers on neck and long creamy stripe over the eye; female has blackish spots on breast but is more drab than male. Difficult to flush; flies low for short distances.

*Fledglings* similar to adult female but fewer spots on breast.

*Hints* you are more likely to hear Quail in arable country in SE. England than elsewhere in Britain. The call has a ventriloquial effect and searching in crops is not very productive when you are limited to the edges of the field. Popularly described as 'wet my lips' it sounds more like 'whit whit whit' and it is easier to hear in the comparative quiet of the evenings, although it can be heard by day; early in the season the Quail are sometimes seen running across a quiet road separating arable fields. There are 'duets' between male and female, the male remaining near the nest during incubation.

**Pheasant** *Phasianus colchicus*. Pl. **53**, *243*

*Breeds* mid April–May (occasionally in autumn), in woods and copses, farmland with cover from long grass, hedge-bottoms, shrubberies, gardens in the country, also in reed-beds, heaths and scrub. (In British Isles, Europe and S. Scandinavia.)

*Nest* usually a hollow scraped in the ground by female, scantily lined with leaves and grass, also in haystacks, trees and on wall.

*Eggs* usually 8–15, olive-brown. Incubated by female for about 3½ weeks. Male has been recorded on eggs.

*Nestlings* marbled effect of buff, chestnut and black down. Leave nest shortly after hatching, tended by female. Fly after about 2 weeks.

*Adults* familiar game bird with long tail; most males have white collar, dark green head with scarlet wattle, burnished copper body plumage; female has shorter tail and soft brown plumage with black mottling. (Introduced varieties have resulted in very varied plumage.) Walk, run fast, and rocket into the air almost vertically from your feet.

*Fledglings* similar to adult female, but long tail-feathers do not develop until autumn.

*Hints* males 'crow' frequently in spring, standing very upright and beating their wings. Two males are often seen facing each other, like sparring partners, raising the feathers on their rumps, spreading the tail-feathers, which are usually depressed but sometimes jerked up, while they make pecking movements with their heads; their heads move up and down, almost in unison, but occasionally one makes a stab at the other and this usually ends in both males leaping off the ground. The male struts round the female with feathers puffed out and the wing nearest her is often spread. The nest is not easy to find but the female can be watched as she returns to incubate. As pheasants are game birds, searching for nests tends to be unpopular.

**Crane** *Grus grus*. Pl. **54**, *244*

*Breeds* mid April–May or May–June, according to latitude, in marshy meadows, reed-beds and swampy ground near shallow water, damp clearings in woods, also beyond upper limits of birch woods in the north. (In Germany and Scandinavia.)

*Nest* varies from no nest material on a hummock to a bulky, flattish heap of grass and local vegetation, built by both sexes, sometimes in shallow water.

*Eggs* 2, pale grey to reddish-brown with dark markings. Incubated by both sexes for about 4 weeks.

*Nestlings* tawny down on upper-parts, paler on crown, chin and under-parts. Leave nest soon after hatching, tended by both parents, run and swim with ease. Fly after about 10 weeks.

*Adults* larger than Heron, male slightly larger than female, sexes otherwise similar; long-legged, long-necked, drooping bushy 'tail', uniform grey at long range; red patch on crown and whitish stripe down sides of head and neck are visible at close range. Graceful walk, neck usually curved but stretched when nervous; neck and legs extended horizontally in flight.

*Fledglings* brown head and upper-parts without pattern on head.

*Hints* during the Middle Ages they bred in East Anglia, but they are now seen as winter migrants, usually in SE. England, and several hundred were seen in October 1963. In their breeding areas, loud trumpeting calls attract attention. 'Dancing' ceremonies take place in which the cranes walk round in circles, bowing and stretching their necks, leaping up into the air with legs dangling. ('Dancing' also occurs outside the breeding season.) A Crane walking in a crouched position may just have left the nest. Calls from a chipping egg have been heard at a distance of 50 ft and the chicks have a piping call. Adult alarm is expressed by a harsh hissing.

**Water Rail** *Rallus aquaticus.* Pl. 55, 245

*Breeds* April–July, in reed-beds and dense aquatic vegetation on banks of rivers and lakes, in overgrown ditches and on marshy ground. (In British Isles, Europe and S. Scandinavia.)

*Nest* built by both sexes in tussock of sedge or reed, often in shallow water and sometimes raised well above the water-level; loosely matted structure of grass, leaves and herbage, well hidden from above, runway at side sometimes visible.

*Eggs* variable, often 6–11, pinkish cream to buff with dark markings. Incubated by both sexes for about 3 weeks.

*Nestlings* black down, similar to Spotted Crake. Leave nest shortly after hatching, tended by both parents. Fly after about 7 weeks.

*Adults* Corncrake-size, long red bill distinguishes it from other Rails; sexes similar but female more drab; bold black and white barred effect on flanks, white near tail, olive-brown upper-parts patterned with black, bluish-grey head, throat and breast. Looks surprisingly long-legged when in the open; flushes like Corncrake.

*Fledglings* under-parts are marked darker than adult.

*Hints* grunts and pig-like squeals, known as 'sharming', are usually the first indication of their presence. The male starts building several nests before one is finally accepted by the female. Courtship feeding on the nest has been observed and there is a record of a female leaving her eggs and walking round the male, making a crooning sound, rubbing her bill against the male's; the male was also seen preening the feathers on the female's neck. They usually sit close when incubating and do not always fly when startled but tend to run along the ground with a sinuous movement through cover. If surprised in the open, they tend to 'freeze', giving you a good view.

**Spotted Crake** *Porzana porzana*

*Breeds* mid May–June or July, in dense vegetation on swampy ground, such as fens, marshes, overgrown ditches and reedy meres. (Local in England. In most of Europe and S. Scandinavia. Absent in Spain.)
*Nest* on boggy ground, often hidden in a tussock of sedge, made of grass, leaves and bits of aquatic vegetation; probably built by both sexes. The tussock may be growing in shallow water.
*Eggs* 8–12, olive-buff with dark markings. Incubated by both sexes for about 3 weeks.
*Nestlings* long black down with greenish tips. Leave nest shortly after hatching, tended by both parents; 7–8 weeks fledgling period recorded.
*Adults* slightly smaller than Corncrake and Water Rail; sexes similar but female more drab; reminiscent of Corncrake but darker and olive-brown upper-parts are patterned with white (not black), grey under-parts with white spots visible at close range, barred flanks but plain buff near tail, yellowish bill with red base. Wings are brown rather than chestnut when seen in flight; dangling legs and weak flight as in Corncrake.
*Fledglings* drab version of adult with fewer white spots on breast.
*Hints* small numbers are usually seen on passage, but it is possible that they stay to breed in Britain and there are a number of counties with

breeding records in England and Wales. During the breeding season they call monotonously from cover; heard most frequently at dusk or dawn, the sound is described as like a sharp stroke of a lash cutting the air. A male has been seen strutting with long steps before a female, wings half-raised and neck stretched out. There are also chases along the ground, in the water and in the air. Owing to its secretive and skulking behaviour it is difficult to track down and the swampy nature of the nest-site makes searching difficult.

**Corncrake** *Crex crex*. Pl. **56**, *247*

*Breeds* late May–August, in hayfields and rough grass, amongst crops and sometimes on comparatively dry marshes. (In British Isles, most of Europe and S. Scandinavia. Absent most of Italy and Spain.)
*Nest* a hollow lined with grass and leaves, probably by female, hidden in rank vegetation which tends to form a tent-like 'roof'.
*Eggs* 8–12, greyish to reddish-brown with dark markings. Both sexes may incubate but female frequently recorded, for about 2 weeks.
*Nestlings* blackish-brown down. Leave nest shortly after hatching, tended by both parents. Fly after about 4 weeks.
*Adults* slightly smaller than Partridge; sexes similar, yellowish-buff upper-parts with dark patterning, some grey on head with a faint streak above the eye, reddish-brown barring on flanks and near tail. Chestnut wings show up in flight; when flushed, usually flies for short distance with legs dangling before flopping into cover.
*Fledglings* less clearly marked than adult.
*Hints* also known as Land Rails, they are so secretive in their habits that

little has been recorded about their display and behaviour at the nest. Constant creaking note 'crek crek', which is exceedingly monotonous, is usually the only sign that Corncrakes are in the neighbourhood, but they are very difficult to locate, even when calling continuously by day or night. Your only chance is to search through rough grass or crops, but if the area is in S. England, leave it undisturbed as they are now rare in the breeding season. Where farming is less mechanised, such as in parts of Wales, N. England, Scotland and Ireland, they are relatively common.

**Moorhen** *Gallinula chloropus.* Pl. **57**, *246*

*Breeds* March–August (occasionally in other months), in dense cover near fresh water, including built-up areas. (In British Isles, Europe and S. Scandinavia.)

*Nest* a platform of aquatic vegetation is built by both sexes in a clump of reeds, sedge, etc., usually close to water; nests are also built in bushes and trees, often overhanging the water. Old nests of other species such as Rook and Magpie are also used.

*Eggs* usually 5–11, creamy-white, greyish-buff or pinkish-buff suffused with reddish-brown. Incubated by both sexes for about 3 weeks.

*Nestlings* bare blue crown, black down with whitish marks round the head, under-parts sooty brown. Fed by both parents. Leave nest after 2–3 days, earlier if disturbed, tended by both parents. Fly after about 6 weeks.

*Adults* smaller than Coot; sexes similar; familiar dark water bird with bold white 'flashes' on either side of black centre to tail which jerks up and down as it swims; bright red frontal shield against forehead, red

bill with yellow tip. When taking off from water, feet patter along the surface.

*Fledglings* browner than adult, greenish bill and frontal shield, red colour develops during first winter.

*Hints* the nest is usually visible from a distance, but it is worth looking at any fallen branches with twigs protruding above the water as well as in clumps of vegetation. A loud 'kur-ruck' is usually heard when the Moorhen is startled. There are elaborate displays, fanning the white parts of the tail, bowing and pecking motions, one bird placing its foot on the back of another while it is bowing. Fights take place in the water, the birds apparently striking at each other with their feet and kicking up a lot of water. Platforms may be built as early as February.

**Coot** *Fulica atra.* Pl. **58**, *248*

*Breeds* March–August (occasionally earlier), in thick cover near large expanses of water, including quiet backwaters of rivers with suitable cover, sometimes by ponds and lakes in built-up areas. (In British Isles, Europe and S. Scandinavia.)

*Nest* both sexes build a bulky structure of aquatic plants, raised above the water-level, well-defined runway often visible. Artificial rafts also used.

*Eggs* usually 6–9, buff with dark markings. Incubated by both sexes for about 3 weeks.

*Nestlings* blackish down with reddish tips round the head, bare forehead, paler under-parts. Tended by both parents, leave nest after 3–4 days, feed themselves after about 4 weeks, independent after 8 weeks.

*Adults* larger and stockier than Moorhen, with rounded silhouette when swimming, apparently tailless; sexes similar, black plumage, narrow white wing-bar shows in flight, bold white frontal shield against forehead and white bill. Jerks head when swimming; patters along surface when alarmed.

*Fledglings* brownish-grey with whitish area near throat, no frontal shield.

*Hints* large winter flocks split up early in the year and there are noisy splashes of water as the Coots display. Fights are frequent, but sometimes the birds rush towards each other with necks extended and wings half raised, and then either shoot past each other or brake violently, churning up the water. They also 'stand up' in the water, striking it with their feet and smacking it with their wings. At the incubation stage it is usually easy to spot the nests as the birds are quite prominent when sitting on the bulky structure. Some nests appear to be floating but are usually firmly anchored. A number of platforms may be built in addition to the nest.

**Oystercatcher** *Haematopus ostralegus*. Pl. **59**, *249*

*Breeds* mid April–July, on sand, shingle and rocky shores; also inland on moors, agricultural land and in forest clearings. (In British Isles, Europe and Scandinavia.)

*Nest* both sexes make scrapes before one is selected by female; it may be scantily lined with small shells, shale or pebbles, rabbit droppings, often on slightly raised site, including stone wall; occasionally more substantial structure of heather or seaweed.

*Eggs* usually 3, buff to light brown with dark markings. Incubated chiefly by female for $3\frac{1}{2}$–4 weeks.

*Nestlings* marbled effect of greyish-buff, blackish-brown and white down. Leave nest after 1–2 days, tended by both parents. Fly after about 4 weeks.

*Adults* sexes similar, large black and

white wader, stockily built, long orange-red bill, crimson eye, pink legs; black head, wings and breast, white rump and under-parts. Bold black and white pattern in flight with broad white wing-bar.

*Fledglings* immature birds have white half-collar.

*Hints* loud piping displays in breeding areas cannot fail to attract attention. The Oystercatchers form a circle on the ground and run with quick, short steps, head and bill pointing down in a hunched attitude; the piping accelerates and often ends in a beautiful trill. Display flights with butterfly-like motion are also seen, accompanied by piping. Males also chase each other in the air, twisting and diving. There are many nests in the same area and the birds usually run off the nest, 'shoulders' hunched, as you appear; it is worth searching several yards back on the same line. Sometimes after running a short distance they squat down suddenly as though sitting on eggs; as you approach, the bird appears to be luring you on, crouching and running with wings half-spread and the tail fanned.

**Ringed Plover** *Charadrius hiaticula*. Pl. **60**, *250*

*Breeds* May–July (occasionally March–August), on sand and shingle beaches, pebbled shores of streams, rivers and lakes; also on arable land and sandy heaths. (In British Isles, Europe and Scandinavia.)

*Nest* male makes a number of scrapes, one of which is lined by female with small stones and shells, sometimes bits of local vegetation; nests are sometimes partially hidden by low plants.

*Eggs* usually 4, greyish-buff with dark markings. Incubated by both sexes for about $3\frac{1}{2}$ weeks.

*179*

*Nestlings* greyish-buff down with dark streaks. Leave nest shortly after hatching, tended by both parents. Fly after about 3½ weeks.

*Adults* small wader, roughly Lark-size; sexes similar, plump build, short orange bill with black tip, orange legs; brown upper-parts, white under-parts, black band contrasts with white breast, white collar, brown crown merges with black band above white forehead. Narrow white wing-bar shows in flight. Runs along the ground.

*Fledglings* less clearly marked than adult, incomplete collar, no black band above forehead; may be confused with young Little Ringed Plover and Kentish Plover.

*Hints* aggressive behaviour accompanied by fast, liquid 'toodle toodle toodle' calls, attracts attention to them in their breeding areas. There is a butterfly-type display flight and males crouch in front of females on the ground, puffing out their feathers, stretching their wings and depressing their fanned tails. Once you are accustomed to spotting them against the background, you sometimes notice them running in a crouched position as you appear; keep in mind where you first saw them, go beyond the point to which they ran and then sit down to watch for their return to the nest. Distraction display includes floundering along the ground.

## Little Ringed Plover *Charadrius dubius*. Pl. **61**, *251*

*Breeds* late April–July, inland on gravel and shingle banks, dried mud or flat waste ground, often near gravel-pits, locally on sandy coasts. (In S. and E. England, Europe and S. Scandinavia.)

*Nest* a depression in bare ground, several scrapes may be made before the female selects one and sometimes lines it with pebbles and bits of local vegetation.

*Eggs* usually 4, similar to Ringed Plover's but smaller. Incubated by both sexes for about 3½ weeks.

*Nestlings* similar to Ringed Plover but cinammon-buff rather than greyish-buff, black line encircles crown. Leave nest shortly after hatching, tended by both parents. Fly after 3–4 weeks.

*Adults* smaller than Ringed Plover with different pattern on head in which the black band on the head is separated from brown crown by narrow white band; yellow ring encircling the eye is visible at close range. No white wing-bar in flight.

*Fledglings* less clearly marked than adult; no wing-bar helps to identify from young Ringed Plover and Kentish Plover.

*Hints* any bare ground surrounding a gravel-pit is worth searching, mainly in southern and eastern counties of England but possibly farther north. There is a butterfly-type display flight and there are frequent 'tirra tirra tirra' calls and a high-pitched 'tee-u' alarm-note, with the emphasis on the second syllable. This becomes particularly emphatic when the parents are warning the young of the approach of an intruder; distraction display is often observed, and it is advisable to watch where you put your feet instead of following the adult as it runs along in a crouched position, flicking its wings and drooping them along the ground. Earlier in the season, an adult often flies over to meet you as you arrive, swerving away before you get too close.

## Kentish Plover *Charadrius alexandrinus*

*Breeds* May–July, on shingle beaches and sandy shores along the coast,

**Kentish Plover**

also on mudflats and saltings a little distance from the sea. (In Channel Isles, Europe and SW. Sweden. Has bred SE. England.)

*Nest* several scrapes may be made before the female selects one, often unlined, sometimes scantily lined with bits of grass and local vegetation; also recorded on low wall and bare rock.

*Eggs* usually 3, buff with black markings. Incubated by both sexes for about 3½ weeks.

*Nestlings* similar to Ringed Plover but paler. Leave nest shortly after hatching, tended by both parents. Fly after about 3½ weeks.

*Adults* slightly smaller than Ringed Plover but appear to be longer legged, legs blackish rather than yellowish and upper-parts paler than Ringed Plover; male's black markings across white breast are confined to two dark patches at the side (collar not entire), black patch above white forehead merges into rufous crown; female lacks black patch above forehead and side patches on her breast are brownish. Narrow white wing-bar shows in flight.

*Fledglings* very similar to young Ringed Plover but legs are darker.

*Hints* aggressive note in breeding area is described as a fast, twanging 'dwee dwee dwee'; the alarm-note is a series of 'kittups', sometimes slurred together. The display flight is similar to Little Ringed Plover's, accompanied by a trill which accelerates. During the early stages of incubation they usually leave the nest quietly, running in a crouched position. The nest is often on a slight ridge and the eggs may be buried in the sand. The parents become much more demonstrative when chicks are present and shamming injury, as a distraction display, is often seen.

**Dotterel** *Eudromias morinellus.* Pl. 63, 253

*Breeds* late May–July, on bare stony ground with grass tussocks and stunted heather on mountain-tops which have broad spurs; also on tundra. (In Scotland and N. Scandinavia. Local in Italy.)

*Nest* both sexes make scrapes before one is selected by the female and sometimes scantily lined with bits of moss, lichen and grass, often on a slight ridge.

*Eggs* usually 3, buff or reddish-brown with dark markings. Incubated almost entirely by male for 3½–4 weeks.

*Nestlings* marbled effect of sandy, greyish-black and whitish down. Leave nest after about 1 day, tended chiefly by male. Fly after about 4 weeks.

*Adults* slightly smaller than Golden Plover; male smaller and more drab than female, broad white eye-stripes join at nape, making a characteristic V-pattern, whitish throat, brown breast separated from rufous under-parts by white band. Faint wing-bar in flight, short-tailed silhouette.

*Fledglings* drab version of adult, patterning rather blurred.

*Hints* now chiefly confined to Scottish Highlands in Britain, they are often remarkably tame during the breeding season, but owing to the blending of their plumage with the background they may be missed unless you happen to be near a nest. The female takes the initiative in display flights, chasing the male and leading him to a ridge where the nest will eventually be made. Display flight includes fast wing-beats alternating with glides, accompanied by penetrating 'wit wit' calls. The alarm-note is described as a twittering whistle or a soft 'peep peep'. The Dotterel usually runs fast along the ground, raising its wings before taking off. To locate the nest it is necessary to watch the male rather than the female. The male has an elaborate distraction display to divert attention from eggs or young, including a crouching run when it looks like a small mammal, flying aggressively towards the intruder and then flopping down and floundering along the ground as though its wings were broken.

## Golden Plover *Pluvialis apricaria*. Pl. **64**, *254*

*Breeds* mid April–June or May–July according to latitude, on moors with rough grass, peat and short heather; on tundra, barren heaths and morasses in pine forests; usually on high ground in British Isles; from sea-level upwards in Scandinavia; also in Denmark and Germany. (Has bred Holland.)

*Nest* scrapes are made by both sexes, the female selects one and lines it with a few twigs, lichen and grass, usually on a slight hummock in peat and often associated with burnt patches of heather.

*Eggs* usually 4, varying from greenish-buff to reddish-brown with dark markings. Incubated by both sexes for about 4 weeks.

*Nestlings* marbled effect of golden, black and white down. Leave nest after 1–2 days, tended by both parents. Fly after about 4½ weeks.

*Adults* roughly Lapwing-size; sexes similar, typical round-headed appearance of Plover, dark upper-parts with golden and black spangled effect. Northern birds have black areas on face and under-parts which contrast sharply with white areas. Southern birds have some black on face and under-parts but patterning is blurred. Sharply angled wings in flight show white undersides.

*Fledglings* paler than adult and less clearly marked; pale underside of wing distinguishes from young Grey Plover.

*Hints* on arrival in the breeding areas there are skirmishes between males, which run at each other, crouching and raising their wings before 'leap-frogging' over one another. Males also hover over females. Display flight includes flying high above the territory with deliberate wing-beats, often ending in a steep dive, accompanied by a wailing note described as 'per-pee-oo'. When walking over a possible breeding area at the incubation stage, the off-duty bird often flies towards you, uttering a piping alarm 'tlee-oo'; try to watch the ground for signs of the other parent slipping off the nest, even though the hummocky terrain makes this difficult. Distraction display from eggs and chicks may include lying on the ground, tail spread and wings thrashing.

## Lapwing *Vanellus vanellus*. Pl. **62**, *252*

*Breeds* late March–June, in ploughed fields, pasture and rough grassland where there is not much cover; also on marshes, moors, dunes and shingle. (In British Isles, most of Europe and S. Scandinavia.)

*Nest* male makes several scrapes, female selects one, lining it with bits of local vegetation, usually on a slight ridge.

*Eggs* usually 4, buff to dark brown with dark markings. Incubated chiefly by female for about 4 weeks.

*Nestlings* marbled effect of brown, black and white down. Leave nest shortly after hatching, tended by both parents. Fly after 4–5 weeks.

*Adults* familiar black and white wader; sexes similar, iridescent greenish-black upper-parts, black breast, white under-parts, black wispy crest, rufous-buff under tail. Broad rounded wings reveal sparkling white undersides in flight.

*Fledglings* short crest, drab version of adult.

*Hints* wheezing 'peewit' calls are heard as the male gives a spectacular display flight, rising with deliberate wing-beats, making a throbbing sound and then diving, rolling and even somersaulting over the territory. On the ground, display includes making scrapes and 'rocking', swaying with wings up and down. There may be several nests in the same area and it is sometimes possible to spot a bird on the nest with binoculars as the site is often on slightly raised ground. Sometimes an intruder is mobbed and there is also a form of distraction display in which the wings are held high, stretched and vibrated, and also flapped when lying on the ground. This species is also known as Peewit and Green Plover.

**Turnstone** *Arenaria interpres.* Pl. **65**, **255**

*Breeds* May–June or June–July according to latitude, mainly on islands off the coast on dry stony ground with or without low-growing cover. (In Denmark and Scandinavia.)

*Nest* varies from a simple depression to a more substantial structure of leaves and grass, usually scantily lined with bits of local plants; also recorded on bare rock and in Puffin's burrow.

*Eggs* usually 4, greenish with dark markings. Incubated by both sexes, probably for about 3 weeks.

*Nestlings* marbled effect of yellowish-grey and black down, dark patches on side of neck, white under-parts. Tended by both parents, fledging period unknown.

*Adults* stockier and slightly smaller than Redshank; sexes similar, 'tortoiseshell' upper-parts, whitish head with black markings, blackish band across white breast; orange legs, stout but pointed black bill. A pattern of black and white Vs in flight.

*Fledglings* drab version of adult.

*Hints* breeding has been suspected but never proved in N. Scotland and Shetland; numbers are seen outside the breeding season along rocky coasts, feeding along the tide-line. The usual note when disturbed in the winter is a twittering 'kitty-kitty-kitty', but in the breeding areas this becomes a rippling song. There are noisy chases in the air and along the ground, but no elaborate display. June is said to be the best month for finding nests in S. Scandinavia, sometimes several pairs nesting in the same area. The incubating bird usually slips off the nest unobtrusively when warned of the approach of an intruder by the mate; they tend to be reluctant to return, but watching from a distance of at least 50 yds is recommended. The adults are recorded as coming very close if the chicks are handled.

**Temminck's Stint** *Calidris temminckii*. Pl. **66**

*Breeds* mid June–July, in short turf and on tundra with low-growing vegetation such as dwarf willow, on banks of fresh water and islets. (In N. Scandinavia. Has bred England and Scotland.)

*Nest* a shallow depression, roughly 2½ in. wide, sometimes scantily lined with grass and a few leaves by female.

*Eggs* usually 4, greenish-grey with dark markings. Incubated by both sexes, period unknown.

*Nestlings* buff and black down with spangled effect. Tended by both parents, fledging period unknown.

*Adults* smaller than Dunlin, slightly smaller than Little Stint; sexes similar, mousey-grey above, greyish-white below; legs vary from greenish to brownish but are not black as in Little Stint. Tends to 'tower' like a Snipe when flushed; faint white wing-bar and white outer tail-feathers show in flight.

*Fledglings* buff 'scaly' appearance on upper-parts at close range.

*Hints* comparatively small numbers are seen on passage in Britain, mainly in the south and east, but attempts at nesting have been recorded in Scottish Highlands and Yorkshire. During the breeding season a high-pitched trilling song is delivered either from a perch, such as a stone or a low bush, or in moth-like display flight. Wings are frequently flicked up and down, showing the pale underside, and are sometimes held above the back while trilling continues. Searching along Norwegian fjords may yield several nests in the same area. Distraction display, simulating a broken wing, has been observed and sometimes both the parents run to within a few yards of the intruder when chicks are present.

**Dunlin** *Calidris alpina*

*Breeds* mid May–June, usually near the coast on marshes and moorland, also in meadows. (In British Isles, Denmark, N. Germany and Scandinavia. Has bred Holland.)

*Nest* a neat little hollow or a simple scrape, lined with grass and leaves, usually well hidden in a tuft of grass near water.

*Eggs* 4, colour varying from bluish-green to buff or olive-brown, often with dark markings. Incubated by both sexes for about 3 weeks.

**Dunlin**

*Nestlings* marbled effect of yellowish-buff, tawny and black down. Tended by both parents which brood them for a few days and then remain within calling distance as the chicks hide in vegetation. Fly after about 3 weeks.

*Adults* much smaller than Redshank, dumpy and 'round-shouldered' in appearance, fairly long bill which may have slight downward curve at tip; sexes similar, chestnut back with black streaks, black 'spade' marking on white breast. White wing-bar and edges of tail show in flight.

*Fledglings* resemble adult but have dark streaks on flanks and breast.

*Hints* trilling song is heard as they circle over the breeding area, several Dunlins twisting and turning as they fly after each other; the male also has a hovering display flight in which it rises and loses height like Skylark. Nests are difficult to find and the chicks tend to hide in little gullies after the first few days when they are brooded by the adults. Adults' attempt to distract your attention by running towards you and then away again when the eggs are either hatched or about to hatch. Breeding records in Britain come mainly from Scotland and northern counties of England, but there are some from West Country moors and from a number of Welsh counties.

**Ruff** *Philomachus pugnax*. Pl. **67**, *256*

*Breeds* May–June or June–July according to latitude; on marshes and damp meadows in southern part of range, among damp birch and willow scrub and dry tundra in the north. (In most of N. Europe and Scandinavia. Has bred England.)

*Nest* a hollow hidden in a tussock of long grass, neatly lined with grass by the female, or in open site in the north.

*Eggs* 4, usually olive-brown or brownish-yellow, with dark markings, but very variable. Incubated by female for about 3 weeks.

*Nestlings* black and pinkish-buff down with golden spangled effect. Leave nest shortly after hatching, tended by female. Fly after 2–3 weeks.

*Adults* roughly Redshank-size, male (Ruff) larger than female (Reeve); male has remarkable ear-tufts and ruff which can be raised; colour combinations include black, purple, chestnut, buff and white, some thoroughly mottled in appearance. Female has no adornments, 'scaly' pattern on upper-parts, buff under-parts. In flight both sexes show narrow white wing-bar and white oval patches on either side of tail.

*Fledglings* somewhat similar to adult female.

*Hints* they used to breed regularly in E. England during the last century, but are now normally seen on passage, chiefly in the south and east. Displaying Ruffs are seen from time to time in East Anglia. In their regular breeding haunts, such as in Holland, displays reach their peak in May. Males gather at a display area and rush towards each other as though going in to attack, raising their ruffs, flapping their wings, often turning aside and crouching, then suddenly sinking down on the ground in a 'frozen attitude'. Sparring can be seen at close range as the Ruffs appear to take no notice of human intruders. Nests are usually some distance from the display areas, hidden in long grass; sometimes a runway in the grass gives away the site. If the female flies around you, calling constantly, there are probably young in the vicinity.

**Redshank** *Tringa totanus*. Pl. **68**, *257*

*Breeds* mid April–June, in damp meadows near rivers, rough grassland, moors and marshes, including saltings. (In British Isles, most of Europe and Scandinavia. Local in France and Italy.)

*Nest* several scrapes are made by both sexes in tufts of vegetation, the female lining one with dry grass; the long tuft usually forms a tent-like structure above the nest.

*Eggs* usually 4, creamy-buff or yellowish-brown with dark markings. Incubated by both sexes for about 3 weeks.

*Nestlings* marbled effect of buff and black down. Leave nest shortly after hatching, tended by both parents; transport of young by adults recorded. Fly after about 4 weeks.

*Adults* considerably smaller than Curlew, medium-sized wader; sexes similar, orange-red legs, long reddish bill with black tip, brown upper-parts marked with black, white under-parts spotted and barred. Dark wings show white hind edge in flight, white rump and barred tail. 'Bobs' when nervous.

*Fledglings* yellow legs, plumage more heavily marked than adult.

*Hints* loud alarm-call, 'tew tew tew', alerts all the other birds in the neighbourhood. A musical whistling version of this call is heard frequently from the breeding areas and these waders are often seen perching on posts. The males usually arrive before the females. Display flight above the territory consists of a fluttering ascent followed by planing down with wings arched. The male runs after the female on the ground and, when she pauses, he raises his wings high above his back, 'fanning' the air with them, then runs towards her with a formal high-stepping action. When walking over a possible breeding area, the Redshank usually rises silently while you are some distance away; it often runs before taking off, but try to mark this place and search every tuft, bearing in mind that it is usually hidden from sight under the tent-like 'roof'. If the adults fly towards you, calling loudly, circling overhead, there are probably chicks squatting in the grass near you.

**Greenshank** *Tringa nebularia*. Pl. **69**, *258*

*Breeds* May–June, on Highland moors, with or without trees, on dead ground with rotting stumps, rock outcrops, heather and peat runnels in N. Scotland; in wooded marshes and forests with lichen growth on forest floor in N. Scandinavia.

*Nest* on the ground, usually near a fallen branch or landmark of some kind; female makes a scrape and lines it with bits of local vegetation, occasionally with rabbit or hare droppings.

*Eggs* usually 4, olive-buff, occasionally reddish-brown, with dark markings. Incubated by both sexes for about 3½ weeks.

*Nestlings* marbled effect of greyish-white, buff and brown down. Leave nest shortly after hatching, tended by both parents. Fly after about 4 weeks.

*Adults* slightly larger and greyer than Redshank; sexes similar, long greenish legs, long blackish bill slightly turned up; grey upper-parts marked with black, dark spots and bars on white under-parts. Extensive area of white shows on back in flight, no wing-bar, legs extend beyond tail, which is faintly barred. 'Bobs' when nervous.

*Fledglings* darker than adult.

*Hints* this nest is regarded as exceptionally difficult to find but if you are determined to see Greenshanks at the nest and can visit the Scottish Highlands, you cannot do better than read a detailed account of the technique for watching and listening described by Desmond Nethersole-Thompson in *The Greenshank* (Collins, 1951). Display flights occur in which both sexes climb high, turn and swerve as though 'pair-skating' in the air, often ending in a steep dive; there are also fast zigzagging pursuits at a low height. The male often perches in a tree or on a stump, flutters up into the air above the female at the nest-site, then lands on another perch and vibrates his wings, held high over his back. During incubation when the sexes change over at the nest, excited 'chip chip chip' calls continue for some time.

Usual call-note when flushed is a ringing 'tew tew tew', pitched lower than Redshank's. Distraction display has been observed.

## Green Sandpiper *Tringa ochropus*

*Breeds* mid April–June or mid May–July, according to latitude, mainly in mature forests which are on swampy ground. (In E. Germany and most of Scandinavia. Has bred England, Scotland and Holland.)

*Nest* usually in old nest of other species, such as Song Thrush, Wood Pigeon, Jay and Crow; moss or lichen may be added as lining. Nests have been recorded on the ground.

*Eggs* 4, greenish or buff with a few dark markings. Incubated by both sexes, apparently chiefly by female, for about 3 weeks.

**Green Sandpiper**

*Nestlings* similar to Wood Sandpiper but under-parts are whiter. Leave nest shortly after hatching, tended by both parents, often chiefly by male. Probably fly after about 3 weeks.

*Adults* slightly larger and much stockier than Common Sandpiper and Wood Sandpiper; sexes similar, characteristic black and white appearance; blackish upper-parts (iridescent green at close range), pure white rump, tail barred with black at tip. No wing-bar, blackish underside of wing shows in flight and legs do not extend beyond the tail. 'Bobs' head and tail.

*Fledglings* dark feathers on upper-parts are 'outlined' in buff.

*Hints* mostly seen on passage in the autumn, but courtship display is seen fairly regularly by lochs with trees in N. Scotland and there is a recent breeding record from this area. The display flight is similar to that of Wood Sandpiper, but gliding descent is said to be particularly steep. Trilling song sounds like 'titti-lool, titti-looi'. A 'leap-frog' display has also been observed in which one bird stood behind another with its wings raised and tail fanned, then fluttered over the other bird which then repeated the 'leap-frog'. When flushed, it usually flies up and 'towers' like a Snipe, calling 'tit tlooet tlooet'. When disturbed from the nest during incubation they usually fly away silently but when young are present both parents make themselves very obvious, dashing from tree to tree and calling in a frenzied fashion.

## Wood Sandpiper *Tringa glareola.* Pl. *70, 259*

*Breeds* May–June, often on marshy ground in forests, also on moors, heaths and tundra. (Local in N. Scotland. In Denmark, E. Germany and Scandinavia. Has bred Holland.)

*Nest* usually a depression on the ground in damp grass, lined with grass and a few dead leaves; also, in trees in nests of other species, such as Fieldfare, Great Grey Shrike and Waxwing.

*Eggs* 4, pale green or buff with dark markings. Incubated by both sexes for about 3 weeks.

*Nestlings* marbled effect of cinammon

and blackish-brown down, broad eye-stripe. Leave nest shortly after hatching, tended by both parents, often chiefly by male. Fly after about 3 weeks.

*Adults* smaller than Green Sandpiper, about same size as Common Sandpiper; sexes similar, delicately built with round head and thin neck; brownish upper-parts with white dotted lines running from either side of black crown down to white rump, barred tail; greyish-white underwing shows in flight, no wing-bar, legs extending well beyond tail.

*Fledglings* faint white speckles on upper-parts, like adult in winter, and some reddish-buff spots on sides of body.

*Hints* a few pairs have recently nested on moors with trees in N. Scotland, but most Wood Sandpipers are seen on passage in SE. England. When flushed it gives a shrill 'chiff chiff chiff', but in high display flight the song is reminiscent of Woodlark. Both sexes wheel about with quivering wings, ending in a glide with tail spread and legs held apart. They sit close when incubating. When young are present, both parents demonstrate at an intruder, flying overhead, constantly calling, and suddenly pitching down.

## Common Sandpiper *Tringa hypoleucos*. Pl. **71**, *261*

*Breeds* May–June, along banks and shores of hill streams, rivers, lakes and sea lochs, less frequently in lowlands, occasionally some distance from water. (In British Isles, Europe and Scandinavia.)

*Nest* a small depression, lined with grass and a few dead leaves, either in shelter of vegetation or in open site, usually near water. Nests also recorded in pollarded willow, old nest of Ring Ouzel, amongst vegetation on cliff ledges, on railway embankment and in rabbit burrow.

*Eggs* 4, greyish-buff with dark markings. Incubated by both sexes for about 3 weeks.

*Nestlings* greyish-buff down marbled with black and brown. Leave nest shortly after hatching, tended by both parents. Fly after about 4 weeks.

*Adults* smaller than Redshank, sexes similar; remarkably trim appearance with uniform dark upper-parts and white under-parts. Frequently 'bobs' head and tail; flies low over the water, wings drooping when gliding, showing white wing-bar, dark rump, dark centre of tail with white sides.

*Fledglings* darker than adult on upper-parts with feathers 'outlined' in buff.

*Hints* usual note when flushed is a shrill 'twee see see' but during courtship display a trilling song is heard. Males run along behind females, wings raised high over the back, sometimes taking off and flying in wide circles with a fluttering wing action; they also pursue females in the air, following an erratic course with deliberate wing-beats. When searching along a bank near water, the Sandpiper usually flushes at close range and flies low over shallow water, landing on some prominent spot and then 'bobbing' its head and tail. When returning to the nest they land some distance from it and run the rest of the way. Distraction display has often been observed.

## Black-tailed Godwit *Limosa limosa*. Pl. **72**, *260*

*Breeds* May–June, in damp meadows, rough grass on marshes, also on moors and dunes. (Local in E. England, Belgium, France and S. Sweden. In Denmark, Germany and

Holland. Has bred Scotland, Spain and Switzerland.)

*Nest* a scrape made by both sexes in grass, heather and rushes; usually in shelter of some kind of vegetation on dunes, lined with leaves and down.

*Eggs* 4, olive-brown, usually with dark markings. Incubated by both sexes for about 3½ weeks.

*Nestlings* marbled effect of buff, reddish and brown down. Leave nest shortly after hatching, tended closely by both parents. Fly after about 4 weeks.

**Black-tailed Godwit**

*Adults* slightly smaller than Curlew, much more elegant; sexes similar, long-legged, long straight bill which is sometimes slightly up-turned; broad white wing-bar shows in flight, tail is black and white, long legs trail behind. (Bar-tailed Godwit has no wing-bar and legs barely show behind the barred tail.)

*Fledglings* brownish-grey upper-parts, reddish tone on neck and breast.

*Hints* small numbers have bred regularly in East Anglia since 1952 and sporadically elsewhere. Every effort is being made to leave suspected breeding sites undisturbed in the hope that this species will re-establish itself. It is well established in Denmark and Holland where the Godwits arrive during March. They are particularly noisy in the breeding areas, circling overhead, climbing rapidly at first, then changing to slow wing-beats and tilting the body, uttering a slower call. There is a

nasal, two-syllable call like a Lapwing's and a more musical 'tittering' sound. There may be several pairs nesting in the same area, spaced out at roughly 10–30 yds. The adults guard their young closely, often giving an alarm-call from a fence-post and then either flying at the intruder, calling loudly, or running round him in circles.

**Curlew** *Numenius arquata.* Pl. **73**, *262*

*Breeds* late April–July, on rough grassland, moors, damp meadows, heaths, dunes, amongst crops and occasionally on shingle by rivers. (In British Isles, Europe and Scandinavia.)

*Nest* a scrape in low vegetation, sometimes scantily lined with dry grass or bits of heather.

*Eggs* 4, olive-green with dark markings. Incubated by both sexes for about 4 weeks.

*Nestlings* blackish-brown and buff down. Leave nest soon after hatching but remain near it for a day or two, closely guarded by both parents. Fly after about 5 weeks.

*Adults* sexes similar, large greyish-brown wader with long legs and long bill which curves downwards; plumage is streaked except for whitish rump. Occasionally perches in bush or tree in breeding areas.

*Fledglings* resemble adult except for shorter bill.

*Hints* melancholy 'coor-li' call is its most familiar note but a bubbling trill is a sign that courtship may be under way. The males appear to arrive in the breeding areas before the females; they fly in wide circles, wing-beats comparatively slow for a wader, then hover briefly and break into trilling song, planing down on extended wings. In possible breeding localities, it is worth watching for the males from early February. When the females arrive, the males walk close behind them in a crouched position, circling round them when they stop. When walking over a likely nesting area, it is worth squatting down every so often as sometimes the bird's head with its characteristic long curved bill can be seen silhouetted against the sky. During early stages of incubation they usually leave the nest silently when you are still about 100 yds away, often running some distance before taking flight. Later, when the eggs are near to hatching, the parents fly round you, calling excitedly. Distraction display has been observed. This species is known locally as Whaup.

## Whimbrel *Numenius phaeopus*

*Breeds* late May–June, on moors amongst boulders, rough grass and poor heather in Shetland; also, meadows and heaths, rough grass on verges of woods and on open ground beyond tree-limit amongst hummocks of peat and stunted vegetation in N. Scandinavia.

**Whimbrel**

*Nest* a scrape on open ground amongst poor vegetation, scantily lined with feathers, grass, moss or bits of local vegetation.

*Eggs* usually 4, olive-brown with dark markings. Incubated by both sexes for nearly 4 weeks.

*Nestlings* similar to Curlew except for patterning on head like adult. Leave nest shortly after hatching, tended by both parents. Fly after about 4 weeks.

*Adults* sexes similar, smaller than Curlew, but very similar in appearance except for pale streak on crown which separates two dark stripes; bill is slightly shorter.

*Fledglings* resemble adult but plumage looks 'brighter'.

*Hints* as soon as the call-note is heard, a rippling 'whinny' made up of seven whistling notes, Whimbrel are easily identified from Curlew. They call repeatedly on arrival in the breeding area. The male has a display flight which is similar to that of the Curlew, accompanied by a trilling song, planing down to earth or tumbling down in a zigzagging descent. During incubation the off-duty bird stands guard on a boulder or prominence of some kind, including the branch of a tree where this is available. In the early stages both birds leave the area of the nest at the first sign of an intruder; in the later stages of incubation or when the chicks have hatched, they are much bolder in defence of their family, approaching within a few yards of the intruder, either hovering or running and fluttering about on the ground.

## Woodcock *Scolopax rusticola*. Pl. 75, *263*

*Breeds* mid March–July, in open woods and rough ground with some cover in secluded areas with dry ground for nesting and marshy patches for feeding. (In British Isles, most of Europe and Scandinavia. Absent most of Italy and Spain.)

*Nest* a scrape lined with plenty of dead leaves, often by a tree in some kind of ground cover.

*Eggs* 4, greyish-white to light brown, with dark markings. Incubated by female for about 3 weeks.

*Nestlings* marbled effect of rufous and buff down with pale forehead and broad streak over eye. Tended by female who often carries them from the nest when danger threatens, apparently clasping them between her thighs. Fly after about 3 weeks.

*Adults* larger than Snipe, sexes similar; plumage is perfectly camouflaged against dead leaves; domed head with stripes running across it, long straight bill which is stouter than Snipe's. Rounded wings in flight with bill pointing down, dumpy silhouette as it dodges between trees.

*Fledglings* resemble adult in the field.

*Hints* very difficult to spot on the nest, although sometimes a round black eye can be seen in a patch of dead leaves. Dusk or dawn are the best times at which to listen for the 'roding' display flight of males over their territories; wing-beats are much slower than in normal flight and there are croaks and high-pitched 'sneezing' calls. During the later stages of incubation the female sits so close that you nearly tread on her as she crouches at your feet, her large eyes set far back in her head. Distraction display takes various forms, including a laboured flight and the bird lying on its side, flapping one wing and 'squeaking'.

**Snipe** *Gallinago gallinago.* Pl. **76, 264**

*Breeds* April–June (occasionally March–August), on marshy ground with rushes and sedges, less frequently on moors amongst heather. (In British Isles, most of Europe and Scandinavia. Absent most of Italy and Spain.)

*Nest* a scrape hidden in clump of rushes or tussock of grass, sometimes on dry ground, lined with grass.

*Eggs* usually 4, olive-brown with dark markings. Incubated by female for nearly 3 weeks.

*Nestlings* marbled chestnut and black down with a silver spangled effect. Leave nest shortly after hatching, tended by both parents; a few records exist of adults carrying young. Fly after about 2 weeks.

*Adults* smaller than Woodcock, sexes similar; richly mottled plumage of black, buff and reddish-brown with golden stripes down the back; stripes on head run lengthways rather than across it as in Woodcock. Zigzagging flight, long slender bill hangs down, some white shows in tail.

*Fledglings* resemble adult in the field.

*Hints* walking through an area where Snipe are breeding you hear a monotonous rhythmic 'chicka chicka' call, delivered both on the ground and in flight, but the most spectacular display is given in the air. The Snipe climbs rapidly and circles, then twists and dives down at an angle, producing a vibrant 'drumming' sound, like a small boy blowing against paper over a comb; this is caused by air passing through the outer tail-feathers. Nests are well hidden in rough ground and you have to look carefully before putting your foot down or you may tread on a chick 'frozen' in the grass, relying on its protective coloration. The female tends to sit close during incubation and may flush at your feet, taking off in a fast zigzagging flight, giving a hoarse call. The drumming display reaches its height in May and June, and may continue after dark. Distraction display has been observed.

**Black-winged Stilt** *Himantopus himantopus.* Pl. **74**, *265*

*Breeds* late April–June, on marshy ground in shallow water or on boggy verges of pools and rivers, also amongst plants on dried mud. (In Spain. Local in France and Italy. Has bred England, Belgium, Germany and Holland.)

*Nest* varies from a shallow depression surrounded by bits of local vegetation to a more bulky structure of stalks, sometimes lined with bits of wool, bents and small white pebbles; usually near or in water, but site may dry out.

*Eggs* 3–4, buffish with dark markings. Incubated by both sexes for 3–4 weeks.

*Nestlings* greyish-brown with black speckles and lines on head and along the body, white under-parts. Leave nest shortly after hatching, tended by both parents. Fly after about 4 weeks.

*Adults* slightly smaller than Avocet, disproportionately long pink legs, long straight black bill; both sexes have dark upper-parts contrasting with white under-parts; female is brownish-black, male is blacker with small black area on back of head. Narrow triangular wings with dark undersides, legs extend well beyond tail in flight.

*Fledglings* browner than adult.

*Hints* every year a few pairs are seen on passage in Britain but in 1945 two pairs bred on a Nottinghamshire sewage bed amongst chickweed. There is a 'dancing' display in which the Stilts prance up and down on one spot and round each other, flapping their wings. In regular breeding areas there are a number of nests in the same neighbourhood. Noisy alarm-calls, 'kik-kik-kik', accelerating into a sound like a puppy yelping, usually greet an intruder while the parents hover and flutter about with legs dangling or 'dance' along the ground. The young skulk in cover during the parents' noisy demonstration.

**Avocet** *Recurvirostra avosetta.* Pl. **77**, **78**, *267*

*Breeds* late April–July, on salt-marshes, mudflats, sand-banks near brackish pools and in low-lying meadows near the coast. (Local in E. England and Italy. In Denmark, S. France, Germany, Holland, S. Spain and S. Sweden. Has bred Belgium and Ireland.)

*Nest* several scrapes are made by both sexes before one is selected by female on raised ground near water; the depression may be unlined, scantily lined or a comparatively bulky structure of reeds.

*Eggs* 4, buff with dark markings. Incubated by both sexes for about 3½ weeks.

*Nestlings* greyish-buff with marbled effect of black and brown down, mainly white under-parts, bill straight at first. Leave nest shortly after hatching, tended by both parents. Fly after about 6 weeks.

*Fledglings* browner than adult.

*Adults* large black and white wader with long, delicately up-curved black bill and long greyish-blue legs; sexes similar. Wades quite deep, 'up-ends' like a duck when swimming; in flight, neck is curved and legs extend beyond tail.

*Hints* the easiest way to see Avocets in Britain is to visit the R.S.P.B. reserves at Minsmere and Havergate in Suffolk. (Apply for permit to R.S.P.B., The Lodge, Sandy, Beds.) Communal ceremonies take place in which Avocets form a circle, bowing towards the centre, swinging their heads from side to side as though feeding in typical manner; these displays usually end in fights, the birds attempting to strike each other with their wings. When nest-building, a pair stands close together, side by side, bowing and pecking at objects, throwing them to one side with a jerk of the head. There are many nests in the same area and if you walk through a colony you are likely to be mobbed. The typical call- and alarm-note is 'kloo-it'. Distraction display includes floundering about in the water.

## Red-necked Phalarope *Phalaropus lobatus*. Pl. **79**, *266*

*Breeds* late May–July, on marshy ground scattered with shallow pools on the shores or lochs and on islets in rivers. (Local in N. Scotland and W. Ireland. In N. Scandinavia.)

*Nest* a scrape, about 3 in. wide, in a tussock near water, lined with grass and leaves; both sexes take part in making scrapes.

*Eggs* usually 4, varying from buff to dark brown, generally with dark markings. Incubated by male for nearly 3 weeks.

*Nestlings* marbled effect of buff and black down. Leave nest shortly after hatching, tended by male, female sometimes present. Fly after about 2½ weeks.

*Adults* smaller than Common Sandpiper, sexes similar but male is more drab than female; delicately built with long fine bill; reddish patch on side of neck contrasts with white throat; grey head, greyish-buff upper-parts with whitish streaks, white under-parts. Frequently seen spinning round in the water, like a top, darting its head sideways.

*Fledglings* rather similar to adult in winter with dark upper-parts, white wing-bar showing up well in flight.

*Hints* Shetland and Orkney are the best-known breeding localities in Scotland and it is worth looking closely at every bird that looks like a small gull swimming on a pool. The female arrives first and occupies a territory, defending a pool against other females, making ceremonial flights in which she rises up from the pool, calling 'whit whit whit', with rapidly beating wings for a few seconds and then lands on the water, neck stretched vertically. The females pursue the males when they arrive and take the initiative in making scrapes. If you see both male and female making scrapes, try to mark these down as one of them is likely to be the nest. Searching the ground on the margins of pools may be successful. Distraction display by the male has been recorded.

A visit to the R.S.P.B. Balranald Bird Reserve on North Uist provides an opportunity of seeing these birds in the breeding season without risk of disturbing them.

## Stone Curlew *Burhinus oedicnemus*. Pl. **80**, *268*

*Breeds* mid April–August, on sandy heaths and dunes, chalk and flint arable land or downs, shingle-banks and in young conifer plantations. (In E. and S. England. In most of Europe. Absent Denmark.)

*Nest* both sexes make scrapes in bare ground, often near a patch of vegetation, lined sometimes with a few stones or rabbit droppings.

*Eggs* 2, creamy to brown with dark markings. Incubated by both sexes for nearly 4 weeks.

*Nestlings* sandy-buff down with black streaks, greyish under-parts. Leave nest shortly after hatching, tended by both parents. Fly after about 6 weeks.

*Adults* Wood Pigeon-size, stockily built, sexes similar; round-headed like a plover, pale yellow legs with thick joint; mainly sandy-brown, appears to have one white wing-bar when standing, but two white bars show in flight; large yellow eye, bill yellow and black.

*Fledglings* similar to adult.

*Hints* take a walk at dusk in likely breeding area in April and listen for rather melancholy 'cooree' calls which are reminiscent of Curlew. There is a bowing display and the males sometimes raise their wings, 'skipping' along in front of the females; fights between males include 'leap-frogging' over one another. During incubation the pair is extremely wary, one bird standing guard in the vicinity of the nest while the other is sitting; the off-duty bird is usually noticed first as it runs fast along the ground before taking flight. You naturally tend to watch this bird and therefore miss the other slipping off the nest, but it is worth marking the spot where the bird was first seen, preferably with a stick as the terrain is usually featureless, and then search in widening circles. Collections of small stones or rabbit droppings are worth examining as possible nest lining before the eggs are laid. Distraction display has been recorded. This species is known locally as Thick-knee and Norfolk Plover.

**Great Skua** *Stercorarius skua*. Pl. 82, 269

*Breeds* mid May–July, on bare moor-land and rough ground with tussocks of grass, usually near the sea, on Fair Isle, Orkney, Shetland, St Kilda and Outer Hebrides, locally on mainland of N. Scotland.

*Nest* both sexes make scrapes, accumulating a lining of bits of dry grass, moss or local material.

*Eggs* 2, greyish-buff or olive-brown with dark markings. Incubated by both sexes for about 4 weeks.

*Nestlings* yellowish-brown down paler on under-parts. Leave nest shortly after hatching, but return to it for several days to be fed, tended by both parents. Fly after about 6 weeks.

*Adults* slightly larger and more bulky than Herring Gull, sexes similar; dark brown plumage, semicircular white patch shows on broad wing (just behind the angle) in flight; short tail, blackish legs, shortish hooked black bill. Decidedly heavy, coarse appearance.

*Fledglings* less white on wing than in adult.

*Hints* a large brown bird flying straight towards you in an alarmingly aggressive manner, as you walk across rough ground, is a sure sign that you are in a breeding area. You need to be adept at ducking and to have eyes in the back of your head as they also come up from the rear. Nests are well spaced out on the moor, perhaps 20 yds or more apart. Bonxies, as they are named locally, return to their breeding areas about mid April where they are often seen standing with wings raised high above the back, calling loudly. There are also aerial chases and throughout the breeding season it is a decidedly aggressive bird. There is a long list of species which Skuas are known to have devoured and they often chase other birds, forcing them to drop their food which is usually caught by the Skua before it reaches the ground.

**Arctic Skua** *Stercorarius parasiticus*. Pl. 83, 270

*Breeds* late May–July, in similar places to Great Skua in N. Scotland and Hebrides; on tundra, shingle, sandy coasts, heaths, moors and damp marshes in Scandinavia.

*Nest* both sexes make scrapes, accumulating a little local material as lining.

*Eggs* 2, olive-green to brown with dark markings. Incubated by both sexes for nearly 4 weeks.

*Nestlings* brown to blackish-brown down, paler on under-parts. Leave the nest shortly after hatching, tended by both parents. Fly after about 3 weeks.

*Adults* smaller than Great Skua, much more streamlined, in flight central tail-feathers extend well beyond the rest of wedge-shaped tail, sexes similar. There are light and dark forms, with intermediate variations. Light form has dark cap, yellowish on cheeks and neck, dark brown upper-parts, dusky band on white under-parts; dark blackish-brown form has no contrasting colours. Exceptionally graceful and agile flight.

*Fledglings* more mottled than adult and shorter central tail-feathers; adult plumage acquired in 3 years.

*Hints* dramatic aerobatic displays, accompanied by wailing calls, take place over the breeding areas. Wings are also raised high above the back and fluttered when on the ground. They make aggressive swoops at human intruders, but strike less frequently than Great Skua; pairs nesting in colonies are more aggressive than when there is a single nest. Distraction display is often seen, the Skua trailing its wings, fluttering and tumbling about. Like Great Skua, it also pursues sea-birds, forcing them to drop their food and then catching it.

## Black-headed Gull *Larus ridibundus* Pl. **84**, *271*

*Breeds* mid April–July, near fresh water and along the coast, on moors, marshes, mudflats, dunes and shingle, occasionally in plantations of trees. (In British Isles, most of Europe and S. Scandinavia. Absent most of Italy and Spain.)

*Nest* usually on damp ground, sometimes on floating vegetation but also in dry sites and occasionally on buildings or in trees; both sexes make a flattened platform of local material, such as sedge or water-weed, or a mere scrape, lining it with a little grass.

*Eggs* 3, varying from greenish-grey or buff to brown, with dark markings. Incubated by both sexes for about 3½ weeks.

*Nestlings* marbled brown and black, long silky down, paler on under-parts. Leave nest after a few days, tended by both parents. Fly after about 5 weeks.

*Adults* sexes similar; smallish gull, but larger than Little Gull which also has a dark head, red bill and legs; dark 'hood' is brown rather than black; long narrow wings with black tips and white leading edge shows in flight.

*Fledglings* mottled brown upper-parts, yellowish bill and legs; much the same as adult by second winter.

*Hints* breeding areas are occupied in March, and the gulls make a lot of noise with raucous calls as they take up their nesting territory. They adopt threatening attitudes in which the bill points at an opponent, head stretched forward; they also stand very upright, the neck looking swollen as the bill points down and the wings are held slightly away from the body. There are various greeting ceremonies. As you approach a colony, there is a tremendous noise as the gulls dive at your head.

## Lesser Black-backed Gull *Larus fuscus*. Pl. **85**, *272*

*Breeds* May–July, on grassy slopes of coastal cliffs, flat-topped islands, shingle and dunes, often on inland marshes and moors. (In British Isles, N. Europe and Scandinavia.)

*Nest* usually on the ground, occasionally on buildings, in low bushes or trees; nests may be in low cover such as heather and bracken or in open site, generally on a gentle slope but also on cliff ledges; built by both sexes, amount of material varying according to local vegetation, often of grass, seaweed or bits of bracken and heather.

*Eggs* 2–3, similar to Herring Gull's, but may be greenish-blue with dark markings. Incubated by both sexes for nearly 4 weeks.

*Nestlings* very similar to Herring Gull. Remain in vicinity of nest, fed chiefly by female, until able to fly after about 5 weeks.

*Adults* sexes similar; smaller than Great Black-backed Gull, roughly same size as Herring Gull, but more finely built and has darker grey mantle and yellow (not pinkish) legs; both gulls have red spot on bill. Scandinavian race has blackish mantle, like Great Black-backed Gull, but colour of legs helps to distinguish them when not seen together.

*Fledglings* easily confused with young Herring Gull; adult plumage acquired after 3 years.

*Hints* there may be a few pairs nesting amongst Herring Gulls, but the main colony is usually in a separate area. It is worth walking over any flattish ground with young bracken or similar low-growing cover. Their noisy calls are deeper than those of Herring Gull, but their behaviour is much the same.

**Herring Gull** *Larus argentatus.* Pl. **86**, *273*

*Breeds* late April–July, usually on coastal cliffs with rocks and turf, also on dunes and shingle, less frequently inland near fresh water, locally on roof-tops and in trees. (In British Isles, Europe and Scandinavia.)

*Nest* usually a fairly bulky structure, built by both sexes, of dry grass, seaweed or local material, sometimes a scantily lined scrape.

*Eggs* 2–3, olive-green or brown, with dark markings. Incubated by both sexes for about 4 weeks.

*Nestlings* greyish-buff with dark marbled effect. Fed by both parents in or near the nest, remaining in the gullery until able to fly after about 6 weeks.

*Adults* sexes similar; familiar seaside gull with 'laughing' call; larger than Common Gull, smaller than Great Black-backed Gull; large yellow bill with red spot, pinkish legs. Black wing-tips have oval white spots which show in flight, often called 'mirrors'.

*Fledglings* mottled brownish with dark bill, gradually becoming paler in plumage, like adult after 3 years.

*Hints* flocks arrive in the breeding areas in March, flying about above the site of the colony, and as they land there is a great deal of noisy calling as they threaten each other in ritualised postures. Various 'meeting ceremonies' are performed, indicating that hostility is being overcome and pairs are gradually formed. Hostility is expressed in various movements of the head and neck, the latter often appearing swollen; at times the gulls seem to 'choke' in between bouts of pulling up grass and pecking at the ground. Later in the season, adults can often be seen attacking eggs and nestlings of their neighbours. Chicks tend to shelter under a stone or flatten themselves on the ground when alarmed. Well-grown chicks will walk slowly ahead of you on a cliff path while the adult flies overhead, calling 'ag ag ag'.

## Great Black-backed Gull *Larus marinus*. Pl. **88**, *275*

*Breeds* May–June, on rocky coasts and islands, occasionally on shingle and dunes, also inland on boggy moorland. (In British Isles, NW. France, Denmark and Scandinavia.)

*Nest* both sexes build a bulky structure of local material, such as sticks, seaweed, grass, heather, sometimes including a few feathers.

*Eggs* 2–3, olive-brown with dark markings. Incubated by both sexes for nearly 4 weeks.

*Nestlings* similar marbled effect to Herring Gull, but the grey areas are paler. Remain in vicinity of nest, fed by both parents, until able to fly after about 7 weeks.

*Adults* noticeably larger than Herring Gull and Lesser Black-backed Gull; blackish mantle, pale pink legs rather than flesh-pink as in Herring Gull, red spot on heavy bill.

*Fledglings* whiter head and under-parts than young Herring and Lesser Black-backed Gulls; adult plumage acquired during fourth winter.

*Hints* the largest gull commonly seen along the coasts with a gruff 'aw-aw' call. Nests are often on bare rock stacks or isolated promontories, either singly or a few in the same area. On lower slopes, the nests are spaced out in rather loose colonies. The displays are much the same as in Herring Gull and it is a bold predator. If you are interested in collecting remains of dead birds, Great Black-backed Gulls will provide you with perfect specimens of wings, bills and feet of such species as Puffin, Manx Shearwater, Storm Petrel and Leach's Petrel.

## Common Gull *Larus canus*. Pl. **87**, *274*

*Breeds* mid May–July, on islets in fresh water or sea lochs, on moors, shingle banks near rivers; less frequently on grassy slopes or dunes on sheltered parts of coast. (In Ireland, Scotland, Denmark, Germany, Holland and Scandinavia. Local in SE. England.)

*Nest* usually on the ground, amongst boulders or vegetation, occasionally in trees, recorded in old nest of Rook and on stone walls; variable amount of material, sometimes substantial structure of heather, grass and reeds, built by both sexes, or a mere hollow scantily lined with grass.

*Eggs* 2–3, brown or bluish-green with dark markings. Incubated by both sexes for about 3½ weeks.

*Nestlings* marbled effect of buffish-grey and blackish-brown down, long and silky, paler under-parts. Leave nest after a few days, tended by both parents. Fly after 4–5 weeks.

*Adults* sexes similar; somewhat similar to a small, delicately built Herring Gull with greenish-yellow legs and bill (no red spot); black wing-tips have white spots, distinguishing from Kittiwake which has completely black wing-tips.

*Fledglings* greyish-brown upper-parts, similar to young Herring and Lesser Black-backed Gulls but dark area of pale tail is more pronounced.

*Hints* colonies are most numerous in SW. Scotland and northwards, large colonies are well established in W. Ireland, very few pairs nest in England, and these should be left completely undisturbed. Some colonies are comparatively small and there may be single nests in one area. Common Gull's calls are higher pitched, although reminiscent of Herring Gull. Behaviour during the breeding season is much the same, but Common Gulls have been seen walking about with their heads right back over the mantle uttering a guttural note. A form of distraction display has been seen in which the Gull ran along the ground, as though on tiptoes, with the wings half-closed.

## Kittiwake *Rissa tridactyla*. Pl. **81**, *276*

*Breeds* late May–July, typically on rocky ledges of precipitous cliffs, but also on low cliffs, flat ground with boulders, shingle and dunes, occasionally on ledges of buildings. (In British Isles, Denmark, NW. France and N. Scandinavia.)

*Nest* a mud cup of seaweed, grass and moss, built by both sexes, usually on inaccessible, narrow ledge of rock.

**Kittiwake**

*Eggs* 2–3, varying from bluish-grey to yellowish-buff or brown, with dark markings. Incubated by both sexes for nearly 4 weeks.

*Nestlings* long silky greyish-brown and creamy-white down. Fed by both parents. Leave nest after about 4 weeks, fly after 5–6 weeks.

*Adults* same size as Common Gull, but more slenderly built, sexes similar; soft grey and white plumage which looks remarkably clean; dark eye, yellow bill, black legs. Entirely black wing-tips distinguish it from Common Gull in flight.

*Fledglings* slightly forked tail, black bands across wings, tail and back of neck make a zigzag pattern in flight;

very similar to adult by second winter.

*Hints* they return to their breeding areas early in the season and characteristic 'kittiwa-ak' calls ring out as more and more birds return to claim nest-sites. There is a lot of bickering as they fly to and from the ledges of the colony, and the displays are much the same as those of Herring Gull. The orange interior of the mouth can be seen as pairs 'choke' when greeting each other, often rubbing bills and 'kittiwa-aking'. It is well worth making an effort to see these elegant gulls at their nest-ledges. One accessible site which is usually occupied by small numbers is on the small island of St Helen's in the Isles of Scilly; boat trips to Men-a-vawr will usually land people on St Helen's where the colony is on low cliffs at the northern end. There is a large colony at Flamborough Head in Yorkshire.

## Black Tern *Chlidonias niger*. Pl. **89**

*Breeds* May–June, in shallow water of fens, marshes, flooded areas and along ditches bordering farmland. (In most of Europe. Local in Italy and SW. Sweden. Has bred Finland and Norway.)

*Nest* a floating platform on aquatic weed, made by both sexes of reeds, sedges, etc., sometimes anchored in comparatively open water; also a scantily lined scrape amongst herbage on firm ground. Nests on artificial rafts recorded.

*Eggs* 3, buff, green or brown, with dark markings. Incubated by both sexes for about 3 weeks.

*Nestlings* yellowish-buff down streaked with black, white area around eye, buff and greyish-white under-parts. Fed by both parents. Leave nest after about 2 weeks. Fly after about 3 weeks.

**Black Tern**

*Adults* sexes similar; small tern with predominantly blackish-grey plumage, white under tail-coverts, pale grey underwing. Fast wing-beats, tail looks square as it flies, often dipping down to take floating insects off the surface of water.

*Fledglings* browner than adult; resemble adult by the winter, white forehead, blackish patch on nape and 'saddle', white under-parts.

*Hints* they used to breed in E. England and it is hoped that colonies will be re-established in East Anglia before very long. Any pairs suspected of breeding should obviously be left undisturbed. Nesting colonies can be seen in the Naardermeer nature reserve in Holland. (Full particulars regarding visitors' access to the reserve can be obtained from Vereeniging tot Behoud van Natuurmonumenten in Nederland, Herengracht 540, Amsterdam-C.) Courtship activities include a high flight, several birds climbing high into the air and then gliding down; there is also a 'fish-ceremony' in which the male flies with a fish in his bill, followed by a female, ending in the female being fed outside the breeding colony. Males also feed females on the nest. The usual note in the breeding season is a repetitive 'kik' or 'kreek'.

**Gull-billed Tern** *Gelochelidon nilotica*

*Breeds* May–June, on mud or sandbanks by brackish pools, islets in saline lagoons and on salt-marshes. (In Denmark, S. France, Holland and S. Spain. Has bred England and Germany.)

*Nest* a scrape in sand or mud, sometimes amongst thick vegetation in bare patches between plants, scantily lined with grass and bits of material, goose droppings recorded.

*Eggs* 2–5, pale buff or brownish with dark markings. Incubated by both sexes for about 3 weeks.

*Nestlings* yellowish-grey or brownish-black with dark streaks, white and grey under-parts. Leave nest shortly after hatching, tended by both parents, but remain in the vicinity. Fly after about 4 weeks.

*Adults* roughly same size as Common Tern, sexes similar; short stout black bill, short forked tail, black legs are markedly longer than in other terns; black-capped head but no crest. Often catches flying insects, feeding inland frequently.

*Fledglings* buffish crown, brownish mottling on back, legs reddish-brown (not black).

*Hints* suspected of breeding in 1949, confirmed in 1950, a pair bred on an islet in a reservoir at Abberton, in Essex. These terns are normally seen in small numbers, mainly in spring. In regular breeding areas the nests may be in a colony or scattered amongst other species, such as Gulls, Avocets and Common Terns. The usual note is a loud 'gaa-waak' and when alarmed a scolding 'za-za-sa'. Display is described as much the same as in other terns, including a high flight, gliding and then diving at speed.

**Sandwich Tern** *Sterna sandvicensis*.
Pl. 90, *277*

*Breeds* May–June, on sand and shingle along the coast, also on islands and locally inland near fresh water. (In British Isles, Belgium, Denmark, Germany and Holland. Local in France, Spain and S. Sweden.)

*Nest* both sexes make scrapes in which bits of grass or seaweed accumulate to form a scanty lining.

*Eggs* usually 2, white to brownish-buff with dark markings. Incubated by both sexes for about 3½ weeks.

*Nestlings* buffish-grey down with dark streaks, matted at tips giving a 'spiky' effect. Remain in or near the nest for 1–2 days, tended by both parents. Fly after about 5 weeks and join up with others of their own age on the shore.

*Adults* sexes similar; large tern with black crest, yellow tip to black bill, black legs; looks whiter than Common or Arctic Terns, tail less deeply forked. Crest is erected into a shaggy tuft when excited.

*Fledglings* browner than adult, mottled on back, may lack yellow on bill until fully mature, white crown with black streaks.

*Hints* harsh 'kirrick' calls attract attention to breeding colonies in which the nests are usually placed very close together. They tend to breed on the same sites as more aggressive species and when watching a colony, it is wise to keep your distance when the chicks have hatched as if the parents leave them for too long there may be heavy losses due to predation. Displays are often seen in April, in the neighbourhood of nest-sites, flying high and swooping down. Males feeding females with fish can be seen during courtship; they usually lead the females to a scrape, after courting them on the ground, adopting various neck-stretching postures with the wings held away from the body. This tern does not dive at your head but relies on its more aggressive neighbours to drive off intruders. There are regular breeding colonies on Farne Islands and at Ravenglass in Cumberland.

**Common Tern** *Sterna hirundo*. Pl. 91, *278*

*Breeds* mid May–July, along the coast on sand and shingle beaches, dunes, salt-marshes and turf; also inland near fresh water. (In British Isles, Europe and Scandinavia. Absent most of Italy.)

*Nest* both sexes make scrapes, often unlined but female sometimes uses seaweed, sticks, grass, shells, etc., when readily available. Nest also recorded on fence-post in lake.

*Eggs* 2–3, buffish-brown, greenish or bluish-white, with dark markings. Incubated by both sexes for about 3 weeks.

*Nestlings* marbled effect of greyish-buff and blackish-brown down, dusky on throat, white under-parts. Remain in or near the nest for a few days, tended by both parents. Fly after 3–4 weeks.

*Adults* sexes similar; easily confused with Arctic Tern, light red bill has black tip (Arctic Tern's is usually entirely blood-red), long tail 'streamers', but they do not project beyond wings when standing; red legs are noticeably longer than those of Arctic Tern when seen side by side. Characteristic slow flight when fishing, looking down at the water, sometimes hovering before plunging for fish.

*Fledglings* browner on back than adult; similar to young Arctic Tern, but in winter legs and bill are red rather than black.

*Hints* noisy 'kikikik' and harsh 'kreeerrr' calls attract attention to colonies. Early in the season there are high display flights, side-slipping and gliding down, and aerial chases carrying fish; displays on the ground include bowing and stretching the neck with bill practically vertical. During incubation the sitting bird is often fed by its mate. Intruders are mobbed, the birds diving down, often striking a human head. When watching a colony it is safer to use binoculars at a distance, not only to avoid aggressive birds but also to ensure that the parents do not leave their nests for too long and so risk predation. Blakeney Point and Scolt Head, in Norfolk, are two places where well-established colonies can be observed.

**Arctic Tern** Sterna paradisea. Pl. **92**, *279*

*Breeds* late May–July, on sand and shingle beaches, islets with bare rock and low vegetation; also inland near fresh water. (In British Isles, N. Europe and Scandinavia.)

*Nest* both sexes make scrapes, one of which is selected by female, often unlined but lining may consist of shells, grass, etc.

*Eggs* 2–3, similar to Common Tern's but usually more boldly marked. Incubated by both sexes for about 3 weeks.

*Nestlings* similar to Common Tern, but dusky patch sometimes extends to forehead. Remain in or near the nest for a few days, tended by both parents. Fly after 3–4 weeks.

*Adults* sexes similar; easily confused with Common Tern, but bill is usually completely red (without black tip), red legs look shorter when standing side by side with Common Tern and tail 'streamers' project slightly beyond folded wings. In flight, wings may look translucent with a dark border along the hind edge, whereas Common Tern may show only a light patch on the wing-tips; slow flight when fishing as in Common Tern.

*Fledglings* similar to young Common Tern, in winter legs and bill tend to be blackish.

*Hints* noisy calls, somewhat similar to those of Common Tern, but described as less drawn-out, cannot fail to attract attention to a colony. The two species are sometimes present in the same colony, the Arctic Tern tending to nest in areas where vegetation is low or sparse rather than thick and long. The display is similar and Arctic Terns are aggressive towards intruders. Care should be taken, as with other terns, not to keep the parents away from the nest for too long. Anglesey and the Farne Islands both have breeding colonies. In Norway nests have been found on small hummocks in pools, surrounded by pine trees in which the Arctic Terns apparently perched without difficulty.

**Roseate Tern** Sterna dougallii. Pl. **93**, *280*

*Breeds* June–July, on sand and shingle along the coast and on rocky islets with turf. (In British Isles and NW. France. Has bred S. France and Denmark.)

*Nest* both sexes make scrapes in sand or pebbles in the open or hidden in a recess under a hummock or in a natural hollow, usually little or no lining, although some scrapes have been found with bracken, flower-heads, moss and rabbit droppings as lining.

*Eggs* 1–2, creamy-buff or pale brown with dark markings. Incubated by both sexes for 3–3½ weeks.

*Nestlings* marbled effect of buffish-grey and blackish-brown down, matted at the tips giving a 'spiky' effect, white under-parts. Remain in or near the nest for a few days, tended by both parents. Fly after about 4 weeks.

*Adults* sexes similar; roughly same size as Common and Arctic Terns but with very long tail 'streamers'; bill mainly black (some red at base), red legs; plumage looks very white, but in some lights a pink flush is visible on under-parts. Wing-beats less pronounced than in Common Tern; tail 'streamers' project beyond wings when standing.

*Fledglings* more speckled than young Common and Arctic Terns, blackish legs become orange-red in winter.

*Hints* colonies of this comparatively rare tern should be left undisturbed. A few pairs are sometimes seen nesting in colonies of other terns where the Roseate Tern's prolonged 'aagh-aagh' call attracts attention; the nest is likely to be where vegetation is thickest. Display includes high flight and carrying fish as well as displays on the ground, much as in Arctic and Sandwich Terns. There are colonies on Farne Islands and in the R.S.P.B.'s reserve at Inchmickery Island in Midlothian.

## Little Tern *Sterna albifrons*. Pl. **94**, *281*

*Breeds* mid May–July, on sand, shingle and mud beaches along the coast; often inland near fresh water in Europe. (In British Isles and Europe; mainly in S. Sweden in Scandinavia.)

*Nest* both sexes make scrapes; occasionally the chosen depression is lined by the female with small stones or bits of local material.

*Eggs* 2–3, pale buff with dark markings. Incubated by both sexes for about 3 weeks.

*Nestlings* marbled effect of sandy and blackish-brown down, white under-parts, throat may be buff. Remain in or near the nest for about 1 day, tended by both parents. Fly after about 4 weeks.

*Adults* sexes similar; small tern with white forehead below black cap, yellow bill with black tip, yellow legs, short tail 'streamers'. Fast fluttering wing-beats, frequently seen hovering before plunging for fish.

*Fledglings* look like Common Tern, but legs are drab yellow.

*Hints* high-pitched 'kikikkik' calls attract attention to a breeding colony where the nests are usually much more scattered than in other terneries, often 12 yds or more apart. Displays are similar to those of Common Tern. Human intruders are mobbed but rarely struck on the head. Care should be taken not to keep the adults away from the nest for too long. All terns are remarkably graceful in flight, but a Little Tern, hovering in the sun, is an outstanding sight. There are more colonies on the east coast than elsewhere in Britain.

## Razorbill *Alca torda*. Pl. **95**, *282*

*Breeds* May–July, on sea-cliffs with rocky crevices and boulder-strewn shores. (In British Isles, NW. France and Scandinavia.)

*Nest* on bare rock, usually in a crevice or cavity in preference to an open ledge on a cliff, also amongst boulders on the shore. No nest material, but bits of shale or debris sometimes accumulate and act as a miniature retaining wall, helping to prevent the egg from rolling.

*Egg* 1, varying from white or bluish-green to brown, with dark markings. Incubated by both sexes for 4–5 weeks.

*Nestling* short silky down, white on top of head, brownish-black and buff marbled effect on upper-parts, whitish under-parts. Fed by both parents, leaves nest-site after 2–3 weeks and joins adults in sea.

*Adults* larger than Puffin, more heavily built than Guillemot, with thick neck and stout bill which has a white mark running across the middle; sexes similar, white under-parts, black mantle has white horizontal line which looks like a small wing-bar when at rest; in whirring flight, the white area comes half-way along the hind edge of wing.

*Fledgling* no white on bill, browner version of adult.

*Hints* they return to the cliffs in February or March, standing near nest-sites in pairs and also swimming in the sea. They rub bills with each other, both on land and when swimming; mixed flocks also swim around together, turning their heads from side to side, then diving suddenly and reappearing with their bills pointing up. Colonies of Razorbills and Guillemots are often seen in the same neighbourhood. It is not always possible to get down to them, but sometimes a route can be spotted with binoculars. A colony on Skokholm Island is accessible and a strong smell greets you as you get down to their level and there is usually a growling protest.

**Guillemot** *Uria aalge.* Pl. **96**, *283*

*Breeds* mid May–August, on sea-cliffs with rocky ledges and on flat-topped stacks. (In British Isles, NW. France, W. Spain and islands off Denmark and in the Baltic; mainly in Norway in Scandinavia.)

*Nest* on bare rock, usually on open ledge, sometimes in rock crevice or sea-cave. No nesting material.

*Egg* 1, very variable in colour; range includes white, cream, bluish-green, shades of brown and red, with dark markings. Incubated by both sexes for 4 weeks or longer.

*Nestling* streaked and spotted effect of blackish-brown, grey and white down. Fed by both parents. Leaves nest-site after about 3 weeks and joins adults in sea.

**Guillemot**

*Adults* same size as Razorbill, but more slimly built, with slender neck and long pointed bill; sexes similar, brown rather than black upper-parts, white under-parts, similar wing-bar effect to Razorbill. Mantle of northern race is as dark as Razorbill; southern race more chocolate-brown. 'Bridled' form has narrow white ring round eye and line running back from the eye.

*Fledgling* similar to adult but has more 'scaly' appearance.

*Hints* they gather in the sea early in the season below the breeding sites and there is a lot of activity. Water splashes as they skid along the surface, they dive a lot and chase each other under water; there are wheeling flights which sometimes rise to a considerable height then diving down and pulling out at the last moment to wheel round again.

When they first take to the ledges, they space themselves out, but as more birds arrive, there is considerable jostling for position, bobbing and bowing, accompanied by growling calls. Like Razorbills they also rub their bills together and nibble each other's feathers. There are large colonies on Farne Islands off Northumberland, Handa Island off Sutherland, and Ailsa Craig off Ayrshire. From a boat rows of Guillemots can be seen standing shoulder to shoulder, looking out to sea, their eggs between their feet; when the chicks have hatched they often stand with their backs to sea.

## Black Guillemot *Cepphus grylle*.
Pl. **97**, *284*

*Breeds* May–July, on mainland coasts or rocky islands, towards the base of cliffs or on boulder-strewn shore. (Local in N. England. In Ireland, Scotland, islands off Denmark and in the Baltic, and in Scandinavia.)

*Nest* in a hole or crevice, usually among boulders, occasionally in a wall. No nesting material but stones are gathered.

*Eggs* 1–2, varying from white to bluish-green and shades of brown, with dark markings. Incubated by both sexes for about 3 weeks, possibly longer in far north.

*Nestlings* blackish-brown down, paler on under-parts. Fed by both parents. Leave nest and go to sea after about 5 weeks.

*Adults* roughly Puffin-size; sexes similar, black plumage except for bold white patch on wing which 'flashes' in whirring flight, bright red legs. Dive frequently and use wings under water.

*Fledglings* mottled brown and white on upper-parts, like adult in winter, but browner and legs are reddish-brown.

*Hints* Tysties, as they are named locally, are not common and there are usually only a few pairs breeding in the same area. Isle of Man, Shetland, Orkney and Fair Isle are some of the places where they are found in the breeding season. Small parties assemble early in the year and there are various communal displays, including swimming in line astern, pattering along the surface of the water and 'leap-frogging' in flight over one another, alighting on the water with wings raised before swimming with head and neck submerged. There is also an 'underwater ballet', the Tysties propelling themselves with their wings below the surface. High-pitched whistling calls are heard. Early in May the pairs come ashore and they have been seen gathering flat stones and laying them in the nest-site. Unlike Guillemots, their nests are well spaced out and they are secretive and silent ashore.

## Puffin *Fratercula arctica*. Pl. **98**, *285*

*Breeds* late April–August, on or near coastal cliffs with turf and boulders, on islands and headlands of the mainland. (In British Isles, NW. France, N. Scandinavia.)

*Nest* burrow excavated by both sexes, earth loosened with bill and shovelled with feet, in turf or scree, also under boulders; rabbit and Shearwater burrows also occupied. Nesting chamber may contain bits of bracken, grass and a few feathers.

*Egg* 1, white with faint markings, soon becomes stained. Incubated chiefly by female for 5–6 weeks.

*Nestling* long down, blackish-brown, grey and white. Fed by both parents for about 6 weeks, then deserted. Leaves the burrow after about 7 weeks, making its own way to sea.

*Adults* smaller than Razorbill and

Guillemot; sexes similar, plump, head appears disproportionately large with stout, vividly coloured triangular bill (orange, blue and yellow); black and white plumage gives 'dinner-jacket' effect, orange legs, webbed feet which look like orange paddles in braking action as they come down to land on the cliff.
*Fledgling* similar to adult in winter with thin blackish bill.
*Hints* if you have never seen Puffins it is worth making a special effort to get to a colony in June. The islands of Skokholm and Skomer, off the Pembrokeshire coast, have colonies which can be watched in lovely surroundings. Puffins stand about in groups, apparently taking a lively interest in all that goes on. Their 'busybody' attitude, upright stance and comical appearance, cannot fail to entertain the human observer. They exchange bows and rub bills when greeting each other. The delicate grey shading on the sides of the bill is a perfect foil for the extraordinary bill and rosette. When there are chicks underground, the parents fly to and fro, sand-eels packed crosswise in their bills. Nesting areas tend to be honeycombed with burrows and it is wise to look where you are going.

## Wood Pigeon *Columba palumbus*. Pl. **99**, *286*

*Breeds* March–September (occasionally other months), almost anywhere with trees and hedgerows, including built-up areas. (In British Isles, Europe and Scandinavia.)
*Nest* height varies from ground-level up to about 40 ft, flattish site in tree, bush, hedge or on ledge of building; male brings material, female builds a flimsy framework of small twigs, sometimes built on top of old nests of other species.

*Eggs* 2, white. Incubated by both sexes for about 2½ weeks.
*Nestlings* straw-coloured tufts of down between bare patches of skin. Fed by both parents. Leave nest after 3–4 weeks.
*Adults* sexes similar; familiar pigeon with bluish-grey plumage and white patch on either side of neck; broad white band across the wings shows in flight.
*Fledglings* drab version of adult with no white on neck.
*Hints* persistent cooing from a conifer early in the season may indicate nest-site and if you look up you may even see the eggs showing through the flimsy structure. Deciduous trees tend to be occupied later in the season when the foliage gives good cover. When prospecting for nest-sites, the male crouches on the branch, as though pecking at it, giving a double 'coo coo'. Twigs are gathered from the ground rather than snapped off living trees. The display includes bowing and mutual caressing, nibbling the plumage and the female sometimes inserts her bill into the male's. The display flight is a familiar sight, with a steep rise into the air and a clapping sound before gliding down.

## Stock Dove *Columba oenas*. Pl. **100**, **101**, *287*

*Breeds* March–September in parks and farmland with mature trees, also on cliffs, dunes and in built-up areas. (In British Isles, Europe and Scandinavia.)
*Nest* in a hole of some kind, in trees, buildings, rabbit burrows and in cliffs; nest-boxes used. There may be no nest material; sometimes dead leaves are used to line the cavity.
*Eggs* 2, white. Incubated by both sexes for about 2½ weeks.
*Nestlings* darker down than Wood

Pigeon's. Fed by both parents. Leave nest after 3–4 weeks.

*Adults* sexes similar; smaller and darker than Wood Pigeon, more blue tone in plumage; no white on neck or wings, iridescent green patch on sides of neck. Faint black marks on wings show in flight.

*Fledglings* drab version of adult, no green on neck.

*Hints* wing-clapping occurs in display flight, but it sounds much fainter than in Wood Pigeon and the birds tend to sweep about in circles; skirmishes take place on the ground, in which they appear to strike each other with their wings. There may be more than 1 pair nesting in the same area and some adults leave the nest with a considerable commotion as you approach, dashing out on the far side. Nests have been recorded in various man-made sites, including the turrets of derelict army tanks.

## Rock Dove *Columba livia*

*Breeds* March–September (main season), occurs in every month; usually along wild rocky coasts where there are fissures, ledges and caves; also on inland cliffs. (In Isle of Man, Ireland, Scotland, S. France, Italy and Spain. Feral stock throughout Europe and Scandinavia.)

*Nest* a few bits of local vegetation, in a hole or on a ledge, often in a cave.

*Eggs* 2, white. Incubated by both sexes for about 2½ weeks.

*Nestlings* sparse yellowish down with rufous tone. Fed by both parents. Leave nest after about 5 weeks.

*Adults* same size as Stock Dove, blue-grey plumage, green and mauve iridescent patches on sides of neck. Ancestor of domestic Pigeon; pure wild stock has white rump, white undersides of wing and two bold black wing-bars. Fast, dashing flight.

*Fledglings* drab version of adult without coloured patches on neck.

*Hints* domestic stock interbreeds with wild stock and usually breeds on buildings in built-up areas. Truly wild Rock Doves nest in inaccessible sites and usually one only catches a glimpse of the bird as it dashes out of a cave or fissure. Cooing note is similar to domestic stock's. Display is much the same as that of Wood Pigeon.

## Collared Dove *Streptopelia decaocto*. Pl. **102**, *288*

*Breeds* March–December (no nests recorded yet in January–February), in parks and gardens in built-up areas. (In British Isles, most of Europe and S. Scandinavia.)

*Nest* at varying heights, mainly 15–30 ft, in trees (apparently favouring conifers), on buildings, telegraph-poles, also old nests of other species; male brings material, female builds platform of sticks, sometimes lined with grass and roots, wire has also been used as nest material.

*Eggs* 2, white. Incubated by both sexes for about 2 weeks.

*Nestlings* no description available. Fed by both parents. Leave nest after 2–3 weeks.

*Adults* smaller than Stock Dove, same size as Turtle Dove; sexes similar, uniform drab greyish-brown upper-parts, narrow black and white collar; blackish wing-tips contrast with rest of drab wing, underside of tail shows white band at the end (white runs right across, not confined to sides).

*Fledglings* black mark on neck is fainter than in adult and there is a slightly patterned effect on plumage.

*Hints* listen for a three-syllable 'coo', with the emphasis on the second syllable. Similar bowing display to other doves. As this is still a comparatively new breeding species in Britain, first recorded in 1955, it is worth making detailed notes of everything to do with their breeding biology; it is thought to be very similar to that of Turtle Dove. Successive broods are often reared in the same nest.

**Turtle Dove** *Streptopelia turtur.* Pl. **103**, *289*

*Breeds* mid May–July, in open country with scattered bushes and untrimmed hedges, copses and fir plantations, large gardens and shrubberies. (In England, S. Scotland, Wales and Europe. Has bred S. Sweden.)

*Nest* usually a few feet above the ground in a bush, tree or hedge, also recorded on the ground and on top of old nests of other species; female builds flimsy platform of twigs, sometimes lined with roots and stems.

*Eggs* 2, white. Incubated by both sexes for about 2 weeks.

*Nestlings* tufts of pale yellow down and patches of bare skin. Fed by both parents. Leave nest after about 3 weeks.

*Adults* smaller than Stock Dove, slenderly built, sexes similar; sandy upper-parts with faint black patterning, black and white patch at sides of neck, pinkish under-parts; blackish tail fans out to show a white 'fringe' at the sides. Fast, dashing flight.

*Fledglings* drab version of adult without neck patches.

*Hints* soft coo-ing or purring note becomes more of a wheezy gasp during the display, which includes steep ascents and gliding descents, usually describing a circle and landing in the tree from which it took off. Bowing display may take place on the ground or in a tree. Hawthorns, blackthorn bushes or quickset hedges

are worth searching; the bird usually breaks from cover on the far side, making quite a commotion. Distraction display, fluttering helplessly along the ground, has been observed. There may be more than one pair nesting in the same area.

**Cuckoo** *Cuculus canorus.* Pl. **106**, **107**, **108**, **109**, *292*

*Breeds* May–July, in wide variety of sites, depending on the species which act as foster-parents, such as Meadow and Tree Pipit, Reed and Sedge Warbler, Dunnock, Robin and Pied Wagtail. (In British Isles, Europe and Scandinavia.)

*Nest* no nest of its own as nests built by other species are used for laying.

*Eggs* 12 or more are laid during the breeding season, normally 1 egg in each nest, often similar in colour to the foster-parents' eggs, although usually larger. Incubated by foster-parent; normal hatching period is 12½ days.

*Nestlings* no down, orange inside mouth, yellow flanges. About 4 days after hatching, the young Cuckoo ejects other eggs or nestlings from the nest; it is fed by the foster-parent and leaves the nest after nearly 3 weeks.

*Adults* sexes somewhat similar, reminiscent of a Sparrowhawk with pointed, not rounded, wings and a long graduated tail with white tips; bluish-grey upper-parts and throat, dark grey barring on pale under-parts; female tends to look browner and there is a rufous variety. Fast wing-beats ending in a glide before perching are characteristic.

*Fledglings* upper-parts either greyish-brown or rufous with black barring and a few white feathers.

*Hints* bubbling call of the female often betrays her presence and it is worth looking at any bird with a

Hawk-like flight, quartering the ground like a Harrier. The female has been seen in this typical 'raptor flight', locating a nest of a future foster-parent. Nests with freshly laid eggs are usually chosen and after laying her own egg, the Cuckoo has been seen to remove one of the other eggs and swallow it. Nests of species listed above are those most frequently parasitised in Britain; look for a clutch with 1 egg larger than the rest. One 'outsize' youngster, begging constantly for food may well be a Cuckoo. The foster-parent often lands on the back of the young Cuckoo when feeding it.

## Barn Owl *Tyto alba*. Pl. 110, *293*

*Breeds* usually late April–May but recorded in every month; on agricultural land near farms and villages, also in quarries and on cliffs and some islands. (In British Isles, Europe and SW. Sweden.)
*Nest* in a hollow tree or hole in derelict building, on floor or ledge in barn and loft, in crevice of quarry and cliff, also recorded in old nests of Jackdaws. No nesting material. Tray-type nest-box used.
*Eggs* 4–6, white. Incubated by female for about 4½ weeks.
*Nestlings* white down with bare patches, replaced by creamy down. Both parents bring food. Fly after about 9 weeks, but may leave the nest earlier.
*Adults* slightly smaller than Tawny Owl, very pale colouring with pure white face and under-parts; male has orange-buff upper-parts, female is greyer, but both sexes look whitish at dusk. Dark breasted form, typical in North and East Europe, is occasionally seen in Britain. Hunts along open country by day. Perches with upright stance; long legs have 'knock-kneed' appearance.

*Fledglings* similar to adults, creamy down tends to cling to feathers.
*Hints* snoring and hissing sounds, coming from the nest-hole, are made by adults and young. Adults seen emerging from a hole early in the season are probably roosting in the nest-site. The male presents food to the female at the nest-site for some time before eggs are laid and any hole littered with prey and shiny black pellets is likely to be occupied through the breeding season. A wing-clapping display has been observed. Weird, long-drawn-out shrieks are also characteristic of Barn Owls.

## Long-eared Owl *Asio otus*. Pl. 111. *294*

*Breeds* late February–June, mainly in woodland with fir trees, but also on dunes and marshes with some bushes. (In British Isles, Europe and S. Scandinavia.)
*Nest* old nests of other species are usually taken over in trees, but nests on the ground are usually built amongst low cover; artificial sites, such as baskets and platforms intended for wild duck are also used abroad.
*Eggs* usually 4–5, white. Incubated chiefly by female, but male has been recorded on eggs; period about 4 weeks.
*Nestlings* white down. Fed by both parents. Leave nest after about 3½ weeks.
*Adults* sexes similar; smaller than Tawny Owl; long ear-tufts are visible at close range, yellow eyes (not black as in Tawny Owl); in flight it looks more slenderly built than Tawny Owl, with longer wings and tail. Plumage is darker than that of Short-eared Owl. Hunts by night, roosts close to tree-trunk by day, looking tall and slim.

*Fledglings* downier appearance than adult.

*Hints* low-pitched 'oo-oo-oo', described as more of a moan than a hoot, helps to locate them at night. Trees used as roosts usually have a collection of pellets and droppings at the base of the trunk. Small birds often mob a roosting owl, drawing attention to it. The nest-site of the previous year is not usually used again the following year. There is a wing-clapping display flight. They are not easy to flush from the nest, but distraction display has been observed.

## Short-eared Owl *Asio flammeus*. Pl. 112, 295

*Breeds* April–June or later if voles are plentiful, on marshes, moors, dunes and rough open country. (In Britain, most of Europe and Scandinavia. Has bred Ireland and Switzerland. Absent Italy and Spain.)

*Nest* a depression in the ground, in some kind of cover, lined with bits of grass and local vegetation, trampled down rather than carried to the scrape.

*Eggs* 4–8, white. Incubated by female for about 4 weeks.

*Nestlings* buff down. Male brings food but young are fed by female. Leave nest after about 2 weeks.

*Adults* slightly larger than Long-eared Owl, paler plumage, ear-tufts hardly show even at close range; sexes similar; barred wings look very long in flight and there is a dark mark on the underside. Diurnal but often seen at dusk, flying low over the ground, slow wing-beats alternating with glides, quartering the ground for food.

*Fledglings* similar to adult but feathers look rather loose.

*Hints* wing-clapping display flight, sometimes rising to a great height,

circling and hovering, then losing height as it plunges down before rising again; this display is accompanied by a hooting 'song'. Dusk is the best time to watch for the male hunting; he may return to the nest with food for the female, flying low over the ground. Walking over a marsh or other open rough country devoid of trees is likely to be productive and when on the wing it often comes quite close, as though taking a look at you. Having confirmed their presence, it is then worth searching by day. When disturbed in the nest area, barking and various raucous cries are heard and the owl may mob you.

## Little Owl *Athene noctua*. Pl. 113, 296

*Breeds* late April–July, mainly on agricultural land with trees and buildings, also on dunes, near quarries and coastal cliffs, sometimes in built-up areas and on treeless islands. (In England, Wales, S. Scotland and Europe. Has bred S. Sweden.)

*Nest* in a natural hole, frequently in a tree, also in walls and on the ground, including burrows; no nesting material. Rarely in nest-boxes.

*Eggs* 3–5, white. Incubated by female for about 4 weeks.

*Nestlings* white down. Fed by both parents. Leave nest after about 4 weeks.

*Adults* sexes similar; noticeably small and plump; broad, flattened head with typical 'scowling' expression. Flies by day but hunts chiefly at dawn and dusk. 'Bobs' when nervous and is often seen perching on a post.

*Fledglings* paler but otherwise similar to adult.

*Hints* favourite perches are usually within a few yards of the nest. Sunny days are particularly good for finding these perches as the owls tend to bask in the sun. In spring, males and females can be heard calling to each other, often in broad daylight. The male flies about in the vicinity of the nest-site and the same holes are used for many years. The call is a rather plaintive 'kiew kiew' and versions of this almost amount to a song. When the young are being fed, the male frequently perches in the favoured spot, dives down for food, returns to the perch and then carries its prey to the nest.

## Pygmy Owl *Glaucidium passerinum*.

*Breeds* April–May, chiefly in coniferous forests but also in mixed woodland. (In Germany, Switzerland and N. Scandinavia.)

**Pygmy Owl**

*Nest* in a hole in a tree. Woodpecker holes are often appropriated. No nesting material.

*Eggs* 3–6, white. Incubated by female for about 4 weeks.

*Nestlings* no description available. Fed by both parents. Leave nest after about 4 weeks.

*Adults* smallest European owl, roughly Skylark-size and flight silhouette is reminiscent of Skylark; sexes similar, less 'scowling' expression than Little Owl and plumage is darker; whitish 'eyebrows', dark brown upper-parts spotted with white, tail barred with white, pale under-parts, whitish feathers on legs. Kills small birds in flight.

*Fledglings* brownish under-parts as well as upper-parts, 'eyebrows' as in adult.

*Hints* although mainly active at dawn and dusk, it is diurnal like Little Owl. It has a whistling call, reminiscent of Bullfinch; 'duets' can be heard, mainly at dusk and at their best in March. Male presents the female with food during courtship and at the incubation stage, each morning and evening. It swings its tail from side to side, cocking it at an angle just after it has landed. This species has not been recorded in Britain.

## Tawny Owl *Strix aluco*. Pl. **114**, 297

*Breeds* March–June, occasionally February, in woods and parks, often near farms, also in built-up areas. (In British Isles, Europe and S. Scandinavia.)

*Nest* usually in a hollow tree, also on buildings and in old nests of other species, from ground-level up to about 70 ft. Chimney-type nest-boxes used. Normally no nesting material.

*Eggs* 2–4, white. Incubated by female for about 4 weeks.

*Nestlings* white down. Male brings food, but female feeds young. They can fly after about 5 weeks, but may leave the nest earlier.

*Adults* larger than other British owls; sexes similar, no ear-tufts, head looks large and body rather plump; mottled brown upper-parts with grey facial disc and black eyes; buff under-parts with dark streaks. A greyish form is said to be more common in the Continental race. Nocturnal, seen flying by day when disturbed or

**Tawny Owl**

perching in a tree, apparently basking in the sun.

*Fledglings* similar to adult, but feathers look rather loose.

*Hints* characteristic hooting, popularly described as 'tu-whit tu-whoo', is often heard in October and November when males are taking up territory, but is at its height in January and February; pairs can be heard answering each other, hooting followed by 'kewick' calls. It is unwise to investigate any likely site during the breeding season owing to the aggressive attacks of these birds in defence of the nest. Eric Hosking lost an eye when photographing a Tawny Owl and he also mentions, as a warning to unwary ornithologists, that he was a member, of a party which was viciously attacked by a Hawk Owl when looking at its nest in Finland.

**Nightjar** *Caprimulgus europaeus.* Pl. **104,** *290*

*Breeds* late May–August, in young plantations and felled areas of woodland and on open rough ground, such as downs, heaths, commons and dunes. (In British Isles, Europe and S. Scandinavia.)

*Nest* on the ground, no nest material, often amongst dry bracken and dead sticks are sometimes found near the nest.

*Eggs* usually 2, greyish-white with marbled effect. Incubated chiefly by female for about $2\frac{1}{2}$ weeks.

*Nestlings* scanty pale buff down, very wide gape compared with size of bill. Fed by both parents, male taking over when female lays second clutch. Short-distance flights after about 2 weeks.

*Adults* same size as Mistle Thrush with remarkably good camouflage patterning in grey, brown and black; this plumage gives them the appearance of dead sticks covered with bark; male has white spots on wings and outer tail-feathers. Flattened head silhouette, long wings and tail.

*Fledglings* similar to adult female.

*Hints* persistent churring, usually the first indication of their presence, may be heard from dusk to dawn from mid May to early August. By day they usually remain on the ground or squatting on a branch; at dusk, watch for a moth-like flight following an erratic course in silence. It is very difficult to spot one on the nest, but sometimes a large black eye gives the bird away. Look carefully at anything which looks like dead bark on the ground. They usually flush just before you tread on them. During the incubation stage it is worth watching at dusk for the male flying in to relieve the female, often uttering typical call described as 'co-ic'. Both sexes have been seen flying as though injured in some way, dragging a wing and leaping into the air, when disturbed at the nest-site.

**Swift** *Apus apus*

*Breeds* late May–August, mainly in built-up areas where there are suitable holes in tall buildings, such as church towers and ruins; also in thatch and on sea-cliffs. (In British Isles, Europe and Scandinavia.)

*Nest* in hole or crevice in buildings, occasionally under eaves in House Martin site and in burrows of Sand Martin; also in trees in parts of Europe. Both sexes gather straw, leaves, seed fluff and bits of vegetation floating in the air and glue them with saliva into a 'saucer'. Artificial nest 'saucers', made of twisted straw and placed at the end of an 18-in. long box, are used as nest-boxes.

*Eggs* 2–3, dull white. Incubated by both sexes for nearly 3 weeks.

*Nestlings* no down, greyish-pink body, pink inside mouth with pale brown spot. Fed by both parents. Flap their wings from day of hatching, fly properly when 5–8 weeks old.

*Adults* larger than Swallow, sexes similar; typical dark flight silhouette with long scythe-shaped wings and short forked tail. Alpine Swift, *Apus melba*, is larger and paler, with a brown band across breast and whitish under-parts; it breeds in mountain areas of central and southern Europe and is occasionally seen in Britain.

*Fledglings* hoary-headed appearance due to whitish tips to feathers.

*Hints* early in May screaming notes overhead are a welcome sign that the Swifts are back. Parties fly round the nesting colonies throughout the breeding season and are particularly noticeable on warm evenings as they scream overhead. During courtship the pairs indulge in vigorous bouts of mutual preening, accompanied by screaming notes. Aerial mating has been seen as well as mating at the nest. When returning to feed the young, the parents pack their throats with a mass of insects, making a visible bulge just below the bill. One-year-old Swifts, form pairs and build a nest which they occupy through the breeding season, but no eggs are laid.

**Kingfisher** *Alcedo atthis*. Pl. **105**, *298*

*Breeds* late March–August, near fresh water where there are banks suitable for excavating nesting burrows. (In British Isles, Europe and S. Sweden.)

*Nest* tunnel sloping slightly upwards, 1½–4 ft length, bored by both sexes in steep bank, usually 2–3 ft above slow-running water; no nesting material, but fish-bones collect round the eggs at end of chamber.

*Eggs* usually 6–7, white; as with other white eggs, they look pink when first laid. Incubated by both sexes for about 3 weeks.

*Nestlings* no down, pink inside mouth, bluish flanges. Fed by both parents. Leave nest after about 3½ weeks.

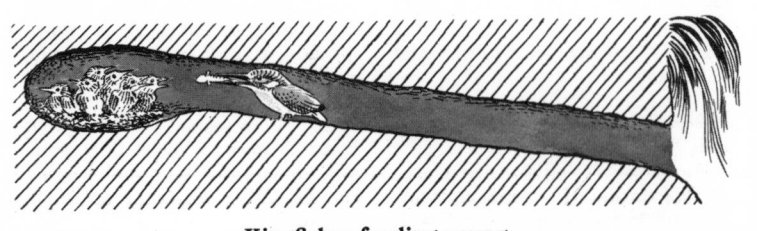

**Kingfisher feeding young**

*Adults* roughly Sparrow-size; sexes similar, but female usually has more reddish-orange at base of black, dagger-like bill; squat silhouette, short tail, vivid bluish-green upper-parts, chestnut under-parts with white throat and patch at sides of neck, bright red feet. Often sits on perch overlooking water, plunges for food, returning to the perch to eat it; fast whirring flight.

*Fledglings* drab version of adult.

*Hints* whistling notes are heard in butterfly-like display flight. Male pursues female in the air; on the ground they bow and stretch their necks so that the bill points up and crouch at an angle to each other, fanning their wings and revealing the blue sheen on back and rump. The best method for locating the nest is to look for favourite perch and search the bank near this spot for a circular hole. Courtship feeding also takes place on the perch. White droppings at the rim of the burrow usually indicate that the young have hatched.

**Bee-eater** *Merops apiaster*. Pl. 117

*Breeds* late May–June, in country with stunted vegetation or with scattered trees and bushes, including open woodlands and roadside verges with suitable perching posts, in banks of rivers and gravel-pits. (In SE. France, Italy and Spain. Has bred Britain, Belgium, Denmark, Germany and Switzerland.)

*Nest* both sexes excavate a burrow, loosening the soil with the bill and kicking it backwards with the feet; the shaft is usually from 3 ft to 9 ft long, sloping downwards. No nest material is carried into burrow.

*Eggs* 4–8, white. Incubated by both sexes for about 3 weeks.

*Nestlings* no down, bright pink body, pink inside mouth. Fed by both parents. Leave nest after about 4 weeks.

*Adults* smaller than Roller, roughly Mistle Thrush-size, with a long curved bill which tapers to a fine point; sexes similar, streamlined silhouette with long central tail-feathers; gold, chestnut and greenish-blue plumage looks vivid in certain lights. Often seen perching in promi-nent position with rather upright stance.

*Fledglings* drab version of adult.

*Hints* when prospecting for nest-sites, the birds fly backwards and forwards, gliding gracefully on long pointed wings; there is a repetitive call-note, 'qui-ick, qui-ick' which becomes very monotonous. They dig in sand rather than clay soil, the earth flying out behind them to make a mound; running down the shaft, there are two grooves made by the constant kicking of the feet. While one bird excavates the mate often stands at the entrance, calling con-stantly, and sometimes the male calls the female out and feeds her on a perch near the burrow. Two pairs bred successfully in a Sussex sand-pit in 1958; a Sand Martin's burrow was occupied in Alderney during 1956.

**Roller** *Coracias garrulus*. Pl. 118

*Breeds* mid May–June, in open wood-land of mature conifers and mixed deciduous species, in orchards, gardens and open country with scattered trees. (In SE. France, Germany, Italy and Spain; a few in S. Scandinavia.)

*Nest* in a hole or crevice of tree, wall, bank or sandy cliff; occasionally in old nest of other species and recorded in rabbit burrow. Nesting material is either scanty or absent, sometimes a few wood chips or grass with feathers or hair.

*Eggs* usually 4–5, white. Incubated by both sexes for about 2½ weeks.

*Nestlings* no down. Fed by both parents. Leave nest after about 4 weeks.

*Adults* roughly Jay-size, sexes similar; bright blue plumage, powerful bill; in flight the blue wings with black tips contrast with rich chestnut back; greenish-blue tail has brown centre and black tips at sides. Often perches in Shrike-like attitude pouncing on insects. Vivid colour pattern in buoyant flight.

*Fledglings* drab version of adult without black tips of tail.

*Hints* tumbling display flight consists of a series of spectacular dives, turns and somersaults. The Rollers dodge between trees as they chase each other early in the breeding season. Harsh Crow-like calls are associated with display flight. Calls of young from the nest-hole are said to be audible at a considerable distance. There are often several nests in the same area. Good views of Rollers have been obtained in pine forests north of Madrid where the trees are tapped for resin, making them comparatively easy for woodpeckers to excavate, thus leaving old sites for Rollers to appropriate. In districts with sandy soil, it is worth looking for burrow nests. Rollers are seen infrequently in Britain, mostly in the south and east.

**Hoopoe** *Upupa epops*. Pl. **119, 299**

*Breeds* late April–June, in parks, orchards and gardens with mature trees, also in walls and ruined buildings, including outskirts of built-up areas. (In Europe except Denmark. Has bred Britain, Finland and Sweden.)

*Nest* at varying heights in a hole of some kind, often in an old tree; normally no nesting material. Nest-boxes used.

*Eggs* 4–8, greyish-white, soon become soiled. Incubated by female for about 2½ weeks.

*Nestlings* scanty white down, pink inside mouth, waxy white flanges. Fed by both parents. Leave nest after about 4 weeks.

*Adults* smaller than Jay, sexes similar; pinkish-brown plumage, black and white wings and tail, pinkish crest tipped black which shows well when erected. Often seen feeding on lawns or short turf.

*Fledglings* drab version of adult with shorter crest.

*Hints* Hoopoes are seen regularly on passage in spring and autumn in Britain, but it is thought that a pair probably breeds somewhere in most years. Typical note during the breeding season is a soft 'hoop poo poo' which carries quite well. In flight they look like large black and white butterflies following an undulating course. The crest is fanned during courtship display and also when alarmed. They are said to be very shy at the nest-site and the hole often looks disproportionately small for the Hoopoe's size. The male feeds the female in the nest-hole during incubation. Both parents make frequent visits to the hole when feeding young. Hissing can be heard from the hole if the young are disturbed.

**Wryneck** *Jynx torquilla*. Pl. **115, 116, 291**

*Breeds* May–July, in orchards and parks, almost anywhere with old trees, including gardens on outskirts of towns. (Local in SE. and E. England. In Europe and S. Scandinavia.)

*Nest* in a natural hole at varying heights, typically in an old fruit tree or pollarded willow and occasionally in walls and banks. Nest-boxes used readily. There is no excavation and rarely any nesting material.

*Eggs* 7–10, white. Incubated chiefly by female for nearly 2 weeks.

*Nestlings* no down, pink inside mouth, pink flanges. Fed by both parents. Leave nest after about 3 weeks.

*Adults* smaller than Song Thrush; sexes similar with mottled greyish-brown plumage, similar to Nightjar and at short range the patterning is remarkably beautiful. Usually perches across a branch, but also clings to tree-trunk like a woodpecker.

*Fledglings* similar to adult.

*Hints* shrill call, reminiscent of a falcon's 'quee quee quee', is usually the first indication of their arrival. This call may be heard from April to mid July, but it is not heard when the first clutch is complete in mid May; this does not mean that the nest has been deserted and watch should be kept later for the adults flying to and from the hole when feeding young, often on ants. There are often 2 broods and calling is resumed before the completion of the second clutch. Courtship includes a display in which both sexes contort their heads backwards and forwards, making a writhing motion with their necks; aerial chases also take place. When disturbed at the nest, a violent hissing sound greets the intruder and the bird looks as though it were having a fit, twisting and turning its neck as it darts its head upwards. Wrynecks are now so scarce in England, even in the east and south-east, that every breeding record is of interest.

## Green Woodpecker *Picus viridis*. Pl. **120**, *300*

*Breeds* late April–June, in open deciduous woods and country with scattered trees, such as farmland, parks, large gardens and occasionally in built-up areas. (In Britain, Europe and S. Scandinavia.)

*Nest* hole in mature tree, excavated by both sexes, from a few feet above ground up to 30 ft or more; the entrance hole is circular to oval; no nesting material is carried into the shaft which is 1–2 ft deep, but wood chips serve as a 'cushion' for eggs. Nest-boxes used.

*Eggs* usually 5–7, white. Incubated by both sexes for nearly 3 weeks.

*Nestlings* no down. Fed by both parents. Leave nest after about 3 weeks.

*Adults* roughly Jay-size, greenish plumage with yellow rump; both sexes have crimson crown and a moustachial stripe which is red (bordered with black) in male and black in female. Markedly undulating flight; hops about the ground, often seen feeding at ants' nest.

*Fledglings* paler than adult with light spots on upper-parts and darkish barring on under-parts.

*Hints* laughing call is usually the first indication that they are in the neighbourhood, heard intermittently in January and frequently from February. Courtship includes chases round tree-trunks, the pair jerking their heads from side to side, revealing crimson patch to each other. The noise of a hole being excavated can be a useful guide to the nest-site, but wood chips lying at the base of the tree are the best sign. During incubation, if you suspect that a hole is occupied, try rubbing a stick along the bark as near to the hole as you can reach, making a soft scratching noise, inducing the woodpecker to look out of the hole and enabling you to identify the species; if you bang the trunk loudly, the bird usually sits tight and does not appear. Loud squealing notes can often be heard when the young are clamouring for food.

**Black Woodpecker** *Dryocopus martius*. Pl. **121**, *301*

*Breeds* April–May in conifer forests and mixed woodland. (In most of Europe and Scandinavia. Absent British Isles, Denmark and most of Italy.)

*Nest* hole in mature tree, excavated by both sexes, usually 15–32 ft above ground; the entrance hole is a long oval shape, the depth of shaft varying between 15 in. and 2 ft, with wood chips at the bottom. Nest-boxes used.

*Eggs* usually 4–6, white. Incubated by both sexes for nearly 2 weeks.

*Nestlings* no down. Fed by both parents. Leave nest after about 3 weeks.

*Adults* Rook-size; plumage is black except for red forehead in male and red patch at back of head in female; ivory-coloured bill and pale yellow eye. Typical undulating flight.

*Fledglings* similar to adult.

*Hints* alleged to be very wary and it is difficult to get close to them except when they are drumming; this may be heard in January, reaching a peak in April and continuing until the young have fledged. During the breeding season the male calls the female with a double-note 'pee-ack', and when this is heard regularly you can be reasonably sure that a pair is breeding in the neighbourhood. They often return to sites occupied in previous years. In Germany these tend to be on the edge of clearings in woods in tall beech, not necessarily in decaying wood. Lime, birch, willow and decaying poplar have been occupied in Norway.

**Great Spotted Woodpecker** *Dendrocopos major*. Pl. **122**, *302*

*Breeds* mid May–July, in deciduous and coniferous woods and copses, also in parks and large gardens with many trees, including built-up areas. (In Britain, Europe and Scandinavia.)

*Nest* hole in mature tree, often in decaying wood, excavated by both sexes, usually at a height of 10 ft or more; the entrance hole is oval, the shaft rising before descending perpendicularly for about 1 ft, with a few wood chips at the bottom. Nest-boxes used.

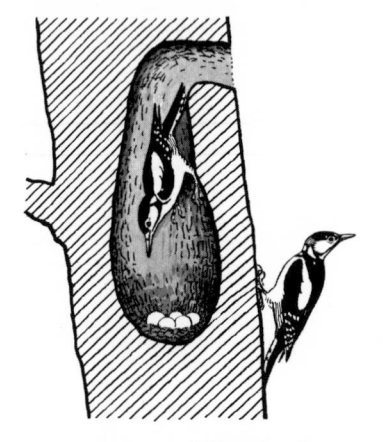

**Great Spotted Woodpecker**

*Eggs* usually 4–7, white. Incubated by both sexes for about 2 weeks.

*Nestlings* no down. Fed by both parents. Leave nest after about 3 weeks.

*Adults* smaller than Green Woodpecker, roughly Song Thrush-size; both sexes have black and white plumage with a large white patch on 'shoulders' and a crimson patch under tail; male has another crimson patch at back of head. Less frequently seen on the ground than Green Woodpecker, but similar bounding flight. Visits bird-tables.

*Fledglings* both sexes have crimson crown.

*Hints* characteristic drumming by both sexes may start as early as January, becoming frequent in March and April. Between bouts of drumming, the pairs chase each other, dodging about in the branches. They also fly with head sunk in 'shoulders', tail slightly raised and wings quivering, calling 'tchick tchick'. Fresh holes are sometimes bored just below an old hole and new chips at the base of a tree are a useful guide. The young give a rapid 'kew kew kew' call when they are nearly ready to fly and peep out of the hole.

## Lesser Spotted Woodpecker *Dendrocopos minor*. Pl. **123**, *303*

*Breeds* late April–June, in open woodlands, copses, parks, orchards and large gardens with mature trees. (In England and Wales, throughout Europe except Denmark, and in Scandinavia.)

*Nest* hole in decaying wood, excavated by both sexes, from just above ground-level up to about 70 ft; the entrance hole is oval and the shaft usually less than 1 ft deep, with a few wood chips at the bottom.

*Eggs* usually 4–6, white. Incubated by both sexes for about 2 weeks.

*Nestlings* no down. Fed by both parents. Leave nest after about 3 weeks.

*Adults* Sparrow-size; both sexes have black and white barring across back and wings, and there is no crimson under the tail; crown of male is crimson, female's crown is whitish. Usually seen fluttering from branch to branch or flying short distances; more shy than other woodpeckers seen in Britain.

*Fledglings* some crimson on crown of both sexes.

*Hints* drumming and 'tchick tchick' calls sound more feeble than Great Spotted Woodpecker. There is a slow, fluttering display flight. A ringing 'kew kew kew' call is often heard during the breeding season and the young have a shrill version of this call when clamouring for food. The nest is usually in a side branch of a deciduous tree in Britain, but conifers are used in Scandinavia.

## Woodlark *Lullula arborea*. Pl. **124**, *304*

*Breeds* late March–August in open country with scattered trees, on un-cultivated ground and outskirts of woods and felled clearings, heaths and downs. (In England, Wales, Europe and S. Scandinavia. Has bred Ireland.)

*Nest* on the ground, usually in depression in grass, sometimes under bramble or bracken; neat structure, built by both sexes, of grass and moss, lined with grass and hair.

*Eggs* 3–4, greyish-white with dark markings. Incubated by female for about 2 weeks.

*Nestlings* dark grey down, yellow inside mouth with three black spots, yellowish-white flanges. Fed by both parents. Leave nest after nearly 2 weeks.

*Adults* sexes similar; smaller than Skylark with much shorter tail; pale stripes run from above the eye to meet at the back of the neck and there is a noticeably dark mark where the wing bends. Crest is only obvious when raised.

*Fledglings* feathers are dotted with black, making them look like a mottled version of adult.

*Hints* remarkably sweet song attracts attention by day and sometimes after dark; it sounds like a flute, 'lu lu lu lu', rising and falling in pitch, with pauses between phrases. The song is delivered from the ground, a bush or tree and also in display flight when the bird circles and loses height, finally plunging to earth. Song-posts give a clear view of its territory which is occupied by late February. During incubation the male tends to perch near the nest and joins the female when she comes off to feed. Distraction display has been recorded.

**Skylark** *Alauda arvensis*. Pl. **125**, *305*

*Breeds* April–July, in open countryside where there are stretches of open ground, such as fields, aerodromes, downs and moors with rough grass; also in dunes and dry areas of marshes. (In British Isles, Europe and Scandinavia.)

*Nest* on the ground in a depression, often in tuft of grass or in crops; female builds a cup of grass, hair sometimes included in lining.

*Eggs* usually 3–4, whitish but closely marked with brown. Incubated by female for about $1\frac{1}{2}$ weeks.

*Nestlings* straw-coloured down, pale yellow inside mouth with three black spots, white flanges. Fed by both parents. Leave nest after about 9 days.

*Adults* sexes look alike; larger than Woodlark with longer tail and less obvious eye-stripe, crest is shorter than Woodlark's but often shows up better. White outer tail-feathers conspicuous in flight and hind edge of wing looks whitish.

*Fledglings* more mottled appearance than adult; may be confused with young Woodlark.

*Hints* males establish their territories before females arrive, often settling in the same place as in the previous year. Soaring in the sky, singing continuously, sometimes for five minutes without pause, the display flight is a familiar sight; the point of descent, however, is not necessarily a guide to the nest-site. Skylarks are so inconspicuous on the ground that it is difficult to follow where they go. Finding a nest is largely a matter of luck, but sometimes there is a runway leading into a tuft which shows up best when you get right down and look along the lie of the grass.

**Sand Martin** *Riparia riparia*. Pl. **126**, *306*

*Breeds* April–August, in open country where there is a steep bank of some kind, such as a sand-pit, quarry, railway embankment, river-bank or soft earth on coastal cliff. (In British Isles, Europe and Scandinavia.)

*Nest* a hole tunnelled into a bank, excavated by both sexes which gather feathers and bits of straw in flight as nesting material; also recorded in drainpipes, walls and heaps of sawdust. Nest-boxes used occasionally.

*Eggs* 4–5, white. Incubated by both sexes for about 2 weeks.

*Nestlings* pale grey down, inside mouth and flanges pale yellow. Fed by both parents. Leave nest after nearly 3 weeks.

*Adults* smaller than House Martin; sexes similar, brown upper-parts, white under-parts, brown band across white breast is distinctive. Fluttering flight, often seen feeding over water.

*Fledglings* similar to adult but with less clean-cut appearance, due to pale edges of feathers on upper-parts.

*Hints* parties of Sand Martins fluttering low above the water, catching insects, are not necessarily feeding near their nesting colonies as they go some distance in search of food. Watch suitable steep banks for any sign of birds clinging to the sides and hovering near holes in the earth face. Sand Martins often return to the same colony and a previously occupied site is worth watching.

**Swallow** *Hirundo rustica.* Pl. **127,** *307*

*Breeds* mid May–September (sometimes early October), near farms and houses with out-buildings which provide suitable rafters as nest-sites, occasionally on industrial sites with girders, etc., in countryside and on outskirts of towns. (In British Isles, Europe and Scandinavia.)

*Nest* on a ledge, usually inside a building with open access, rarely on outer side of building; a saucer-shaped nest is built by both sexes of mud and grass or straw, lined with grass and feathers. Tray-type nest-boxes used. Tree nests recorded.

*Eggs* usually 4–5, white with dark markings. Incubated by female for about 2 weeks.

*Nestlings* scanty grey down, yellow inside mouth, whitish flanges. Fed by both parents. Leave nest after about 3 weeks.

*Adults* larger than House Martin; both sexes have dark blue upper-parts, whitish under-parts, red patch at throat and forehead, and conspicuously long outer tail-feathers (slightly shorter in female). Swooping flight, often changing direction.

*Fledglings* more drab than adult with shorter tail 'streamers'.

*Hints* familiar twittering song in dashing flight, sweeping in and out of out-buildings, indicates that they are prospecting for nest-sites. They frequently return to the same site year after year; check places where one rafter meets another as the nest needs support at the side as well as at the base. Sometimes they build in chimney-stacks or under the eaves of a roof in typical House Martin's nest-site; where buildings are not available, they nest in caves. Several pairs frequently nest in the same area.

**House Martin** *Delichon urbica.* Pl. **128, 129,** *308*

*Breeds* mid May–October, in suburban areas and country districts where there are buildings with suitable eaves and a supply of mud, often near water, also on coastal cliffs and inland quarries. (In British Isles, Europe and Scandinavia.)

*Nest* typically under eaves of houses or out-buildings and under bridges; both sexes gather mud and grass, plastering them into a deeper cup than Swallow's, lining it with bits of straw and feathers. The cup is stuck against the wall and has a small entrance towards the top at one side. Artificial nests made out of clay and cemented to suitable site are used; nest also recorded on attic floor.

**House Martin's nest**

*Eggs* 4–5, white. Incubated by both sexes for about 2 weeks.

*Nestlings* scanty greyish-white down, yellow inside mouth, paler flanges. Fed by both parents, late broods are sometimes fed by young of earlier brood. Leave nest after about 3 weeks.

*Adults* sexes similar, smaller than Swallow with short forked tail and distinctive white rump; dark blue upper-parts, white under-parts. Often seen perching on wires or wheeling about under eaves; when going somewhere, flight is more fluttering than that of Swallow.

*Fledglings* browner version of adult.

*Hints* they usually arrive a few days after Swallows and are then often seen with them, hawking for insects over water, before returning to nest-sites. Twittering song is heard in flight and when perching. The white feathers on their legs show up well when gathering mud for making the nest. Constant flights up to the eaves make the location of sites easy; there are often several nests in the same area.

## Tawny Pipit *Anthus campestris*

*Breeds* May–June, on dry stony ground, both cultivated and un-cultivated, dunes and barren regions with poor vegetation. (In most of Europe. Has bred Switzerland. Local in S. Sweden and the Baltic. Absent British Isles and most of Scandinavia.)

*Nest* on the ground in a depression sheltered by a tuft; made of grass and roots, lined with a little hair, some nests thickly lined.

*Eggs* 4–5, whitish, often densely marked. Incubated by both sexes for about 2 weeks.

*Nestlings* pale buff down, deep yellow inside mouth, yellowish-white flanges. Fed by both parents. Leave nest after about 2 weeks.

*Adults* a large but slender pipit, reminiscent of a wagtail, long legs and upright stance; sexes similar, pale sandy plumage with creamy eye-stripe, faintly streaked upper-parts with a row of blackish 'diamonds' looking like a wing-bar and under-parts streaked at the sides. (May be confused with Richard's Pipit, *Anthus richardi*, but the latter has no black 'diamonds'.)

*Fledglings* greyish-brown, streaked upper-parts, spotted under-parts.

*Hints* there is a popularly held theory that a pair bred in Sussex in 1905.

Male has a fluttering display flight, uttering a monotonous, metallic 'chivee' as he loses height. During incubation the male often perches near the nest, pursuing the female and driving her in various directions when she comes off to feed. Distraction display, the bird appearing to be lame, has been observed when disturbed off the nest.

## Tree Pipit *Anthus trivialis*. Pl. **130**, *309*

*Breeds* May–July, on rough ground with scattered trees or suitable perching posts, on heaths and commons, along railway embankments, outskirts or open rides in woods and felled clearings. (In Britain, most of Europe and Scandinavia. Absent most of Italy and Spain.)

*Nest* on the ground, usually hidden under a tussock, sometimes in a bank with a 'mousehole' entrance; made of grass and moss, lined with grass and hair.

*Eggs* usually 4–6, very variable in colour, mainly reddish-brown or grey with dark markings. Incubated by female for about 2 weeks.

*Nestlings* grey down, orange and yellow inside mouth, pale yellow flanges. Fed by both parents. Leave nest after nearly 2 weeks.

*Adults* easily confused with Meadow Pipit as colour distinctions are difficult in poor light; sexes similar, upper-parts more warm brown than greyish-green, breast yellowish-buff and heavily streaked, white belly and streaked flanks. (Meadow Pipit's under-parts are of more uniform colour and streaks are diffused.) Tree Pipit's legs are pale flesh colour rather than brown and the hind claw, when visible, is noticeably shorter than in Meadow Pipit; both species have white outer tail-feathers.

*Fledglings* more buff than adult and streaks are darker.

*Hints* late April is the easiest time at which to locate future nests by watching where the male gives his display flight; fluttering up from one of several tall perches, silent at first, he then breaks into song as he floats down, wings half-closed and tail spread, landing on the original perch and finishing the song with a shrill 'seea seea seea'. The nest should be built somewhere in this area. During incubation, if you see one bird pursuing another, watch where they go as the male may be driving the female back to the nest.

## Meadow Pipit *Anthus pratensis*. Pl. **131**, *310*

*Breeds* late April–July, in open country on hills and moors, rough uncultivated ground, heaths and dunes. (In British Isles, most of Europe and throughout Scandinavia. Absent Spain and most of Italy.)

*Nest* on the ground, usually invisible from above, beside or under a tussock; made of grass, lined with finer grass and sometimes hair. Nests in banks and in ruined building have been recorded.

*Eggs* 4–6, very variable in colour, mainly whitish or brownish with dark markings. Incubated by female for nearly 2 weeks.

*Nestlings* brownish-grey down, crimson inside mouth with whitish spurs, pale yellow flanges. Fed by both parents. Leave nest after nearly 2 weeks.

*Adults* sexes similar; very like Tree Pipit (refer to Tree Pipit for differences in appearance). Perches on trees when they are available, but in breeding habitat is usually seen flitting about the ground.

*Fledglings* resemble adult.

*Hints* fluttering song flight is similar to Tree Pipit's, but the bird usually rises from the ground instead of from a perch. When walking across moors and fells, you are more likely to put up a Meadow Pipit than any other species; characteristic, thin 'tseep' note is usually heard as it flushes. If you linger in one spot and the alarm note persists, the chances are that the nest is within a few yards of you; squat down low and look at the sides of tussocks for a 'mouse-hole' entrance. Nests are always worth examining because the Cuckoo often lays an egg in the nest of this species. Distraction display has been recorded.

## Rock Pipit *Anthus spinoletta petrosus*. Pl. **132**, *311*

*Breeds* late April–June (occasionally July), near the sea on rocky coasts and islands. (In British Isles, locally in Denmark, NW. France, N. Spain and on Scandinavian coasts; also inland on high ground in Europe.)

*Nest* usually in a recess of rocky cliff overlooking the sea or in grassy bank or burrow, at varying heights above the sea; also on rough moorland near the sea in the Outer Hebrides. Female builds nest of grass, seaweed sometimes included, lining it with finer grass and sometimes hair.

*Eggs* 4–5, greyish-white, thickly covered with dark markings. Incubated by female for about 2 weeks.

*Nestlings* greyish-brown down, reddish inside mouth, pale yellow flanges. Fed by both parents. Leave nest after about 2 weeks.

*Adults* larger than Meadow Pipit, slightly longer bill and much darker legs; sexes similar, dark olive-green plumage with grey outer tail-feathers. Water Pipit, *Anthus spinoletta spinoletta*, has white outer tail-feathers. Often seen flitting about on a rock cliff.

*Fledglings* more streaked than adult.

*Hints* the song flight, rising from the cliff or shore, is very similar to Meadow Pipit's, but the song has a more ringing quality, often enhanced by the echo from the cliff. It is comparatively easy to locate the nest-site, particularly when feeding young, but very difficult to find the actual nest owing to the nature of the terrain.

## Yellow Wagtail *Motacilla flava flavissima.* Pl. **133**, *312*

*Breeds* mid May–July, chiefly in low-lying meadows and arable fields near rivers, also on marshes, dunes, shingle, heathland and moorland. (In England and Wales, throughout Europe and Scandinavia. Local in S. Scotland. Has bred Ireland.)

*Nest* on the ground, usually sheltered by herbage in a slight hollow; female builds nest of grass and roots, lining it with hair.

*Eggs* 5–6, greyish or pale brown with yellowish-brown markings. Incubated chiefly by female for about 2 weeks.

*Nestlings* buffish-white down, orange-yellow inside mouth, pale yellow flanges. Fed by both parents. Leave nest after about 1½ weeks.

*Adults* very slender and elegant with long tail which constantly moves up and down, typical of wagtails with their brisk actions; male has bright yellow head, greenish crown, yellow-ish-green upper-parts, yellow under-parts; female is more drab, browner above and paler below. Blue-headed Wagtail, *Motacilla flava flava* (Central European race), has bluish crown and white chin, the male brighter coloured than the female.

*Fledglings* browner above, paler below, with dark markings at throat, like an untidy bib.

*Hints* undulating flight tends to catch the eye and a rather penetrating 'swee ou, swee ou' makes you look round. Watch likely breeding areas from late April for courtship display in which the plumage looks fluffed out; the male runs round the female on the ground, quivering his wings and also has a fluttering display flight. During the incubation the male sometimes calls the female off the nest as you approach and when this happens move a little farther away and watch for the return of the female; she tends to hover over the nest-site, but wait for her to settle as she may hover in several places before diving into the herbage. Distraction display has been observed.

## Grey Wagtail *Motacilla cinerea.* Pl. **134**, *313*

*Breeds* late March–July, usually near fast-running streams in hilly districts but also near slower water in lowlands. (In British Isles, most of Europe and SW. Sweden. Has bred Norway.)

*Nest* in a hole in bank or wall, including drainage pipes, usually close to water, occasionally in old nests of Dipper and in burrows of Sand Martin; female builds solid nest of twigs, moss, leaves and grass, lined with hair and occasionally a few feathers.

*Eggs* 5–6, pale brown with marbled or streaked effect. Incubated by female for about 2 weeks.

*Nestlings* golden-buff down, orange inside mouth, pale yellow flanges. Fed by both parents. Leave nest after about 1½ weeks.

*Adults* conspicuously long black tail with white outer feathers, yellow under-parts and bluish-grey upper-parts; male has pale eye-stripe and black throat; female's throat is whitish or slightly smudged. Frequently seen standing on boulders in streams, lifting tail up and down. *Fledglings* some dark marks at the throat; some yellow on under-parts distinguish from young Pied Wagtail, which has greyish-buff flanks.

*Hints* follow the course of a likely hill-stream and you may see this elegant bird flit ahead of you to perch on another boulder, giving a shrill 'tchipp' or double note 'tchissckk' which is reminiscent of Pied Wagtail. There is a butterfly-like display flight and the male runs towards the female on the ground with head held low, wings fluttering and tail partially spread, the feathers on the rump fluffed out. The nest entrance is often hidden under a fern or in ivy. Try searching any culvert or bridge for likely ledges. Even a sight of this beautiful bird, darting into the air to catch an insect, makes an expedition worth while.

### Pied Wagtail *Motacilla alba yarrellii*. Pl. **135**, *314*

*Breeds* mid April–August, usually in the country, often near water, around farms, villages, houses with large gardens, roadsides of stone wall country and outskirts of towns. (In British Isles, Europe and Scandinavia.)

*Nest* in some kind of cavity, often hidden by a creeper, sometimes in nest of other species. Nests have been recorded in greenhouses and on the ground. Open-type nest-boxes used. Female builds solid nest of twigs, moss, grass and leaves, lining it with hair, wool and feathers.

*Eggs* 5–6, greyish-white with grey markings. Incubated chiefly by female for about 2 weeks.

*Nestlings* grey down, orange-yellow inside mouth, pale yellow flanges. Fed by both parents. Leave nest after about 2 weeks.

*Adults* familiar black and white

wagtail, also known as Water Wagtail; the black back of male distinguishes Pied Wagtail from White Wagtail, *Motacilla alba alba*, which has light grey back and rump. Female Pied Wagtail is greyish on back, but this darkens to black on rump.

*Fledglings* easily confused with White Wagtail, brownish-grey above and greyish-buff below with blackish crescent marking across breast.

*Hints* loud 'tchissick' call is usually heard as wagtail moves off in typical bounding flight. This call is also given during courtship display which includes males pursuing females and standing face to face with them, stretching their necks to show off the black patch at the throat and constantly changing direction. Creepers on walls, rambler roses and fruit trees are always worth investigating, but the nest cavity is usually well hidden and you may have to wait until the young are being fed before finding the nest.

### Red-backed Shrike *Lanius collurio*. Pl. **136**, *315*

*Breeds* late May–July, in untrimmed hedgerows and thickets, on commons and heaths with patches of bramble and scattered thorn bushes. (In E. and SE. England, N. Spain, rest of Europe and S. Scandinavia.)

*Nest* in a tangle of thorns in bush or hedge, usually from 1–8 ft above ground; nest of dry grass and moss, sometimes decorated with a few feathers, lined with fine roots, hair and sometimes with bits of wool. Built chiefly by male.

*Eggs* 4–6, varying from creamy to pinkish-brown or greenish, usually with dark markings. Incubated chiefly by female for about 2 weeks.

*Nestlings* no down, orange-yellow inside mouth, pale yellow flanges.

Fed by both parents. Leave nest after nearly 2 weeks.

*Adults* smaller than Song Thrush, Hawk-like appearance; male has bold black streak through eye, female usually lacks eye-stripe; male has chestnut back, female usually more russet with dark crescent markings; graduated tail which expands and swings up and down and from side to side. Often perches in exposed position, waiting to pounce on prey which may then be stuck on a thorn, making a 'larder'.

*Fledglings* dark 'scaly' appearance; in autumn they may be confused with young Woodchat Shrikes on passage which have similar 'scaly' appearance but are paler.

*Hints* you are most likely to see this species during the breeding season in East Anglia or Hampshire; they tend to nest in the same locality for several years and then move on. Harsh 'chack chack' attracts attention and the male spends a lot of time on exposed perch. Courtship display includes bowing and presenting food to female. When taking food to the female during incubation, the male may be seen diving into cover; this gives a general location of the nest, but it is easier to pinpoint the site when the male breaks from cover as he leaves the nest. Although most records indicate that the male builds the nest, a female was observed building a nest in Finland by Bruce Campbell.

**Waxwing** *Bombycilla garrulus*. Pl. **137**, *316*

*Breeds* May–July, in conifer forests, favouring pine and spruce in N. Scandinavia.

*Nest* on a horizontal branch a few feet from the trunk, height from 5 ft to 30 ft above ground; both sexes probably take part in building the nest which is made of twigs, moss and lichen, the lining may include grass, hair, fur and feathers.

*Eggs* usually 5, ashy-grey with fine dark markings. Incubated chiefly by female for about 2 weeks.

*Nestlings* red inside mouth with violet patches. Fed by both parents. Leave nest after about 2 weeks.

*Adults* roughly Starling-size; sexes similar with a crest that looks windswept and is longer in the male; pinkish-brown plumage, tail tipped yellow, wings patterned in yellow, white and red.

*Fledglings* shorter crest and more drab than adult.

*Hints* when displaying aggression, the Waxwing becomes very sleek and looks tall; in courtship display the crest is raised and the body feathers are fluffed out, making it look much larger. The male performs a momentary 'swagger', as though pushing the female to one side; bits of food and other objects are passed backwards and forwards between the pair in a 'gift-passing' ceremony. (This has also been seen in winter.) Nests are not easy to find as they are frequently hidden by trailing strands of lichen. Parties of Waxwings arrive in Britain from October onwards, some years in considerable numbers, and they can be watched at close range, feeding on bushes with berries.

**Dipper** *Cinclus cinclus*. Pl. **138**, *317*

*Breeds* late February–June, near swift streams and rivers, mainly in hilly districts. (In British Isles, most of Europe and Scandinavia. Has bred Denmark. Absent Holland.)

*Nest* a few feet above shallow, fast-flowing water, in a crevice or on a ledge, often on the underside of a bridge; sometimes near a waterfall and occasionally in branches overhanging the water. Bulky domed structure of dry moss, lined with dead leaves, built by both sexes working from the inside.

*Eggs* usually 5, dull white. Incubated by female for 2–2½ weeks.

*Nestlings* grey down, orange inside mouth, whitish-yellow flanges. Leave nest after about 3 weeks.

*Adults* reminiscent of a large Wren, with a white throat and some chestnut on breast, sexes look similar in the field. Has characteristic bobbing action when perched on a boulder; white eyelid often covers the eye, as though winking. Wades and submerges when walking along the beds of shallow streams, searching for food under stones.

*Fledglings* throat is mottled grey, not white as in adult.

*Hints* Dippers tend to lurk under banks and when trying to locate a pair, it is worth walking along the bed of the stream. As you come round a bend, the bird usually flies low ahead of you, often perching round the next bend until you put it up again; eventually, when you have 'pushed' it to the limit of its territory it will double back. The usual note is a loud 'zit zit zit', but the male often sings from a boulder below the nest-site; listen for a Wren-like song on your way back and look in any crevices near this spot, but do not disturb the nest as they readily desert. Courtship display includes wing-shivering and bowing. Traditional sites for the nest can be located outside the breeding season as dry moss is left from year to year. If the moss has leaves in it at the start of the breeding season, it is probably already occupied.

**Wren** *Troglodytes troglodytes*. Pl. **139,** *318*

*Breeds* mid April–July, in almost any habitat with low cover. (In British Isles, Europe and most of Scandinavia.)

*Nest* usually in a hole or crevice; various sites include bramble, tree-stump, ivy on walls and banks, bushes, hedges, inside buildings and in old nests of other species. Nest-boxes used occasionally. Nest is domed in an exposed site; shape varies from elongated to nearly spherical, with a side entrance. Male builds several nests of dead leaves, bits of bracken, moss, grass or straw; female lines one of these with feathers.

*Eggs* usually 5–6, white with dark markings. Incubated by female for about 2 weeks.

*Nestlings* scanty greyish-black down, bright yellow inside mouth, pale yellow flanges. Fed by both parents. Leave nest after about 2½ weeks.

*Adults* sexes similar; a very small brown bird which looks like a plump 'triangle' with its tail cocked up at an angle. Active and restless, appearing briefly and then disappearing into cover; flies for short distance with whirring wings.

*Fledglings* more mottled version of adult.

*Hints* when the male displays there is a remarkable volume of sound from such a small bird; his wings and tail appear to vibrate with the vehement spate of notes. During the early stages of incubation the nest is often deserted if disturbed, and it is wiser not to put your finger inside to feel for the feathered lining; if it is occupied, you should eventually see both parents flying in and out when feeding the young. There are several island races and one of these, larger and paler than the mainland Wren, nests on precipitous turf and boulder slopes on the cliffs of St Kilda, as well as in stone walls in the area of the deserted village; down the cliffs, the St Kilda Wren looks more like a mouse than a bird as it creeps about, seldom flying in such a windswept habitat.

**Dunnock** *Prunella modularis*. Pl. **140, 141**, *319*

*Breeds* April–July (sometimes March and August, occasionally during the winter), in town and countryside alike, providing thick low cover is available. (In British Isles, most of Europe and Scandinavia. Absent most of Spain.)

*Nest* usually from 1 ft to 4 ft above ground, in thick hedge, bush or dense undergrowth; male accompanies female while she builds neat nest of twigs and moss, lining it with fur, wool and sometimes feathers. Nests on the ground have been recorded.

*Eggs* usually 4–5, blue. Incubated by female for nearly 2 weeks.

*Nestlings* black down, orange inside mouth with two black spots, whitish-pink flanges. Fed by both parents. Leave nest from 1½ to 2 weeks.

*Adults* smaller and much more trim build than House Sparrow; sexes similar, at first sight a rather drab brown bird with slender bill but looked at in detail, it is beautifully marked with blackish streaks on back and wings; head and throat are grey. Has characteristic action of flicking wings.

*Fledglings* spotted with brown crown instead of grey.

*Hints* they are easily overlooked as they hop along the ground, searching for food, but quick flicking of wings tends to catch your eye and a sweet warbling song usually betrays their presence. The song has been heard in every month of the year, sometimes after dark. Sexual chases occur from January onwards, the birds flitting along a hedge, flicking their wings and spreading them. Display includes much quivering of wings and tail; male is sometimes seen pecking at cloaca of female while she raises her tail and quivers. Garden hedges are worth searching; squat down low in order to get the dark silhouette of the nest against the light. This species is also known as Hedge Sparrow.

**Savi's Warbler** *Locustella luscinioides*

*Breeds* mid April–July, in extensive reed-beds and on marshes with scattered bushes. European breeding range includes France, Germany, Holland, N. Italy and S. Spain. (Has bred England. Absent Scandinavia.)

*Nest* at low height amongst dead reeds and sedges, just above shallow water; loosely woven cup of dead sedge built by female.

*Eggs* 3–6, greyish-white with dark markings. Incubated by female for nearly 2 weeks.

*Nestlings* reddish-brown down. Fed by female in early stages, later by both parents. Leave nest after nearly 2 weeks.

**Savi's Warbler**

*Adults* slightly larger and darker than Reed Warbler; sexes similar, no spots or streaks, reddish-brown above (wings and back uniform), paler below (palest at throat), graduated tail may be indistinctly barred. Skulks in tangled aquatic vegetation when not singing from tops of reeds.

*Fledglings* similar to adult.

*Hints* reeling song may be confused with Grasshopper Warbler's; it has a similar ventriloquial effect but the bursts of song are shorter and louder, and often start with a series of low ticking notes. The nest is invisible from above, hidden in tangled dead stems, and there are often several nests in the same area. During the last century these warblers bred regularly in East Anglia before the Fens were drained, arriving about mid April. In 1960 they returned to breed in Kent.

## Grasshopper Warbler *Locustella naevia*. Pl. **142**, *320*

*Breeds* mid May–July, in either dry or damp sites where there are scattered bushes or trees with plenty of low cover, including young plantations, heaths, moors and dunes. (In British Isles, most of Europe and S. Sweden. Absent Denmark, most of Italy, Scotland, Spain and Scandinavia.)

*Nest* on or near the ground in long grass, rushes, bramble or similar low cover, often with a visible runway to the nest; built by both sexes, on foundation of dead leaves, made of grass or stems and lined with finer grass, sometimes hair and flowering heads.

*Eggs* 6, creamy white with reddish markings. Incubated by both sexes for about 2 weeks.

*Nestlings* greyish down, yellow inside mouth with black spots and greenish sides of roof, yellowish flanges. Fed by both parents. Leave nest after about 2 weeks.

*Adults* sexes similar, mouse-like as they creep about undergrowth, round-shouldered and longish tail which is graduated; olive-brown upper-parts with black streaks, pale buff or whitish under-parts with faint streaks on breast.

*Fledglings* reddish-brown upper-parts, more dingy on under-parts than adult.

*Hints* listen for characteristic reeling song which sounds like a fishing-line running out, both by day and night. It is not easy to locate the bird as there is a ventriloquial effect, but sometimes the male can be seen with his bill wide open, turning his head from side to side and apparently shaking all over his body. The nest should be somewhere in low cover below one of these song-posts. While searching, watch the undergrowth rather than the bird singing, as the female may slip off the nest as you approach. Distraction display has been recorded.

## Moustached Warbler *Lusciniola melanopogon*

*Breeds* April–June, in reed-beds and low bushes or saplings in swampy ground. (In S. France, Italy and S. Spain. Has bred England.)

*Nest* often suspended in reeds 2 ft above water or at side of ditch near water; female builds a loosely woven structure of wide weeds and rotting vegetation, sometimes lining it with flower-heads and a few feathers.

*Eggs* 3–4, greyish-brown with dark markings.

*Nestlings* orange-yellow inside mouth. Fed by both sexes.

*Adults* sexes similar, easily confused with Sedge Warbler but upper-parts are darker, crown almost black, and the eye-stripe looks white (not creamy) and is squared at the nape. Skulks in reed-beds, sliding up the stems and often perches with tail cocked vertically.

*Fledglings* resemble adult but mantle is paler and bill nearly white (not brown as in adult).

*Hints* a pair bred in Cambridgeshire in 1946 and there have been a few records from eastern counties of England since then. They breed regularly in the Mediterranean area, and if you are taking a holiday in Majorca, Sicily or the Camargue, it is worth looking closely at any bird resembling a Sedge Warbler. The song is said to start with a cry like a Redshank's and to contain phrases that are reminiscent of Woodlark and Nightingale; a subdued warbling is less harsh than that of Sedge Warbler. Some nests are built on the foundation of old nests and the same sites are apparently used year after year. There is a harsh alarm-note described as 't-chik', repeated rapidly, accompanied by cocked tail. Details regarding incubation and fledging have not yet been recorded.

**Sedge Warbler** *Acrocephalus schoenobaenus*. Pl. **144**, *325*

*Breeds* mid May–June, sometimes in July, in rough vegetation near water and on dry ground with bushy cover, in straggling hedgerows, occasionally in crops. (In British Isles, most of Europe and Scandinavia. Absent Spain.)

*Nest* well hidden in tangled vegetation, often about 2 ft from ground; firmly built structure, chiefly by female, made of grass, stalks and moss, lined with hair, plant down and sometimes a few feathers.

*Eggs* 5–6, yellowish but heavily marked with brown. Incubated chiefly by female for about 2 weeks. *Nestlings* no down, orange-yellow inside mouth with two black spots, pale yellow flanges. Fed by both parents. Leave nest after 1½–2 weeks.

*Adults* same size as Reed and Marsh

Warbler; sexes similar with conspicuous creamy stripe above the eye, blackish streaks on crown and mantle, rufous rump shows in flight, creamy-buff under-parts. Often skulks in cover but will perch in the open.

*Fledglings* yellower-brown than adult.

*Hints* vigorous chattering song, phrases often repeated, a jumble of harsh and musical notes containing phrases of other species, is heard early in May when dancing display flight makes them conspicuous. As the breeding season advances they tend to remain in cover, making a scolding note, but sometimes noisy parties involving several individuals are heard. Notice where the males sing before incubation starts, as the nest should be somewhere in tangled vegetation below one of these song-posts.

**Marsh Warbler** *Acrocephalus palustris*. Pl. **107, 145,** *326*

*Breeds* late May–July, locally in western and southern counties of England, in withy beds and rank vegetation, often near water and occasionally in crops; sometimes in gardens in Europe. (Absent Ireland and Scotland, most of Italy and Scandinavia. Has bred Spain.)

*Nest* usually at height of about 2 ft, attached by 'handles' to a bush or several stems of plants, such as nettle, willow herb, charlock; built chiefly by female, loosely woven shallow cup of grass and stalks, lined with finer grass, roots, hair and sometimes wool.

*Eggs* 4–5, bluish or greenish-white with dark markings. Incubated by both sexes for nearly 2 weeks. *Nestlings* no down, bright yellow inside mouth with two black spots, yellowish-white flanges. Fed by both parents. Leave nest after 1½–2 weeks.

*Adults* sexes similar, same size as Sedge Warbler and easily confused with Reed Warbler, but plumage is more grey-brown than rufous and legs are pink, not dark brown. Less skulking than Reed Warbler, often singing in the open, perching on tall plant.

*Fledglings* similar to young Reed Warbler but less rufous.

*Hints* song is more musical than Reed Warbler's, more varied and liquid; it also contains many phrases of other species, including a nasal 'zwee'. Displaying male sways from side to side, flicks wings above back and jerks his tail, singing energetically. He also sings from an exposed perch near the nest-site. Nettles are always worth searching for the characteristic nest, slung from several stems to which it is attached by 'handles'.

**Reed Warbler** *Acrocephalus scirpaceus.* Pl. **108, 146,** *327*

*Breeds* May–August, nearly always in reed-beds near water, but sometimes some distance from water in low bushes. (In England and Wales, throughout Europe and parts of S. Scandinavia. Has bred Ireland.)

*Nest* usually attached to reeds at height of 3 ft; deep cylindrical cup, built round several stems of reeds, woven of grass, stems and flowerheads, lined with grass, wool and feathers; built chiefly by female but male sometimes accompanies female, carrying bits of material.

*Eggs* 4–5, greenish-white with dark markings. Incubated by both sexes for about 1½ weeks.

*Nestlings* no down, orange-yellow inside mouth with two black spots, pale yellow flanges. Fed by both parents. Leave nest after 1½–2 weeks.

*Adults* roughly Robin-size, sexes similar; slenderly built with high forehead appearance; brown upperparts (no streaks), whitish throat, no eye-stripe, pale buff under-parts; dark legs distinguish it from Marsh Warbler. Often seen clinging to reeds, one foot tucked under the body and the other down at an angle on a neighbouring stem.

*Fledglings* more reddish-brown than adult.

*Hints* song can be heard by day and night, a monotonous churring sound, altering in pitch every so often and sometimes containing phrases of other warblers; it sounds less excitable and more conversational than Sedge Warbler's song. Display includes fluffing out feathers, spreading and lifting the tail, but there is no song flight; noisy parties of a number of individuals chase each other about reed-beds later during the breeding season. They usually slip off the nest before you get to the site but the nest, binding several reeds together, is not difficult to see in accessible places.

**Icterine Warbler** *Hippolais icterina.* Pl. **147**

*Breeds* late May–June, in gardens, parks, hedgerows and woods. (In most of Europe and S. Scandinavia. Attempted breeding in England. Absent Italy, Spain and most of France.)

*Nest* usually at height of 4–8 ft above ground, in a bush or fork of tree, often in lilac; both sexes build a finch-like nest of grass, moss and wool, woven together with bits of bark and roots, lined with hair and a few feathers, sometimes bits of paper or rag.

*Eggs* 4–5, pinkish-white with dark markings. Incubated by both sexes for nearly 2 weeks.

*Nestlings* no down, pale orange inside mouth with two black spots. Fed by

### Icterine Warbler

both parents. Leave nest after about 2 weeks.

*Adults* larger than Willow Warbler, easily confused with Melodious Warbler, but has longer pointed wings (not rounded) which show a pale patch when closed; sexes similar, olive-brown upper-parts, yellowish under-parts. Moves restlessly amongst foliage, difficult to see but in the open it has a high forehead appearance and rather upright stance when perching.

*Fledglings* more brown than olive on upper-parts, paler under-parts than adult.

*Hints* song helps to distinguish from Melodious Warbler where these two species overlap. Icterine Warbler has a louder song, with a lot of chuckling and grating notes mixed with more musical 'dideroid' phrase; there is a lot of repetition, whereas the Melodious Warbler's song is more musical, more varied and less vehement. Display includes song flight, rising and then floating down like a parachute. The female is said to sit close when incubating and to scold when the nest is approached. In Britain they are regarded as scarce and irregular visitors on passage. One pair attempted to nest near Marlborough in Wiltshire in 1907.

**Melodious Warbler** *Hippolais polyglotta.*

*Breeds* mid May–July, mainly in bushes near water, but also in trees and shrubs, including built-up areas and scrubs of hill-sides. (In France, Italy, Spain and occasionally in Switzerland. Absent British Isles and Scandinavia.)

*Nest* in a bush or tree, often at height 1–5 ft above ground; neat nest of grass and feathers, built chiefly by female, lined with plant down, sometimes with hair and roots.

*Eggs* 4–5, difficult to distinguish from Icterine Warbler's. Incubated by female for nearly 2 weeks.

*Nestlings* no down, deep yellow inside mouth with two dark spots, pale yellow flanges. Fed by both parents. Leave nest after nearly 2 weeks.

*Adults* sexes similar, easily confused with Icterine Warbler, but wings have a more rounded silhouette in flight and look uniform colour when closed (without any pale patch); brownish above, yellowish below. Same high forehead appearance, tends to move restlessly in cover of higher bushes than Icterine Warbler.

*Fledglings* similar to young Icterine Warbler.

*Hints* display flight is similar to that of Icterine Warbler, rising up and parachuting down while singing. Song is more musical, more subdued and less vehement than Icterine Warbler's. Small numbers are seen on passage along coasts of Britain, mainly in the autumn. Breeding was reported in Sussex and Surrey at the end of the last century, but owing to difficulty of distinguishing between Icterine and Melodious Warbler, there is some doubt as to identification.

**Garden Warbler** *Sylvia borin.* Pl. **148**, *323*

*Breeds* mid May–June, in woods where there are gaps in leaf canopy and plenty of undergrowth; also in large gardens which have some un-cultivated patches, on commons and heaths with scattered trees and undergrowth, sometimes in withy-beds away from trees. (In British Isles, most of Europe and Scandinavia.)

*Nest* from ground-level up to about 3 ft, under brambles or in thick cover; loose structure, built chiefly by female, of dry grass and lined with rootlets and hair. Male also builds 'trial' nest.

*Eggs* 4–5, variable colour, usually whitish with brown marbled effect. Incubated by both sexes for about $1\frac{1}{2}$ weeks.

*Nestlings* no down, bright red inside mouth with two purple spots, white flanges. Fed by both parents. Leave nest after about $1\frac{1}{2}$ weeks.

*Adults* same size as Blackcap and Whitethroat; sexes similar, rather plump and drab with round-headed appearance but no distinguishing features of any kind; brown above, pale buff below. Hardly ever seen in the open, but active in cover of leaves and undergrowth.

*Fledglings* similar to adult.

*Hints* their movements are so secretive that their presence is only revealed by a subdued warble which is easily confused with Blackcap's song. The male sings close to the nest which is hidden in dense cover, usually at lower level than Blackcap's nest. Various 'trial' nests are built before the final site is occupied. Brambles below places where the song is heard are worth searching and a hard 'tacc tacc' alarm-note, like two pebbles being rubbed together, is often heard as you approach the nest-site. A bird with tail spread and fluttering its wings near the nest is a sign of alarm, but these postures are also part of courtship display.

## Blackcap *Sylvia atricapilla*. Pl. **149**, *328*

*Breeds* late April–July, in open woodland with plenty of undergrowth, also in gardens and shrubberies with bushy growth and trees. (In British Isles, Europe and most of Scandinavia.)

*Nest* usually from 2 ft to 8 ft above ground, often in evergreen shrubs, nettles and brambles, sometimes in ivy against a wall; neat structure, built chiefly by female, slung by 'handles', made of stems, grass and roots and lined with fine grass and hair. The rim of the nest is often decorated with cobwebs.

*Eggs* 4–6, greyish-buff with brown marbled effect. Incubated by both sexes for $1\frac{1}{2}$–2 weeks.

*Nestlings* no down, pink inside mouth with two faint brown spots, white flanges. Fed by both parents. Leave nest after about $1\frac{1}{2}$ weeks but earlier if disturbed.

*Adults* roughly Sparrow-size; drab greyish-brown and featureless except for cap which is glossy black in male and reddish-brown in female. Less secretive than Garden Warbler.

*Fledglings* slightly darker on breast than adult female and young males have a darker crown.

*Hints* a rich warbling song, more vehement than Garden Warbler's, announces their arrival, usually early in April. The male sings above the nest-site, often from cover but you may catch sight of him with his feathers fluffed out, especially on the crown. Normal flight is rather jerky but during courtship and when other males are being pursued it is much more fluttering. The nest tends to be at a higher level than that of Garden Warbler. Distraction display, flapping along the ground, has been observed. Harsh 'tacc tacc' alarm-note is similar to that of Garden Warbler.

**Whitethroat** *Sylvia communis*. Pl. 150, *329*

*Breeds* May–July, in tangled vegetation of hedgerow, edges of woodland, bushes on commons, edges of moorland and in withy-beds. (In British Isles, Europe and most of Scandinavia.)

*Nest* hidden in dense cover, usually 1–2 ft above ground; male builds 'trial' nests, female may accept one or they may both build another; similar deepish cup to Garden Warbler's, often lined with black hair and decorated with white down.

*Eggs* 4–5, variable colour, usually yellowish-green with variable markings. Incubated by both sexes for about 1½ weeks.

*Nestlings* no down, pink and yellow inside mouth with four dark spots, pale yellow flanges. Fed by both sexes. Leave nest after about 1½ weeks.

*Adults* same size as Blackcap with triangular capped effect, grey in male, brown in female; reddish-brown along the wing when closed, white throat, grey tail with white outer feathers. Tends to dart in and out of cover instead of skulking persistently.

*Fledglings* brown capped like adult female.

*Hints* a rapid warble of grating notes and harsh churring from thick cover announces their arrival, usually early in April. The male has a dancing song flight which is reminiscent of Tree Pipit. Both sexes raise the feathers on crown and back, quivering their wings, looking thoroughly excited. Males also rush towards females as though going in to the attack, swerving up at the last minute. Several nests may be built before the final one, and searching under the canopy of low vegetation in places where the song is most frequently heard is usually successful. Harsh scolding and 'tacc tacc' alarm-note helps to warn you that you are near the nest. Distraction display, fluttering along the ground or in bushes, has been recorded.

**Lesser Whitethroat** *Sylvia curruca*

*Breeds* May–July, on commons, in shrubberies and along lanes with overgrown hedgerows and tall bushy growth. (In England and Wales, most of Europe and Scandinavia. Absent Spain and most of Italy.)

*Nest* in centre of thick cover, such as thorn bush or hedgerow, festooned with creepers, also in young conifers and evergreen shrubs, usually from 2 ft to 5 ft above ground; neat shallow nest, built by both sexes, decorated with cobwebs and sometimes containing some dead leaves, otherwise similar to Whitethroat's. Male also builds 'trial' nests.

**Lesser Whitethroat**

*Eggs* 4–6, white with yellow and brown markings. Incubated by both sexes for about 1½ weeks.

*Nestlings* no down, orange inside mouth with two dark spots, pale yellow flanges. Fed by both parents. Leave nest after about 1½ weeks.

*Adults* slightly smaller than Whitethroat; sexes similar, white throat, dark patch behind eye, greyish upper-parts (no suggestion of red) and white under-parts. More secretive habits than Whitethroat.

*Fledglings* similar to adult but browner.

*Hints* rattling notes which stop suddenly, coming from dense cover, are usually the first indication of their presence. There is also a very subdued warble. Feathers on breast and crown are fluffed out during display; there is a lot of wing-fluttering and a pair are sometimes seen tumbling to the ground, as though fighting. Male sings from several song-posts, but nest should be near one of them. Harsh 'tacc tacc' alarm-note usually indicates that you are near the site. Distraction display, in which the bird appears to fall to the ground and run about with wings and tail held loosely, has been observed.

**Dartford Warbler** *Sylvia undata.* Pl. **151**, *330*

*Breeds* late April–June, locally on heaths and commons with heather and gorse, in very few localities in S. England; allied races breed in France, Italy and Spain.

*Nest* usually just above the ground in long heather or up to 3½ ft in gorse; compact nest of grass, roots, bits of heather and gorse, sometimes lined with hair and a few feathers, built chiefly by female. Male also builds 'trial' nests.

*Eggs* 3–4, whitish with dark markings. Incubated chiefly by female for about 1½ weeks.

*Nestlings* no down, pale yellow inside mouth with two black spots, pale yellow flanges. Fed by both parents. Leave nest after nearly 2 weeks.

*Adults* small, very dark warbler with long, graduated tail; male has dark brown upper-parts, grey head, dull red throat and breast; female looks more drab; both sexes have red eye and a dark tail with a narrow white border which is frequently cocked up. They tend to skulk in cover, but will perch briefly on an exposed spray. Allied races in S. Europe tend to be paler above and below.

*Fledglings* rather similar to adult female.

*Hints* song which is reminiscent of Whitethroat can be heard from late March, often from cover but also, when undisturbed, from the top spray of a gorse bush. There are several song-posts and the nest should be below one of them. Both sexes flirt and fan their tails and expand their wings; there is also a dancing display flight. There are so few breeding pairs that it is not worth risking disturbance by searching likely areas. A few pairs breed in the R.S.P.B.'s reserve at Arne in Dorset.

**Willow Warbler** *Phylloscopus trochilus.* Pl. **152**, *322*

*Breeds* late April–July, in woods and in other places where there are trees and bushes and plenty of ground cover, including hedgerows and large gardens. (In British Isles, most of Europe and throughout Scandinavia. Absent most of Italy and Spain.)

*Nest* usually on the ground hidden by herbage or ground cover, sometimes in the open under tuft of grass, occasionally in disused nests of other species; domed structure with side entrance which is often masked by trailing stems or grass, built by female, of grass and moss and lined with feathers.

*Eggs* 6–7, white with dark markings, often densely marked. Incubated by female for nearly 2 weeks.

*Nestlings* scanty whitish down, orange-yellow inside mouth with two faint brown spots, yellow flanges. Fed by both parents. Leave nest after about 2 weeks.

*Adults* sexes similar, easily confused with Chiffchaff when silent, but greenish-yellow plumage looks brighter and legs are light brown, not blackish; similar flitting about twigs and undergrowth.

*Fledglings* similar to adult.

*Hints* the alarm-note, 'hweet', is similar to Chiffchaff's, but the song is quite different, rising in pitch and then descending in a sweet cascade of notes, ending in a flourish 'sooeet sooeetoo'. As the female returns to incubate, she often calls 'hweet'; watch her as she gets lower and lower in the undergrowth; the nest is often at the edge of a track. Distraction display has been recorded and a hissing sound has been heard from the nest. Courtship display is similar to Chiffchaff's.

## Chiffchaff *Phylloscopus collybita*. Pl. **153**, *321*

*Breeds* late April–June, mainly on edges of woods but also in copses and hedgerows where there are well-grown trees or bushes and plenty of ground cover. (In British Isles, Europe and most of Scandinavia. Absent parts of Scotland and S. Scandinavia.)

*Nest* low down in undergrowth, rarely on the ground, often in bramble or tangled herbage; female builds rounded structure with side entrance, made of dead leaves, grass and moss, lined with feathers.

*Eggs* usually 6, white with dark markings. Incubated by female for nearly 2 weeks.

*Nestlings* scanty grey down, dull yellow inside mouth, pale yellow flanges. Fed chiefly by female. Leave nest after 2 weeks.

*Adults* smaller than Sparrow, easily confused with Willow Warbler when silent, but greenish-yellow plumage looks more drab and the legs are blackish, not light brown; sexes similar, streamlined silhouette, constantly flitting about.

*Fledglings* similar to adult.

*Hints* monotonous double note 'chiff chaff' is the best means of identification when warblers arrive, usually in March. Courtship display includes fluffing out feathers, spreading the tail and a butterfly-like display flight. The nest is easiest to find at the building stage. Note song-posts of males and watch for any sign of movement in the undergrowth below these places; edges of paths and tracks seem to be favourite sites. The alarm-note, an emphatic 'hweet', is often heard as you approach the nest.

## Wood Warbler *Phylloscopus sibilatrix*. Pl. **143**, *324*

*Breeds* mid May–June, in mature beech woods where the leaf canopy is close and there is little undergrowth, also in scrub woodland. (In Britain, most of Europe and S. Scandinavia. Has bred Ireland. Absent most of Spain.)

*Nest* on the ground, often on a slight slope in a comparatively open site, the domed nest just visible; built by female of dry grass, leaves and fibres, lined with grass and hair (no feathers).

*Eggs* 5–7, white, usually with dark markings. Incubated by female for nearly 2 weeks.

*Nestlings* long grey down, yellow inside mouth, paler yellow flanges. Fed by both parents. Leave nest after about 1½ weeks.

*Adults* larger and brighter coloured than Chiffchaff and Willow Warbler; sexes similar, yellow breast contrasts with white belly, greenish-yellow upper-parts, yellow streak above eye. Wings tend to droop when perching.

*Fledglings* drab version of adult with greyish-brown tone on upper-parts.

*Hints* song is best means of identifying from other warblers; it has two types of phrase – a drawling 'piu' and a markedly sibilant trill. Male has a parachute-like display flight, losing height with legs trailing, above the nest-site. The alarm-note is similar to Chiffchaff's but rather softer, and the female often gives a repetitive, piping note as she returns to incubate, making it comparatively easy to follow her back to the nest. If disturbed off the nest she may hover near you, just above the ground, making a hissing sound. Distraction display has been observed.

**Goldcrest** *Regulus regulus.* Pl. **154,** *331*

*Breeds* April–June, in woods and countryside with scattered trees, favouring conifer and yew; also in large gardens and parks with cypress and cedar trees. (In British Isles, most of Europe and Scandinavia. Absent most of Italy and Spain.)

*Nest* usually hanging below end of branch, hidden by foliage, also in creeper near trunk, occasionally in gorse bush; both sexes build a 'hammock' of moss and spider's webs, lined with many feathers, and attached by 'handles'.

*Eggs* 7–10, white or pale buff with darker markings. Incubated by female for just over 2 weeks.

*Nestlings* scanty sooty-grey down, orange inside mouth, pinkish-white flanges. Fed by both parents. Leave nest after about 2½ weeks.

*Adults* tiny and plump, colouring suggests a warbler, actions are tit-like; olive-green above, whitish-buff below; both sexes have black stripes on either side of crown which is golden in male and yellower in female. Goldcrest may be confused with Firecrest, but the latter has white 'eyebrow' and black stripe through the eye; Goldcrest has a pale area round the eye but no stripe. *Fledglings* no crest or stripes on head until winter.

*Hints* very high-pitched 'zee zee zee' makes you look towards the top of trees where a diminutive bird seems to be always on the move, often visible for a moment at the tips of branches. The male's crest is raised and spread sideways during courtship and in aggressive displays at other males while twittering. Nests in trees in parks or gardens, as distinct from woods, are easier to find as you can get the undersides of branches against the light to see if there is any festoon hanging towards the end. The nest is delicately made, and if you touch it when the young are about to emerge you may find chicks floating down over your head.

**Firecrest** *Regulus ignicapillus*

*Breeds* May–July, in similar habitat to Goldcrest but also in some marshy areas with bushes. (In most of Europe. Has bred England. Absent Denmark and Scandinavia.)

**Firecrest**

*Nest* often in similar site to Goldcrest but also in juniper bushes and in ivy-clad alders in swamps; nest is slightly smaller than Goldcrest's, made of moss and feathers. Built by female, accompanied by male.

*Eggs* 5–12, pinkish with dark markings. Probably incubated by female for about 2 weeks.

*Nestlings* no description available. Probably fed by both parents. Leave nest after about 2½ weeks.

*Adults* very similar behaviour and appearance to Goldcrest except for distinctive white 'eyebrow' which extends almost to nape, contrasting with black stripe on crown, and a black streak through the eye; in some lights sides of neck look bronzed. Sexes look similar in the field.

*Fledglings* no crest, similar 'eyebrow' and eye-stripe to adult.

*Hints* similar call-note to Goldcrest's but pitched lower. The majority of Firecrests in England are seen in the autumn, in eastern and southern counties, mainly near the coast. A pair was stated to have bred in Lancashire in 1927, but the first breeding records to be accepted during this century were from Hampshire in the early 1960s. They are said to desert readily if the site is disturbed.

**Pied Flycatcher** *Ficedula hypoleuca*. Pl. **156,** *333*

*Breeds* late April–June, on wooded slopes of hilly country, chiefly in north and west of Britain, also in gardens and orchards with mature deciduous trees; nests are found in towns as well as woods in Scandinavia and in conifer as well as deciduous forests on the Continent. (In Britain, Scandinavia and most of Europe. Absent Italy.)

*Nest* from ground-level up to about 40 ft in a natural hole of tree, also in walls and rock crevices; female builds nest of dead leaves, fibres of honeysuckle and bracken, bark and moss, lining it with fine grass. Nest-boxes used.

*Eggs* 5–8, pale greenish-blue. Incubated by female for nearly 2 weeks.

**Pied Flycatcher**

*Nestlings* scanty grey down, orange-yellow inside mouth, pale yellow flanges. Fed by both parents. Leave nest after just over 2 weeks.

*Adults* slightly smaller and more rounded silhouette than Spotted Flycatcher; same darting flight for insects, but does not return as frequently to the same perch. Male looks brownish-black above, white below, white forehead and white wing-bar conspicuous; female is more drab and wing-bar less obvious.

*Fledglings* white wing-bar distinguishes from young Spotted Flycatcher.

*Hints* when they arrive in breeding areas they are very active and their flashing black and white plumage makes them conspicuous. Males frequently chase females and fight other males for possession of nestholes. A number of holes may be visited before the female accepts one. While the female is building, the male is constantly seen near the site and sings a simple song, described as 'tchee tchee tchee cher cher'. He also feeds the female while she is incubating. Constant visits to the hole when feeding young should make the nest easy to find. In Britain they are found mainly in western counties during the breeding season.

**Collared Flycatcher** *Ficedula albicollis*

*Breeds* May–June, in similar habitat to Pied Flycatcher, in parts of

France, Germany, Italy, Switzerland and on islands of Oland and Gotland in the Baltic.

*Nest* similar to Pied Flycatcher, built by female in a hole in a tree; nest-boxes used.

*Eggs* 4–7, pale to dark blue. Incubated by female for about 2 weeks.

*Nestlings* no description available. Fed by both parents. Leave nest after about 2 weeks.

**Collared Flycatcher**

*Adults* easily confused with Pied Flycatcher as behaviour and appearance are somewhat similar; male has distinctive white collar, larger white patch on forehead and more white at base of wing-tips than Pied Flycatcher; female has only a suggestion of a white collar.

*Fledglings* brown rather than black and white pattern on forehead, brownish shading on collar.

*Hints* its song is simpler than Pied Flycatcher's and is often interrupted by a call-note described as 'seeb'. Males sing during display flight when showing females possible nest-holes. The females visit a number of holes and appear to be fastidious in their choice. The male enters a hole, but reappears immediately should the female slip in behind him. If the female remains inside for several minutes it is likely that she will nest there, although holes are sometimes changed after apparent occupation. The male continues to display by neighbouring holes while the female

is building the nest. Nests have been found in old woodpecker holes. Collared Flycatchers are said to be relatively common in the woods out-side Budapest. In Britain there are very few records of them seen on passage. The white collar is almost obscured outside the breeding season and it is possible that one or two are mistaken for Pied Flycatchers.

**Spotted Flycatcher** *Muscicapa striata*. Pl. **155**, *332*

*Breeds* mid May–July, on outskirts of woods and felled clearings, in parks and gardens, including built-up areas. (In British Isles, Europe and Scandinavia.)

*Nest* on a ledge or in a natural hollow between forks of trees or where branch has been removed, often against a garden wall covered with creeper or shrub growing against it, usually from 5 ft to 15 ft above ground; both sexes build rather un-tidy, loose nest of moss, hair, wool and feathers. Exceptionally on top of nest of other species. Open-type nest-boxes used.

*Eggs* usually 4–5, pale blue with dark markings. Incubated by both sexes for nearly 2 weeks.

*Nestlings* scanty grey down, orange-yellow inside mouth, whitish-yellow flanges. Fed by both parents. Leave nest after nearly 2 weeks.

*Adults* roughly Sparrow-size but more slender; sexes similar, drab greyish-brown above with spots on head, white below with faint streaking on breast. Often perches in same place, standing very upright with tail hanging down; suddenly darts into the air to catch an insect and then returns to the same perch.

*Fledglings* more spotted effect than adult.

*Hints* they usually arrive early in May when their characteristic darting flight, returning to the same perch, attracts attention. A rather thin call-note is also unmistakable once you are familiar with it. Courtship chases in flight take place and the birds frequently flick their wings when perching. At this stage you often become over-confident, noting the places where they are most frequently seen to perch, but when nest-building starts, you tend to lose them and you may have to wait until incubation starts before locating the nest. The incubating bird sits rather high and a beady eye keeps watch. If they nest successfully, they often use the same site the following year.

## Whinchat *Saxicola rubetra*. Pl. **157,** *334*

*Breeds* late May–July, in rough grass on hill-sides with cover from bracken, bushes or young conifers, also on commons, heaths and along railway embankments. (In British Isles, most of Europe and Scandinavia. Absent most of Italy and Spain.)

*Nest* on the ground in a tussock of grass, sometimes with a tunnel runway to the nest which is made of grass and moss, lined with finer grass and hair; male accompanies female while she builds the nest.

*Eggs* 5–6, greenish-blue, usually with fine markings. Incubated by female for nearly 2 weeks.

*Nestlings* pale grey down, orange-yellow inside mouth, yellowish-white flanges. Fed by both parents. Leave nest after about 1½ weeks.

*Adults* roughly Robin-size, often seen perching on top spray, flicking wings and tail; short tail with white sides at the base, distinguishes from Stonechat; male has bold white eye-stripe, female less clearly marked; plumage of both sexes is paler than Stonechat, but the females of both species may be confused, the males

being easily identified by black head of Stonechat.

*Fledglings* similar to adult female but without white patch on wing.

*Hints* notice where the male sings and try searching below one of these song-posts. The male tends to hover near the nest-site and to call 'tick tick utick'. During incubation the female comes off the nest fairly often and is accompanied by the male, giving you a chance to watch where she goes down, providing you are not distracted by the male at the last minute. When young are present, there is often a soft 'chup' as you approach.

## Stonechat *Saxicola torquata*. Pl. **158,** *335*

*Breeds* late March–July, in similar habitat to Whinchat but favours areas of scattered gorse. (In British Isles and throughout Europe, except parts of Denmark. Absent Scandinavia.)

*Nest* often on the ground, sometimes with a tunnel runway to the nest, but also up to about 2 ft in a low bush; built by female, mainly of grass and moss, lined with fine grass and sometimes fur, hair, wool and feathers.

*Eggs* 5–6, paler but similar to Whinchat's eggs. Incubated usually by female, but male has been observed taking a share; period about 2 weeks.

*Nestlings* brownish-grey down, yellow inside mouth, whitish-yellow flanges.

*Adults* may be confused with Whinchat, but slightly stockier and more round-headed appearance; male has black head which contrasts with white collar at sides of neck; female has no eye-stripe and no white on tail. Similar habit of perching in prominent place, flicking wings and tail.

*Fledglings* rather similar to adult

female but very mottled and variable in colour.

*Hints* before nest-building starts, the male chases the female about the territory, but they become less conspicuous after this and song-posts of male are then the best indication of the nest-site. When searching a likely area, the male usually gives a warning 'chuck' as you are getting near the site, but when you are practically on top of it, he attempts to distract your attention by hovering in a very conspicuous manner, calling a loud and continuous 'whit whit whit'.

## Wheatear *Oenanthe oenanthe*. Pl. 159, 336

*Breeds* late April–June, on rough open ground of downs, dunes, moors and mountains, often associated with stone walls and rocky outcrops. (In British Isles, Europe and Scandinavia.)

*Nest* in a hole on the ground, including rabbit burrows and in crevices of stone walls and rocks; built chiefly by female, made of grass and moss, lined with fur, feathers and hair.

*Eggs* 6, pale blue, usually unmarked. Incubated chiefly by female for about 2 weeks.

*Nestlings* dark grey down, pale orange inside mouth, pale yellow flanges. Fed by both parents. Leave nest after about 2 weeks.

*Adults* slightly larger than Stonechat; both sexes have white rump and white sides to base of tail; male has black patch round the eye with a white streak above it, blackish wings contrast with grey upper-parts, giving a very dapper appearance; female is more drab, a combination of buff and brown, less boldly marked round the eye. Often seen on the ground, bobbing and flirting the tail.

*Fledglings* similar to adult female but spotted on body.

*Hints* male is usually much more in evidence than female, either singing from a boulder or in a short song flight, dancing up a few feet and landing again, bobbing and lifting tail up and down. The song is a jumble of notes, like stones being rubbed together. There is also a harsh 'chack chack' call. The nest is easiest to find during incubation as the male often perches facing the exit from the nest and joins the female as she comes off to feed. Keep your eye on the female as she usually returns after only a few minutes; try to mark the area where she goes down, probably within a few yards of where the male originally perched, and then wait for another spell of roughly 20 minutes until she comes off again. Having seen two returns to the nest, you should be able to locate the burrow or hole the next time that she leaves it.

## Black Redstart *Phoenicurus ochrurus*. Pl. 160, 337

*Breeds* late April–July, locally in England, mainly on derelict buildings and industrial plant along the south-east coast; also throughout Europe on buildings, cliffs, rocky ground in mountainous districts, lower down on cultivated land, including gardens and vineyards. (Has bred Norway.)

*Nest* in a hole or on a ledge, sometimes inside farm buildings abroad; built by female of grass, moss and local vegetation, lined with hair and feathers. Nest-boxes used abroad.

*Eggs* 4–5, white, occasionally faintly marked. Incubated by female for nearly 2 weeks.

*Nestlings* dark grey down, yellow inside mouth, whitish flanges. Fed by both parents. Leave nest after about 2 weeks.

*Adults* same size as Redstart with similar shimmering, chestnut-red tail, rest of plumage is much darker than Redstart; male usually has black throat and breast and a whitish patch on wing; female is greyer with no orange or buff on under-parts. More frequently seen on the ground than Redstart.

*Fledglings* darker than young Redstart.

*Hints* from late March, listen for a fast warbling song, with some grating notes towards the end of the phrase. In England singing males have been recorded from many counties, apparently holding territory but not necessarily breeding. Most breeding records since the last war have come from the south-east coast, with a few pairs regularly in the City of London and in the area of Dover. As the bombed sites disappeared, power stations, docks and other industrial installations have been taken over; cliff sites as well as ledges on tall buildings have been recorded.

**Redstart** *Phoenicurus phoenicurus.* Pl. **161**, *338*

*Breeds* mid May–July, in woodlands, orchards, parks and gardens with trees, heaths and hilly country with scrub, stone walls and rocks. (In Britain, Europe and Scandinavia. Has bred Ireland.)

*Nest* in a hole, from ground-level up to about 25 ft, in trees, buildings, crevices of rocks and stone walls and on banks; built by female of grass, roots and moss, lined with hair and feathers. Nest-boxes used.

*Eggs* 5–8, greenish-blue, occasionally faintly marked. Incubated by female but male has been recorded on eggs; period about 2 weeks.

*Nestlings* dark grey down, pale orange inside mouth, yellowish-

white flanges. Fed by both parents. Leave nest after about 2 weeks.

*Adults* Robin-size, both sexes have bright chestnut-red tail which shimmers as the tail flicks up and down; orange breast of male distinguishes from male Black Redstart; the females of these two species are easily confused but female Redstart shows some orange on under-parts. More frequently seen flitting about trees than on ground.

*Fledglings* mottled, like young Robin, but tail is chestnut-red.

*Hints* during courtship the male chases the female from perch to perch, both sexes quivering their tails and making a shimmer of orange which is a remarkable sight. The song is reminiscent of Robin, but seems to fade out rather than come to a concluding phrase. When prospecting likely holes, the male flies in and out and this is the easiest stage at which to locate a breeding pair. Ground nests are not reported as frequently as holes in trees and in walls. The alarm-note sounds like 'wheet tuck'. In Britain they tend to concentrate in hilly districts of the west and north during the breeding season.

**Robin** *Erithacus rubecula.* Pl. **162**, *339*

*Breeds* late March–June, occasionally in July, and eggs have been found in nearly every month; in town and countryside alike, providing some cover is available. (In British Isles, Europe and most of Scandinavia.)

*Nest* from ground-level up to about 10 ft, in a depression or hole, often on a bank, but various sites recorded, including many artificial ones, such as old tins and occasionally indoors. Open-type nest-boxes used. Nest is always well hidden, built by female of dead leaves and moss, lined with hair.

*Eggs* 4–6, white with reddish markings. Incubated by female for about 2 weeks.

*Nestlings* blackish down, yellow inside mouth, whitish-yellow flanges. Fed by both parents. Leave nest after about 2 weeks.

*Adults* sexes similar, orange-red breast and forehead make the Robin familiar to anyone who notices birds, however casually.

*Fledglings* spotted appearance and without full red breast.

*Hints* territorial fights between Robins start in September and continue until May. Males sing a rather melancholy song to attract the attention of a female and pairs are formed from December to February when typical aggressive postures can be seen, both birds swaying face to face with necks stretched upwards. (Both sexes sing in winter.) Courtship feeding usually starts late in March and continues throughout the season, both on the nest and off it. Nests are notoriously difficult to find, but sometimes the female can be followed back to the nest after she has been fed by the male during incubation. When both parents are feeding young, there is a better chance of seeing where they go. A soft 'peep' is often heard as you approach the nest-site. Distraction display has been seen, the female fluttering along the ground. The continental race is less tame, more skulking, and usually nests in open woodland, far away from human habitations.

**Nightingale** *Luscinia megarhynchos.* Pl. **163**, *340*

*Breeds* May–June, in countryside with thicket type of growth, including copses, commons, heaths and tangled hedgerows, with plenty of ground cover of brambles, tall grass and nettles; mainly in southern half of England and at higher altitudes in Europe. (Absent Ireland, Scotland, Scandinavia and most of Denmark.)

*Nest* on the ground or a few feet up, hidden in undergrowth; female builds a rather loose and deep nest of dead leaves, grass and hair.

*Eggs* 4–6, olive-brown. Incubated by female for about 2 weeks.

*Nestlings* dark grey down, orange inside mouth, whitish-yellow flanges. Fed by both parents. Leave nest after about 1½ weeks.

*Adults* reminiscent of a large Robin with a reddish tail which quivers when singing, usually in thick cover; sexes similar, rufous-brown upper-parts with whitish throat, greyish-brown under-parts.

*Fledglings* mottled like young Robin but with redder tail.

*Hints* location of a breeding pair is nearly always by the unique song which has a remarkable variety of liquid notes, often with phrases repeated, some of which become louder and louder. Sings by day and night from a number of perches, usually in thick cover and not necessarily above the nest-site. Try searching the nearest 'open' site to where the song is heard, such as the undergrowth along a track bordering the hedge or copse. The nest is often in brambles or nettles with long grass growing up into them. Distraction display has been recorded.

**Red-spotted Bluethroat** *Cyanosylvia svecica.* Pl. **164**, *341*

*Breeds* late May–June, in open woodland or scrub amongst birch and willow, often near fishing villages in Arctic. (In N. Scandinavia.)

*Nest* female enlarges a natural hollow to make a Robin-like nest on the ground, of grass and moss, lined with finer material.

*Eggs* 4–7, varying from greenish-blue

to reddish-cream with dark markings. Incubated by female for nearly 2 weeks.

*Nestlings* probably similar to White-spotted Bluethroat. Fed by both parents. Leave nest after about 2 weeks.

*Adults* Robin-size but more rotund; male has bright blue patch on throat with bordering of chestnut and black and chestnut spots in the centre of the patch; female has whitish throat. Tail frequently cocked and spread, revealing chestnut base.

*Fledglings* darker and more streaked than young Robin, with dark base of tail as in adult.

*Hints* they have a pipit-like display flight. Song is delivered either from a perch or in display flight. Some of the notes are reminiscent of Nightingale, but not as varied or as rich in tone; a metallic 'ting ting ting' is said to be like a triangle being struck. In some areas they appear to sing mainly after nightfall while the female is incubating the eggs. Some nests are in comparatively open sites; some are hidden under tussocks below a bush. When flushed from the nest, their behaviour also varies from skulking in cover to flitting about the bushes near the nest, scolding with a chat-like 'tacc tacc'. In Britain they are normally only seen passing along the east coast; small numbers, for instance, occur regularly on Fair Isle in May and September.

## White-spotted Bluethroat *Cyanosylvia svecica cyanecula*

*Breeds* May–June, on damp ground at the edges of lakes amongst willow and alder scrub, also on dry hillsides with scattered bushes and on cultivated land without bushes. (In Belgium, France, Germany, Holland and Spain, occasionally in Denmark during the last century.)

*Nest* on marshy ground near water, made of stalks, grass, moss, hair and down; on dry ground below bush of broom, made of twigs, grass and roots; presumably built by female.

*Eggs* 4–6, greyish-green with dark markings. Both sexes have been seen sitting on eggs; period nearly 2 weeks.

*Nestlings* dark grey down, orange inside mouth, whitish-yellow flanges. Fed by both parents. Leave nest after about 2 weeks.

*Adults* very similar in appearance and behaviour to red-spotted form, but male has a white spot in centre of blue throat-patch.

*Fledglings* similar to young Red-spotted Bluethroat.

*Hints* the display and song are similar to Red-spotted Bluethroat's. Central Spain is one of the few areas where these birds have been described during the breeding season. Pipit-like song flight was seen in the 1920s on the western slopes of high ground in the Sierra del Gredos, the birds perching on dead sprays of broom protruding from the average height of the bushes. In Britain a few males have been trapped on Fair Isle between mid March and mid May; sight records from other places suggest that it is only a chance visitor to Britain.

## Fieldfare *Turdus pilaris*. Pl. **165**, *342*

*Breeds* April or May–July, in birch and mixed woodland, pine and spruce forests, in scrub or open country beyond the tree-limit; also in parks and gardens in built-up areas. (In E. France, Germany and Scandinavia. Has bred Denmark, Holland and Switzerland.)

*Nest* usually at height from 6 ft to 15 ft, but recorded from ground-level up to 40 ft, often in a tree, but also in bushes, on ledges of rocky outcrop or open ground and occasionally on ruined buildings; nest built chiefly by female, made of mud, roots and grass, on foundation of twigs and moss.

*Eggs* usually 5–6, greenish with dark markings. Incubated chiefly by female for about 2 weeks.

*Nestlings* long buff down, yellow inside mouth, yellowish-white flanges. Fed by both parents. Leave nest after about 2 weeks.

*Adults* slightly smaller than Mistle Thrush, but more brightly coloured; sexes similar, pale grey head and rump contrast with chestnut back and very dark tail. Noisy and aggressive at breeding sites.

*Fledglings* drab version of adult.

*Hints* there are often many nests in the same area and there is so much restless activity that a colony can scarcely be missed. They dash after intruders and outbursts of harsh chattering notes are frequently heard. Courtship display includes strutting about with wings drooping, tail fanned and depressed. It is said that tourists cannot fail to notice them around Trondhjem Cathedral. In Britain they are usually seen in large flocks, moving through open country during the winter, perching in hedgerows and feeding on berries, or flying overhead in loose formation, uttering their characteristic harsh 'chack chack' calls.

## Ring Ouzel *Turdus torquatus.* Pl. **166**, *343*

*Breeds* mid April–July, in moorland districts of hilly country associated with heather, juniper and rocks. (From SW. England to N. Scotland in Britain; locally in Ireland. In Norway and W. Sweden. Has bred Denmark and France. Alpine form breeds within tree-limit in France, S. Germany, Italy and Spain.)

*Nest* usually on or near the ground in clump of vegetation, such as long heather; often on a bank, recorded in stone walls, cliffs, old mine shafts and in trees. Both sexes build nest of heather, bracken and grass, coarse grass protruding at various angles, lining it with grass.

*Eggs* usually 4, greenish-blue with dark markings. Incubated by both sexes for about 2 weeks.

*Nestlings* buff down, deep yellow inside mouth, yellowish-white flange. Fed by both parents. Leave nest after about 2 weeks.

*Adults* slightly smaller than Blackbird and rather similar except for white half-collar at front; male is dark grey rather than black, female is brownish with less obvious collar. Often perches on rock or exposed site; dashing flight when disturbed, dodging along gullies. Alpine form has very pale wings.

*Fledglings* no collar, more mottled than adult.

*Hints* pairs are usually located by a ringing 'pew pew pew' call, heard some distance away as the Ouzel perches in a prominent place. It is not easy to get close to them, but they have been known to attack intruders near the nest. Distraction display, described as reeling and tumbling about on the ground, has been observed.

## Blackbird *Turdus merula.* Pl. **167**, *344*

*Breeds* late March–July, in woodlands, hedgerows, parks and gardens, including built-up areas and valleys of hilly districts. (In British Isles, Europe and S. Scandinavia.)

*Nest* from ground-level up to about 40 ft, usually in a bush or ivy against a wall, but also on buildings and in trees; bulky cup of stems, grass and moss, plastered with mud with an inner lining of grass which normally distinguishes it from Song Thrush's nest; built by female but male also gathers material sometimes. Nest made entirely of seaweed recorded in Shetland.

*Eggs* 3–5, greenish with dark markings. Incubated by female for nearly 2 weeks.

*Nestlings* buffish-grey down, yellow inside mouth, yellowish-white flanges. Fed by both parents. Leave nest after nearly 2 weeks.

*Adults* familiar 'black bird'; male is jet-black with orange bill; female is brown with a mottled effect on under-parts.

*Fledglings* more rufous and mottled than adult female.

*Hints* both male and female are aggressive and territorial disputes occur from September onwards and are particularly noticeable from January; both sexes fluff out their plumage, stretch their necks upwards and droop their wings, the tail slightly fanned and depressed. Noisy skirmishes and low 'tchook tchook' calls, heard mainly at dusk and often ending in an excited clamour, make the presence of Blackbirds obvious. Flute-like notes of the song, at its best from late February, sound rather nonchalant and relaxed. Courtship displays may be seen as early as January, the female standing with her bill and tail almost vertical. Nesting sites are prospected from late February, the birds often appearing nervous, flicking their wings and jerking their tails. Nest-building is usually the easiest stage at which to locate sites.

**Redwing** *Turdus iliacus*. Pl. **168**, *345*

*Breeds* mid May–July, chiefly in wooded country (birch and mixed woodland, pine and spruce forests), but also in parks and gardens of built-up areas. (Throughout Scandinavia except parts of S. Sweden. Has bred Belgium, France, Germany and Scotland.)

*Nest* on or near the ground up to about 12 ft, often at the foot of a tree or in low bush, also recorded on ledge of building; probably built only by female, grass cup is often strengthened with mud on foundation of twigs, stalks and earth, inner lining of fine straw.

*Eggs* 5–6, greenish-buff with dark markings. Incubated by both sexes for about 2 weeks.

*Nestlings* long buff down, yellow inside mouth, whitish flanges. Fed by both parents. Leave nest after about 2 weeks.

*Adults* slightly smaller than Song Thrush; sexes similar, well-defined creamy stripe over the eye and reddish patches on flanks and under the wing.

*Fledglings* similar to young Song Thrush except for eye-stripe and faint red patches.

*Hints* flute-like notes and a rather feeble twittering are heard during the breeding season. In autumn and winter, when flocks pass overhead in Britain, the usual call-note is a sighing 'seep'. The few pairs which nested in Scotland were in low bushes near houses. In Scandinavia there is often more than one nest in the same area. They are said to sit close during incubation, flushing when you are only a few feet from the nest.

**Song Thrush** *Turdus philomelos*. Pl. **169**, *346*

*Breeds* late March–July (sometimes February–August), in towns and countryside where there are bushes and trees; often in hedgerows, parks and gardens but also in rough open country in more remote upland areas. (In British Isles, most of Europe and Scandinavia.)

*Nest* usually in bush or tree up to about 25 ft above ground, also in creepers on walls and banks, sometimes on ledges of buildings, occasionally on the ground; female builds nest of twigs, grass and moss, plastering the cup with mud, dung and saliva; the hard lining normally distinguishes it from Blackbird's nest which has inner lining of grass.

*Eggs* 3–5, blue, usually scantily marked. Incubated by female for about 2 weeks.

*Nestlings* golden-buff down, bright yellow inside mouth, pale yellow flanges. Fed by both parents. Leave nest after about 2 weeks.

*Adults* sexes similar; roughly Blackbird-size, markedly smaller than Mistle Thrush; brown rather than grey upper-parts, small spots on breast, yellowish patches on flanks and under the wing, no white in outer tail-feathers.

*Fledglings* mottled version of adult.

*Hints* musical song is often confused with Blackbird, but its chief characteristic is the constant repetition of short phrases. Courtship postures are not elaborate, but there are noisy chases. Notice where the male perches when singing as the nest will be in this area. It is easily located at the building stage. Distraction display is not often seen but has been recorded.

**Mistle Thrush** *Turdus viscivorus*. Pl. **170**, *347*

*Breeds* March–June (occasionally February), in woods, orchards, parks and gardens, including built-up areas and valleys in hilly districts. (In British Isles, Europe and most of Scandinavia.)

*Nest* height varying from 3 ft to 50 ft, usually in a tree, either close to the trunk or well out on a bough, also recorded in low bush and on ledges of building and rocky cliff; built chiefly by female, untidy deep cup of grass, roots, moss and mud, sometimes decorated with rag, paper, lichen and feathers.

**Mistle Thrush**

*Eggs* 3–5, greenish-blue with dark markings. Incubated by female for about 2 weeks.

*Nestlings* buff down, bright yellow inside mouth, pale yellow flanges. Fed by both parents. Leave nest after about 2 weeks.

*Adults* larger than Song Thrush with longer tail which has white outer feathers; sexes similar, greyish-brown upper-parts, boldly spotted under-parts and pale underwing shows in flight. Often holds wings closed when flying, bounding flight similar to Green Woodpecker.

*Fledglings* more mottled and spotted appearance than adult.

*Hints* on windy, wet days during January it is often the only bird singing, perched high in a tall tree. After the nest-site has been chosen, adults are often seen dashing at other species, such as members of the crow family, driving them from the site and chattering excitedly, virtually rousing the neighbourhood. After gathering nest material, the female usually flies fast back to the site, making it easy to watch where she goes. In evergreens, the nest tends to be on a horizontal bough, at least half-way along it; in deciduous trees it is often close to the trunk where it forks. During incubation the female usually sits close, even when there is a cat climbing about in the same tree.

**Bearded Tit** *Panurus biarmicus*. Pl. **171**, *348*

*Breeds* April–July (occasionally later), locally in extensive beds of reed and sedge, chiefly confined to East Anglia in Britain; similarly local in Europe, including S. France, Germany, Holland and Italy.

*Nest* usually near the ground at the edge of reed-bed where stems are broken down; both sexes build an open nest of dead reeds and sedge, the male lining it with flowering heads and a few feathers.

*Eggs* 5–7, white with brown markings. Incubated by both sexes for nearly 2 weeks.

*Nestlings* no down, red and black inside mouth with 'peg-like' projections, yellow flanges. Fed by both parents. Leave nest after about 1½ weeks.

*Adults* larger than other tits; tawny above, pinkish-grey below, long graduated tail; male has grey head with bold black 'moustaches' and black patch under tail; female is more drab and has no 'moustaches' or black under tail. They slither up and down reeds, legs wide apart and tend to fly just above the reeds, wings beating rapidly and tail fanned out.

*Fledglings* resemble adult female but are darker on back and tail.

*Hints* display includes the pair soaring up together and then dropping down into the reeds. A ringing 'ping ping' can be heard as they move about in the reeds and you tend to hear them more often than you see them. They nest in such few numbers in Britain that even if you think you know the precise location of breeding pairs, you should be satisfied with a brief and distant view of them. After hard winters, numbers are particularly low and rather than risk any disturbance by searching for them it is worth visiting a reserve such as at Minsmere, in Suffolk, where the R.S.P.B. warden will be able to give you the latest information about facilities for seeing them. This species is also known as Bearded Reedling.

**Long-tailed Tit** *Aegithalos caudatus*. Pl. **172**, *349*

*Breeds* April–May (nest-building may start in late February) in wooded districts, hedgerows, commons, heaths and roadside verges with scrub growth, sometimes in gardens and orchards. (In British Isles, Europe and most of Scandinavia.)

*Nest* in forks of trees or bare twigs, thorny bushes, brambles, trailing creepers, at heights varying from 2 ft to 70 ft; both sexes build an oval-shaped nest (working from the inside) of moss, cobwebs and hair, decorated with lichen and lined with huge numbers of feathers. Has used a hole in the ground and nest-boxes.

*Eggs* 8–12, white with reddish markings. Usually both sexes share incubation for about 2 weeks.

*Nestlings* no down, yellow inside mouth and yellow flanges. Both sexes bring food but female feeds them. Leave nest after about 2 weeks.

*Adults* very small tit with disproportionately long tail; sexes similar, pinkish plumage combined with black and white. Races in Britain, western and southern Europe have blackish eye-stripe; race in northern Europe has pure white head.

*Fledglings* shorter tail and more drab than adult.

*Hints* nests built in a narrow fork of tree are easily missed as the lichen acts as camouflage; those in prickly sites are more easily seen if you get the long oval silhouetted against the light. The small entrance hole is usually at one side towards the top of the nest. Display includes a butterfly-like flight and fast chases. The nest usually takes more than a week to complete and the birds may have to go some distance for feathers, but you can usually follow them back in stages. A rather low 'tupp' and a rippling 'tsirrup' are characteristic notes.

**Marsh Tit** *Parus palustris.* Pl. **173**, *350*

*Breeds* late April–June, in wooded districts with scattered trees, including orchards and large gardens. (In Britain, Europe and S. Scandiavia. Absent most of Scotland and Spain.)

*Nest* in a natural hole in a tree, wall or fence-post, from ground-level up to about 40 ft; male accompanies female while she builds nest of moss, 'felted' lining may include fur, hair and down. Nest-boxes are not used readily.

*Eggs* usually 7–8, white with reddish markings. Incubated by female for nearly 2 weeks.

*Nestlings* scanty brownish-grey down, brownish-yellow inside mouth, pale yellow flanges. Fed by both parents. Leave nest after just over 2 weeks.

*Adults* roughly Blue Tit-size, sexes similar; black cap (without white patch as in Coal Tit), difficult to distinguish from Willow Tit, but in some lights Marsh Tit's black cap looks glossier. Familiar acrobatic actions.

*Fledglings* greyer than adult with sooty, not glossy, black cap.

*Hints* watch for pairs visiting nest-holes from February to April; they give a 'tchaying' note near the nest-site, bob their heads and flick their wings, both sexes pecking at the hole. During nest-building, the male keeps close to the female, often pursuing her as she comes out of the hole. Loud 'pitchou' calls and a scolding 'chickabeebeebee' are often heard. In spite of its drab colour, their plumage invariably looks very neat in the breeding season. Look for knots in trees, particularly in ash, elder and willow, as these species often decay into small holes.

**Willow Tit** *Parus montanus.* Pl. **174**, *351*

*Breeds* mid April–June, in wooded districts with scattered trees, often but not always in damp sites, including hedgerows and gardens. (In Britain, Scandinavia and most of Europe. Absent Denmark, most of Italy, Scotland and Spain.)

*Nest* hole in decaying wood is excavated by both sexes, usually at a height of 2 ft to 10 ft above ground; natural holes and nest-boxes are used sometimes. Nest material may include a little moss, but consists chiefly of wood chips and fibres with a pad of fur, wool, feathers or hair.

*Eggs* 5–10, white with reddish markings. Incubated by female for nearly 2 weeks.

*Nestlings* similar to Marsh Tit. Fed by both parents. Leave nest after about 2½ weeks.

*Adults* sexes similar and very like Marsh Tit; in some lights a pale patch at the edge of the wing shows up when the bird is at rest and the black cap looks matt and smudgy, not glossy. Plumage tends to look less dapper than in Marsh Tit. Northern race, found in N. Europe, is a paler grey with pure white cheeks.

*Fledglings* indistinguishable in the field from young Marsh Tit.

*Hints* harsh 'tchaying' note is often started by a high-pitched 'zi zi zi' or 'zit' and is not accompanied by the 'pitchou' note of the Marsh Tit. Courtship display includes bowing and wing-shivering. Chips of wood or sawdust lying on the ground are often left either below or in the vicinity of the nest. A tree-stump is a favourite place, but rotting wood is the chief characteristic of the site. Tapping the side of a likely tree usually brings the female off the nest during incubation.

**Crested Tit** *Parus cristatus*. Pl. **175**, *352*

*Breeds* late April–May, locally in pine forests and some other conifers in Scottish Highlands; also in mixed deciduous woodland as well as conifers in Europe and Scandinavia. (Absent England, Ireland, Wales and most of Italy.)

*Nest* usually in a hole or crevice in trees from 2 ft to 8 ft above ground, but also recorded at ground-level and in fence-posts; hole is excavated by female, but male sometimes helps to gather material which includes moss and hair. Nest-boxes are used in western Europe.

*Eggs* 5–7, white with reddish markings. Incubated by female for about 2 weeks.

*Nestlings* dark grey down, dull yellow inside mouth, pale yellow

flanges. Fed by both parents. Leave nest after about 2½ weeks.

*Adults* roughly Blue Tit-size; sexes similar with prominent pointed crest which is speckled black and white; greyish-brown above, dingy white below. They are often seen searching crevices of bark for insects, behaving rather like a Treecreeper.

*Fledglings* crest is shorter and darker than adult.

*Hints* a walk through the old pine forests of Speyside will give you the best chance of finding a pair; listen for a purring sound, described as a spluttering trill, as they search for food. Keep your eye on the tree-trunks for any sign of movement. During display, they tend to be up in the twig canopy, the male chasing the female and trilling. As in other members of the same family, the male feeds the female during incubation. The male accompanies the female during nest-building, but constant visits with food when there are young are more likely to direct you to the nest-site.

**Coal Tit** *Parus ater*. Pl. **177**, *354*

*Breeds* mid April–June, in wooded districts of all kinds, but shows preference for conifers; mature trees, young plantations and scrub, sometimes in orchards and gardens. (In British Isles, Europe and most of Scandinavia.)

*Nest* usually on or near the ground in a hole, often in a bank or tree-stump, but also in walls and trees. Nest-boxes used. Both sexes carry moss into hole, lining it with 'felted' hair or down, feathers may be included.

*Eggs* 7–12, white with reddish markings. Incubated by female for about 2 weeks.

*Nestlings* grey down, pinkish-orange inside mouth, pale yellow flanges.

Fed by both parents. Leave nest after just over 2 weeks.

*Adults* smaller than Great Tit with a white oblong patch running up into black cap from back of neck; black bib, white cheeks, rest of plumage rather dingy; sexes very similar. Familiar acrobatic actions.

*Fledglings* white parts of adult have yellowish shade.

*Hints* calls are less harsh than those of other tits and these rather drab-coloured birds are altogether more self-effacing than other members of the tit family. A favourite place for the nest is amongst tree-roots under an overhanging bank. The male feeds the female while she is incubating and, as with other tits, the easiest time to find the nest is when young are being fed.

**Blue Tit** *Parus caeruleus*. Pl. **176**, **353**

*Breeds* April–June (occasionally late March), in similar habitat to Great Tit, but extends right into built-up areas. (In British Isles, Europe and S. Scandinavia.)

*Nest* both sexes carry material into a hole in the same kind of site as Great Tit, using similar materials, and feathers are often used in the lining. Nest-boxes used.

*Eggs* varying in number, often 8–15, white with reddish markings. Incubated by female for about 2 weeks.

*Nestlings* scanty whitish down, dull orange-red inside mouth, pale yellow flanges. Fed by both parents. Leave nest after about 2½ weeks.

*Adults* smaller than Great Tit with blue crown and yellow under-parts; male brighter coloured than female. Familiar acrobatic actions.

*Fledglings* greenish-brown rather than blue on upper-parts, cheeks look yellow rather than white as in adult.

*Hints* sibilant as distinct from ringing quality in call-notes. Courtship display includes much wing-shivering and raising of crest. The male flies into the hole with food for the female while she is incubating (similar to Great Tit), but the nest-hole is most easily found when both parents are feeding young.

**Great Tit** *Parus major*. Pl. **178**, **355**

*Breeds* late April–June (sometimes July), in deciduous woods and districts with trees, including hedge-rows, parks, orchards, gardens and outskirts of built-up areas. (In British Isles, Europe and Scandinavia.)

*Nest* in a hole of some kind, height usually 3 ft to 15 ft, often in a tree-stump or wall, also in various artificial sites such as letter-boxes, pumps, drain-piping and flower-pots. Nest-boxes used. Both sexes carry material into hole, mainly moss, lining it with 'felted' hair, wool and down.

*Eggs* varying numbers, often 9–12, white with reddish markings. Incubated by female for about 2 weeks.

*Nestlings* grey down, orange inside mouth, pale yellow flanges. Fed by both parents. Leave nest after about 2½ weeks.

*Adults* black-capped tit with black band running down centre of yellow breast; black band is broader in male. Familiar acrobatic actions.

*Fledglings* drab version of adult with yellowish cheeks.

*Hints* 'teacher teacher' phrase is the most easily recognised of its many calls, all of which have a ringing quality. Courtship includes wing-shivering while begging for food, accompanied by 'zeedling' call ending in a 'zee'. Several holes may be examined before the female finally accepts one and nest-building is started. Nest-hole is most easily detected when the parents are feeding young, keeping up an almost continuous airlift at certain times; one parent often has to wait for its mate to vacate the hole before flying in with the next load of food.

## Nuthatch *Sitta europaea*. Pl. **179**, *356*

*Breeds* late April–June, in woods, copses, parks and gardens with mature oak and beech trees. (In England and Wales, throughout Europe and in S. Scandinavia.)

*Nest* hole in tree-trunk or large branch is plastered with mud, reducing the size of entrance hole, and is then lined with bark fibres and dead leaves, both sexes taking part; at varying heights, holes in walls and sides of haystack also recorded. Nest-boxes used, holes plastered to suitable size.

**Nuthatch**

*Eggs* 5–12, white with reddish-brown markings. Incubated by female for about 2 weeks.

*Nestlings* scanty grey down, dark pink inside mouth, ivory flanges. Fed by both parents. Leave nest after about $3\frac{1}{2}$ weeks.

*Adults* slightly larger and much stockier than Treecreeper, with heavier bill, climbs up and down and sideways with equal facility. Blue-grey upper-parts, black eye-stripe, buff under-parts with chestnut flanks; male is more brightly coloured than female. Scandinavian race has whiter under-parts and central European race has slightly darker buff under-parts.

*Fledglings* drab version of adult without chestnut on flanks.

*Hints* ringing 'chwit chwit chwit' call is the most frequent note heard in March and April; location of a pair at this stage is useful because they become more silent during incubation and foliage tends to mask likely holes by the time that the young are being fed. Display includes expanding the tail to reveal white spots and fluffing out chestnut feathers on flanks. Look at any holes for signs of caked mud; splits in bark are also plastered and sometimes a 'starfish' effect round the hole attracts your notice.

## Treecreeper *Certhia familiaris*. Pl. **180**, *357*

*Breeds* mid April–June, in woodlands and country with scattered trees, including gardens. (In British Isles, most of Europe and Scandinavia. Local in Spain.)

*Nest* both sexes carry material (twigs, moss, grass, bark fibres, hair and feathers) into a crevice, usually behind rotting bark, often between roots of ivy on a tree-trunk or in cracks of sheds and old walls, at a height varying usually from 3 ft to 10 ft. Nest-boxes are used.

*Eggs* 4–7, white with dark markings. Incubated chiefly by female for about 2 weeks.

*Nestlings* dark grey down, yellow inside mouth, yellowish-white flanges. Fed by both parents. Leave nest after about 2 weeks.

*Adults* smaller and much more slender than Sparrow with a long delicately curved bill; sexes similar, mottled brown above, pure white below. Often seen climbing in jerks up tree-trunk, tail pressed against the bark, looking like a mouse, then flying down to base of next tree before climbing up again. Short-toed Tree-creeper, *Certhia brachydactyla*, which breeds in most of Europe, has brownish flanks and shorter claws.

*Fledglings* more spotted and more rufous-yellow than adult.

*Hints* its song is remarkably sweet-sounding, rather faint and high-pitched and unmistakable once it has registered with you. Although frequently on the move, the upper-parts provide good camouflage and it is easily overlooked against tree-trunks. A flash of white, from the under-parts, sometimes attracts attention, particularly in April when males fly in spirals round trunks, chasing females and 'squeaking'. Look carefully at any fissure of bark for bits of nesting material protruding. Wellingtonia trees, with their soft bark, are favourite nesting sites and Scots pines are worth examining.

## Corn Bunting *Emberiza calandra*. Pl. **181**, *358*

*Breeds* late May–September, on farmland, downs and rough waste ground with low bushes, both inland and near the coast. (In England and Europe. Local in Ireland, Scotland and Wales. Has bred Norway.)

*Nest* on or near the ground, hidden in tuft of vegetation or in low bush; loosely constructed out of grass, lined with fine roots and grass or hair, built by female.

*Eggs* usually 3–5, greyish or light brown with dark markings. Incubated by female for nearly 2 weeks.

*Nestlings* yellowish down, pink inside mouth, yellow flanges. Fed chiefly by female. Leave nest after about 1½ weeks.

*Adults* larger than Sparrow, female slightly smaller than male but sexes look alike; stockily built, nondescript brown with streaks and no white in outer tail-feathers; stubby yellow bill and yellowish legs which dangle in flight. Often seen perching on wire.

*Fledglings* slightly paler but more streaked than adult.

*Hints* it is such a nondescript bird that it is difficult to spot unless you hear the characteristic 'jangling keys' song; this appears to be coming from the middle of a field, but the singing male is usually perched at the side of the field, often on a fence. Their distribution is very local and you can be in a Corn Bunting area one minute, as you drive along a road between arable fields, and only a short distance away, there is not a single male to be heard in an apparently similar habitat. The male sings as much as 100 yds from his nest, but always keeps it in view from various song-posts. You may have to wait for an hour before the female leaves the nest, the male accompanying her; try to keep your eye on the female as they return because she breaks away from him before reaching the nest. This is not easy because the male tends to divert your attention by bursting into song from one of his perches as she goes down on to the nest.

## Yellowhammer *Emberiza citrinella*. Pl. **182**, *359*

*Breeds* May–June (occasionally April–September), on rough ground with bushes, roadsides and hedge-rows along arable land, heaths, commons and felled clearings in woods. (In British Isles, most of Europe and Scandinavia. Absent most of Spain.)

*Nest* on or near the ground, often in hedge-bottom or long grass growing up into a bush, sometimes in a tree;

made of grass, straw and moss, lined with hair, built by female.

*Eggs* 3–5, white, may have pink flush, with mauve 'scribbles'. Incubated chiefly by female for nearly 2 weeks.

*Nestlings* grey down, pink inside mouth, pale yellow flanges. Fed by both parents. Leave nest after nearly 2 weeks.

*Adults* roughly Sparrow-size, yellow and brown plumage, white outer tail-feathers show up well in flight; male has yellow head and under-parts, black streaks on chestnut back, unstreaked chestnut rump; female has darker head.

*Fledglings* dark version of adult female.

*Hints* listen for song, popularly described as 'little bit of bread and no cheese', which can be heard from late February. As the breeding season approaches, note the places where males sing and search the ground below these song-posts. During incubation the female flushes when you are near, leaving the nest with an abrupt alarm-note and continues to protest while you remain. Courtship includes a dashing flight in which the male pursues the female, usually ending in what appears to be a fight, both birds tumbling down. This species is also known as Yellow Bunting.

**Rock Bunting** *Emberiza cia.* Pl. **186**

*Breeds* April or May–June, usually on hill-sides and mountains, on rough stony ground with a little scrub and scattered trees, also on outskirts of woods. (In France, Germany, Italy, Spain and Switzerland.)

*Nest* from ground-level up to about 2 ft, hidden amongst stones or in low bush; probably built by female, made of grass, bark fibres and moss, lined with fine roots and hair.

*Eggs* usually 4, greyish-white or purplish-brown, with dark markings. Incubated chiefly by female for about 2 weeks.

*Nestlings* no description available; probably leave nest after about 2 weeks.

*Adults* roughly same size as Yellow-hammer with similar chestnut rump and white outer tail-feathers; pale grey throat and head which has black patterning of stripes running through the eye and along the crown; black streaks on chestnut back but not on rump; reddish-buff under-parts. Female less clearly marked than male. Both sexes have narrow whitish wing-bar.

*Fledglings* easily confused with young Yellowhammer but under-parts are more reddish-buff than yellowish.

*Hints* described as unobtrusive in its habits, this bunting can easily be missed on rough ground where the terrain is broken up with stones and low bushes. It spends most of the time on the ground but will take cover in a tree when disturbed. The song is reminiscent of Reed Bunting and is usually delivered from a prominent rock, stone wall or bush. This species is rarely recorded in Britain but visitors to Gibraltar might find it worth climbing to the upper slopes of the Rock, where a few pairs may breed amongst the scrub growth.

**Ortolan Bunting** *Emberiza hortulana.* Pl. **183**, *360*

*Breeds* May–June on stony ground with scrub growth on hills and mountains; also in lowlands, outskirts of woods, cultivated fields and roadsides with scattered bushes. (In most of Europe and Scandinavia. Absent British Isles and Denmark.)

*Nest* usually on the ground, often hidden amongst growing crops or sheltered by a bush, also in vineyards; made of dry grass and fine roots, sometimes lined with a little hair, built by female.

*Eggs* 4–6, varying from ashy-grey to russet with dark markings. Incubated chiefly by female for about 2 weeks.

*Nestlings* whitish-grey down with buff tinge, pink inside mouth, pale yellow flanges. Fed by both sexes. Leave nest after nearly 2 weeks.

*Adults* roughly Yellowhammer-size, female paler and more drab than male; greenish-grey head, pale yellow throat with greenish-grey moustachial stripe, brownish back with dark streaks, pinkish-buff underparts. Lemon-coloured ring round eye and pink bill are visible at close range.

*Fledglings* pale rufous with dark streaks.

*Hints* song is described as slower than Yellowhammer's, with the last note prolonged. The male often uses a prominent song-post which may be up to 50 yds from the nest. At the incubation stage it is worth watching where the male goes as he feeds the female on the nest; you may have to search some distance from where he goes down as he invariably walks to the actual nest. The female flushes easily and the nest is said to be hard to find. In Britain, Ortolan Buntings are seen regularly in small numbers on spring and autumn passage at Fair Isle; they are also seen along the south-east coast, off Wales and Ireland, and on the Isles of Scilly.

**Cirl Bunting** *Emberiza cirlus*. Pl. **184**, *361*

*Breeds* mid May–August (occasionally September), in tall hedgerows and belts of trees on verges of cultivated and rough ground, on sheltered slopes of hill-sides and downs, also in garden hedges; mainly in limestone and chalk districts. (In S. England and Wales, Belgium, France, Italy and Spain. Local in SW. Germany and Switzerland.)

*Nest* from ground-level up to about 8 ft, usually in hedge or bush; built by female, made of grass and fine roots with much moss under the cup, lined with hair and grass.

*Eggs* 3–5, greenish-blue with black 'scribbles'. Incubated by female for nearly 2 weeks.

*Nestlings* long greyish-brown down, pink inside mouth, pale yellow flanges. Fed almost entirely by female. Leave nest after nearly 2 weeks.

*Adults* more compact than Yellowhammer, both sexes have olive-brown rump (not chestnut) and white outer tail-feathers; male has black stripe through eye, edged above and below with yellow, black throat with greenish breast-band below it; female is a drab version of male.

*Fledglings* resemble adult female.

*Hints* courtship display is not very obvious and location of pairs is easiest by listening for a monotonous rattling song, somewhat reminiscent of Whitethroat and Greenfinch. The male sings from a number of song-posts, usually in exposed sites and not necessarily above the nest. There may be more than one pair in the same area and as the females do not flush easily, every inch of the ground needs walking over. A rattling alarm note should indicate when you are near a nest and distraction display may be seen.

**Reed Bunting** *Emberiza schoeniclus*. Pl. **185**, *362*

*Breeds* late April–July, in damp places, including margins of rivers, lakes and ponds, rank vegetation and wet fields, fens and marshy ground. (In British Isles, Europe and Scandinavia.)

*Nest* usually hidden in a tussock, on or close to the ground but has been recorded at height of 12 ft and in an open site; female builds nest of coarse grass, lined with finer grass and hair.

*Eggs* usually 4–5, drab brown with dark markings. Incubated chiefly by female for nearly 2 weeks.

*Nestlings* longish black down, dark pink inside mouth with whitish spurs and tip of tongue, yellowish-white flanges. Fed by both parents. Leave nest after about 1½ weeks.

*Adults* roughly Sparrow-size; male has white collar which contrasts with black head and throat; female has brown crown, pale streak over eye and dark moustachial stripe. When perching both sexes often flick wings and expand tail, showing white outer tail-feathers.

*Fledglings* drab version of adult female.

*Hints* a ringing, metallic call-note often makes you look round. Males take up territory some time during February; the females arrive during March and are chased by the males, often ending up in what appears to be a fight, with male and female tumbling about. The nest is easiest to find when the young are being fed. Distraction display at the nest has been seen, the bird apparently crawling along the ground, with one or both wings partially spread over its back.

**Lapland Bunting** *Calcarius lapponicus*. Pl. *363*

*Breeds* late May–July, on rough ground with scattered birch and willow scrub, also beyond the tree-limit where there are hummocks of moss and peat with creeping plants. (In N. Scandinavia.)

*Nest* in a hollow or tussock; female builds a deepish cup of grass and moss with feathers often worked into the lining.

*Eggs* usually 6, varying from greyish-white to pale brown with dark markings. Incubated chiefly by female for 1½–2 weeks.

*Nestlings* no description available. Fed by both sexes. Leave nest after about 9 days, fly about 4 days later. Fed by both parents.

*Adults* roughly Sparrow-size; male has black head and bib, a zigzag buff and white streak from the eye down the side of the cheek, chestnut band across the nape, creamy under-parts; female is browner and less conspicuously marked with whitish throat. Both sexes have yellow bill and show some white at sides of tail.

*Fledglings* rather similar to female Reed Bunting but with shorter tail.

*Hints* male sings either from a bush or in display flight, fluttering high into the air and then planing down with wings quivering slightly; the song has something of a Skylark's quality. The most frequently heard sound during the breeding season is an anxiety-note, described as a monotonous piping, starting with an odd little catch of breath. In Britain, where they are seen mainly on

**Lapland Bunting**

*254*

autumn passage, the typical call-note is a repetitive 'tik tik a tik', ending in a high-pitched 'teu'; more birds are seen in the autumn than in spring. They pass through Fair Isle regularly, usually in September.

## Snow Bunting *Plectrophenax nivalis*. Pl. *364*

*Breeds* late May–June (Scotland), May–July (N. Scandinavia), amongst loose scree, boulders and rocky outcrops; occasionally in deserted buildings in the Arctic.
*Nest* in scree of barren mountaintops, built by female; made of grass, moss and lichen, lining may include wool and hair.
*Eggs* 4–6, varying from yellowish white to greenish or bluish, with dark markings. Incubation chiefly by female for 1½–2 weeks.
*Nestlings* dark grey down, yellow flanges of mouth. Fed by both parents. Leave nest after 1½–2 weeks.
*Adults* slightly larger than Chaffinch, a stockily built bunting that looks white when seen overhead; male has some black on wings and centre of tail, rest of plumage white; female has drab greyish-brown head and back. (In autumn both sexes are much browner above but white under-parts and white areas on wings and tail are obvious.)
*Fledglings* resemble adult female.

**Snow Bunting**

*Hints* a few pairs breed in desolate parts of the Cairngorm mountains where the mist often shrouds the tops even in summer, making the location of pairs difficult in such terrain. Keep your eyes on the scree as the birds spend a lot of time on the ground. Display includes the male walking slowly away from the female, partially spreading his wings and tail, and then running back to her. There is also a song flight in which the male descends with wings fluttering, losing height slowly. The song is slightly reminiscent of Dunnock and easily confused with Lapland Bunting. A rippling twitter is a familiar sound from flocks on passage in autumn and winter. Small numbers are seen regularly in winter along the east coast of Britain, but in September 1949 a flock of 2,000 was seen on Fair Isle.

## Chaffinch *Fringilla coelebs*. Pl. **186**, *365*

*Breeds* mid April–June, almost anywhere that there are hedges, bushes and trees, including built-up areas. (In British Isles, Europe and Scandinavia.)
*Nest* usually at height of 4 ft to 12 ft in a hedge, bush or tree, sometimes against a wall or fence in creeper or shrub; both sexes gather material, but female builds remarkably neat nest of grass, moss, bark fibres, bits of paper and roots, decorated with lichen and cobwebs, lined with hair.
*Eggs* usually 4–5, varying from greenish-blue to brown with dark markings. Incubated by female for nearly 2 weeks.
*Nestlings* pale grey down, carmine and orange inside mouth, white flanges. Fed by both parents. Leave nest after about 2 weeks.
*Adults* familiar finch with broad

white patch on 'shoulder', narrow white wing-bar and white outer tail-feathers; male has greyish-blue head with pinkish-brown sides, chestnut mantle, greenish rump and pinkish-brown breast; female is drab green-ish-brown with paler under-parts. Scandinavian male has pink breast. Western European male has more wine-coloured breast.

*Fledglings* drab version of adult female.

*Hints* a short phrase ending in a flourish which sounds like 'choo-ee-oo', heard as early as the end of January, is a welcome reminder that song-birds are establishing terri-tories after the long winter months in which comparatively little song is heard. There are vigorous bursts of song as the males occupy their terri-tories. The nest is eventually built near one of the regular song-posts and during nest-building and subse-quent stages, you often hear anxious calls of 'pink pink'. Some females will remain on the nest, in spite of the male's alarm notes, when you are only a few feet away, providing you do not stare hard at them. Wait until the female is out of sight before examining the nest, which is beauti-fully constructed.

## Brambling *Fringilla montifringilla*. Pl. **188**, *366*

*Breeds* May–July, in birch and mixed woodlands, on outskirts of conifer forests and in birch and willow scrub. (In N. Scandinavia. Has bred Den-mark and Scotland.)

*Nest* usually in a birch tree, height from 5 ft to 10 ft but also much higher. Chaffinch-like nest but larger and less neat, a deep cup camou-flaged with lichen and often lined with many feathers. Probably built by female.

*Eggs* usually 6–7, darker and greener

than Chaffinch. Incubated by female for about 2 weeks.

*Nestlings* white down. Fed by both parents. Probably leave nest after about 2 weeks.

*Adults* reminiscent of Chaffinch but with distinctive white rump; male has black head and mantle, orange 'shoulders', white wing-bar and orange breast; female is more drab than male with paler under-parts.

*Fledglings* rather similar to adult female.

*Hints* song is somewhat similar to Greenfinch's, embodying long-drawn-out 'twanging' notes. In Scandinavia it is said to be a persis-tent singer and to have an abrupt alarm-note similar to Chaffinch's 'pink'. Song flight with shivering wing-beats has been seen in Britain, but most of the winter-visitor popu-lation are seen passing through arable land or feeding in woods on beechmast; at this time of year, the males look mottled rather than glossy black on the head and mantle. There are several reports of breeding in Scotland but only one confirmed, in Sutherland.

## Greenfinch *Carduelis chloris*. Pl. **189**, *367*

*Breeds* late April–July (sometimes August–September), in bushes and shrubs, hedgerows, gardens and woods. (In British Isles, Europe and S. Scandinavia.)

*Nest* usually at height 6 ft to 15 ft in bush or hedgerow, less frequently in tree; loosely constructed of grass, moss and wool, on foundation of twigs, lined with fine roots and hair; built by female, male accompanying her. Old nests of other species sometimes adapted.

*Eggs* 4–6, whitish with a few dark markings. Incubated by female for about 2 weeks.

*Nestlings* whitish down, pink inside mouth, yellowish flanges. Fed by both parents. Leave nest after about 2 weeks.

*Adults* Chaffinch-size but more rotund shape; olive-green with yellowish rump and bright yellow patch on wings and sides of tail which is distinctly cleft. Female more drab than male.

*Fledglings* browner than adults.

*Hints* long-drawn-out nasal 'tswee-e-e' is heard frequently during breeding season; also a twittering song from the male, either perching at top of tree or flying in circles with butterfly-like motion of wings. Nest should be somewhere near this area. Try to get at sufficiently low angle to look up at the bush so that the nest is silhouetted against the light. There may be more than one nest in the same area.

## Siskin *Carduelis spinus*. Pl. **190**, *368*

*Breeds* April–June, in woodlands with a preference for conifers. (In British Isles, most of Europe and Scandinavia. Local in France, Italy and Spain.)

*Nest* usually towards the end of a conifer branch, 15 ft or more above the ground; both sexes build a neat structure, similar to Goldfinch's nest, of twigs, lichen, moss and wool; lining sometimes includes hair, fur and plant down.

*Eggs* 4–5, bluish-white with dark markings. Incubated by female for nearly 2 weeks.

*Nestlings* no description available. Fed by both parents. Leave nest after about 2 weeks.

*Adults* roughly Goldfinch-size; male has yellowish-green upper-parts with pale wing-bar, yellow under-parts, black bib and crown distinguish male from female, the latter looking much more drab. Tit-like

actions; fine bill and short tail show up well when hanging upside-down, feeding in the top canopy of twigs. *Fledglings* similar to adult female but more streaked appearance.

*Hints* display flight above nesting territory is reminiscent of Greenfinch and the twittering song has the same nasal quality. Siskins are said to favour spruce and pine, but unless you have seen the display flight, searching is largely a matter of luck. In Britain they nest mainly in Scotland but are now spreading into England.

## Goldfinch *Carduelis carduelis*. Pl. **191**, *369*

*Breeds* May–July (sometimes August), in orchards, gardens, hedgerows, open woodland and avenues in parks. (In British Isles, Europe and Scandinavia.)

*Nest* in spreading type of tree or bush, height varying from 6 ft to 40 ft; male accompanies female while she builds neat nest of rootlets, grass, moss and lichen, lined with wool, hair and plant down. Nests in brussels sprout top and in creeper on wall recorded.

*Eggs* 5–6, bluish-white with darkish markings. Incubated by female for nearly 2 weeks.

*Nestlings* dark grey down, purplish and red inside mouth, cream flanges. Fed by both parents. Leave nest after about 2 weeks.

*Adults* smaller than House Sparrow, sexes similar; red, black and white pattern on head, black wings with bright yellow band and white spots, black and white tail. Undulating flight with a dancing motion.

*Fledglings* rather similar to adult but without coloured pattern on head.

*Hints* call-note 'tswitt witt witt' becomes a liquid twittering during March. Courting male 'flashes' the yellow on his wing at the female, swaying from side to side; if you see this display, notice where the pair go as the nest is likely to be in this area. A favourite site for this compact nest is at the end of a spreading bough.

**Twite** *Acanthis flavirostris*. Pl. **193**, *370*

*Breeds* April (Ireland), May–August (N. England and Scotland), in open country, such as moorland, rough grassland and hill-sides. (Also in N. Scandinavia.)

*Nest* on the ground or a few feet up, usually sheltered in a cranny or in low vegetation; male accompanies female while she constructs nest of a few twigs, grass and moss, lining it with wool and sometimes feathers.

*Eggs* 5–6, bluish with dark markings. Incubated by female for about 1½ weeks.

*Nestlings* buffish-grey down, purplish inside mouth, whitish flanges. Fed by both parents. Leave nest after about 2 weeks.

*Adults* Linnet-size and easily confused with female Linnet; darkish brown streaked upper-parts, warm buff throat, paler under-parts; male has pink rump. Forked tail and white border on wings and tail are similar to Linnet but Twite is more slenderly built.

*Fledglings* similar to adult.

*Hints* call-note and song is reminiscent of Linnet but has more of a twanging quality. Male displays by holding wings out, thus revealing his pink rump. There may be several nests close together, often in heather, and nest-building is the easiest stage at which to locate them, but they readily desert before the incubation stage and it is best to leave them undisturbed. On Fair Isle they are regarded as regular breeders, nesting in strips of cultivated land near the crofts.

**Linnet** *Acanthis cannabina*. Pl. **195**, *371*

*Breeds* mid April–August, on rough ground with bushes, frequently on commons with gorse and thorn scrub, also in young plantations, hedgerows, gardens, occasionally on dunes and in heather. (In British Isles, Europe and S. Scandinavia.)

*Nest* usually in a bush or hedge, but also on banks and in low vegetation, such as heather, tufts of grass and rush, from ground-level up to about 10 ft. Female builds substantial structure of grass and moss, lining it with hair, wool, fur and occasionally feathers.

*Eggs* 4–6, bluish-white with dark markings. Incubated chiefly by female for about 1½ weeks.

*Nestlings* greyish down, pink inside mouth, pale pink flanges. Fed by both parents. Leave nest after about 1½ weeks.

*Adults* slightly smaller than Sparrow; reddish-brown back, dark wings with pale wing-bar; white edges to wings and tail which is forked. Both sexes have grey head, but male has crimson crown and red flush across breast; female is more drab and streaked. Undulating flight; usually sings from exposed perch.

*Fledglings* resemble adult female.

*Hints* constant twittering song usually attracts attention. Male displays by drooping wings and spreading tail. More than one pair may build in the same area and if you notice small brown birds diving into cover, it is worth remembering this site. If you squat down when searching, you will have more chance of seeing the nest silhouetted against the light as it is often towards the top of a bush or hedge. Gorse bushes are always worth examining.

**Redpoll** *Acanthis flammea.* Pl. **192**, *373*

*Breeds* May–July, in birch, alder, willow, larch and fir plantations, also in bushes in gardens and parks. (In British Isles, the Alps and N. Scandinavia. Has bred Holland.)

*Nest* in bush or tree, height variable but usually from 4 ft upwards; dead stalks stick out from foundation of twigs, making an untidy silhouette, but inside it is neatly lined with white plant down, hair and feathers; male accompanies female while she constructs the nest.

*Eggs* 4–6, blue with dark markings. Incubated by female for about 1½ weeks.

*Nestlings* dark grey down, red inside mouth with two pale spots, yellowish flanges. Fed by both parents. Leave nest after about 1½ weeks.

*Adults* there are several races which differ slightly. **Lesser Redpoll**, *Acanthis flammea cabaret*, native of Britain, is slightly smaller than Chaffinch and has reddish-brown upper-parts, red forehead, black chin and buff double wing-bar; male has pink breast and rump. Mealy Redpoll, *Acanthis flammea flammea*, native of Scandinavia, seen in Britain on passage, is slightly larger and noticeably paler with double white wing-bar. Greenland race, *Acanthis flammea rostrata*, seen in Britain on passage and may have bred Scotland, is larger and darker than Mealy Redpoll, the bill being heavier. These distinctions are only helpful when one or more races are seen together. Short forked tail and tit-like acrobatics.

*Fledglings* young Lesser Redpoll has small greyish patch on chin, no red on head and under-parts more heavily streaked than adult.

*Hints* the easiest way of locating a pair is by recognising a metallic twittering flight-note, described as 'chuch uch uch uch'. This call is embodied in a trilling song and from late March males can be seen circling in a dancing flight above the trees; this butterfly-like display is given above the nesting site. There may be several nests in the same area.

**Scarlet Grosbeak** *Carpodacus erythrinus.* Pl. **194**, *374*

*Breeds* May–July, in copses of willow, birch and alder, in juniper and bushy vegetation on marshy ground. (In E. Germany and S. Finland. Local in S. Sweden.)

*Nest* usually near water in bush or tree, height up to about 10 ft above ground. Female builds a warbler-like nest of grass, lined with fine roots and hair.

*Eggs* 4–6, deep blue with dark markings. Female known to incubate for about 1½ weeks.

*Nestlings* no description available. Fed by both parents. Leave nest after about 1½ weeks.

*Adults* Bullfinch-size with heavy conical bill and pale double wing-bar; male has crimson head, rump and breast, shading to white on belly, dark brown wings and tail which is cleft; female has drab brown upper-parts and paler under-parts. They adopt parrot-like attitudes when feeding. Dumpy stance with head retracted.

*Fledglings* resemble adult female.

*Hints* call-note heard at breeding site is described as a piping 'twee-eek'. An irregular visitor to northern Scotland, mainly in the autumn. Fair Isle regards this species as an annual visitor in small numbers, usually in September when they are often in the company of House Sparrows and Twites. This species is also known as Common Rose Finch.

**Pine Grosbeak** *Pinicola enucleator*.
Pl. **196**

*Breeds* May–July, in conifer forests, also in mixed woodlands and more open country with birch, willow and juniper scrub, in N. Scandinavia.

*Nest* usually from 3 ft to 20 ft above ground in fir, birch or juniper. Female builds Bullfinch-like nest of twigs, fine roots, moss and hair.

*Eggs* 3–4, deep greenish-blue with dark markings. Incubated chiefly by female for about 2 weeks.

**Pine Grosbeak**

*Nestlings* greyish-green down, mouth with purplish flanges. Fed by both parents. Probably leave nest after about 2 weeks.

*Adults* distinctly larger and heavier than Scarlet Grosbeak, with longer tail which counterbalances the clumsy head. Both sexes have two narrow white wing-bars on brown wings; male is mainly rosy-pink and female mainly bronze-green. Markedly undulating flight, clambers about branches like a parrot.

*Fledglings* resemble adult female.

*Hints* flute-like whistling notes are heard from late March. While watching near a nest one observer described a soft piping which was constant but inaudible at more than 20 yds from the nest. The female

does not flush easily, and one with nestlings has actually been lifted from the nest. This species is rarely seen in Britain.

**Crossbill** *Loxia curvirostra*. Pl. **196**, **372**

*Breeds* February–March (sometimes January–July), in larch, spruce and pine, in woods and on heaths with belts of conifer. (Local in Britain; has bred Ireland. In most of Europe and Scandinavia. Absent Belgium and Holland.)

*Nest* usually out on a side branch, less frequently near the trunk, at height of 10 ft or more. Male accompanies female while she builds nest of grass, moss and wool on a foundation of twigs; lining may include bits of bark and lichen.

*Eggs* 4–5, whitish with dark markings. Incubated by female for about 1½ weeks.

*Nestlings* dark grey down, pinkish mauve and yellow inside mouth, pale yellow flanges. Fed by both parents. Leave nest after about 3 weeks.

*Adults* roughly Chaffinch-size with parrot-like actions; crossed bill is usually clearly visible and deeply cleft tail of a rather stocky finch is a useful guide to identification in flight. Male is brick-red with dark wings, female is yellowish. Scottish Crossbill, *Loxia pytyopsittacus scotica* may be regarded as a race of the Continental Parrot Crossbill but it cannot be distinguished in the field from the Common Crossbill, *Loxia curvirostra*. The Two-barred Crossbill, *Loxia leucoptera*, is smaller and has a double white wing-bar.

*Fledglings* greenish-grey with streaks on under-parts; young males become orange.

*Hints* the best opportunity for finding nests is in the mature pine forests of Speyside in Inverness-shire, although scattered Scots pines in East Anglia also provide a chance and there are breeding records from a number of counties. Frayed fir cones lying on the ground are a useful guide to the presence of Crossbills. There may be more than one pair nesting in the same area. Listen for characteristic 'tchook tchook' call-note. Male often sings near the nest in jerky phrases and feeds the female while she is incubating. As she is not easily flushed, it is possible to get a close view. Try searching the area where the cock sings and look for whitening of branches, due to droppings near the nest.

**Bullfinch** *Pyrrhula pyrrhula*. Pl. **197**, *375*

*Breeds* late April–July (occasionally September), in woods, garden shrubberies, thickets and tall hedgerows. (In British Isles, N. Spain and rest of Europe, in most of Scandinavia.)
*Nest* in thick cover, often in evergreens and thorn bushes, usually from 4 ft to 7 ft above ground; female builds a light but firm structure of twigs, moss and lichen, lined with blackish roots and hair. Male occasionally gathers material. Nests have also been found in reeds and sedges a few feet above water.
*Eggs* 4–6, deep blue with dark markings. Incubated chiefly by female for nearly 2 weeks.
*Nestlings* long grey down, pink inside mouth with puce spots, pale yellow flanges. Fed by both parents. Leave nest after about 2 weeks.
*Adults* slightly smaller than Chaffinch and more stockily built; both sexes have black wings and tail, greyish back and white rump, black cap and bib, noticeably squat black bill; male has bright pinkish-red under-parts, female much greyer below. Rather shy, often disappear into cover.

*Fledglings* browner than female, no black cap.
*Hints* plaintive 'teu teu' call-note betrays their presence, but they tend to be wary and it is seldom that one gets a complete view of them before they flit into cover. The male displays his pink breast, moving his tail from side to side. Subdued twittering from an evergreen bush may indicate a likely site for nest. Female sits close when incubating and in Germany females have been lifted off the nest, ringed and replaced on the nest.

**Hawfinch** *Coccothraustes coccothraustes*. Pl. **198**, *376*

*Breeds* late April–July (August also recorded), in woodlands, orchards, gardens, trees along roadsides and bushy commons. (In Britain, Europe and S. Sweden. Has bred Ireland, Finland and Norway.)
*Nest* at height varying from 4 ft to 80 ft, often far out on a branch towards the top canopy. Shallow, untidy structure of roots and grass on foundation of twigs; lichen, grass and hair may be added. Male accompanies female and has been recorded carrying material, but nest is constructed by female.
*Eggs* 4–5, variable colour, including bluish-white, greenish-grey and pinkish-buff, with dark markings. Incubated by female for nearly 2 weeks.
*Nestlings* long bluish-white down, pink and purple inside mouth with whitish spurs, yellow flanges. Fed by both parents. Leave nest after nearly 2 weeks.
*Adults* slightly larger and much stockier than Chaffinch with bullnecked appearance and large head; conical bill has blue sheen; reddish-brown upper-parts, peach underparts; black bib, black wings with

white 'shoulders'; short tail with white tips. Female slightly more drab than male. They hop and waddle on the ground and tend to perch in the top canopy.

*Fledglings* upper-parts have black scalloped effect, under-parts mottled and barred; black bib not acquired until autumn.

*Hints* 'tzic' call-note is usually the first indication that they are in the vicinity. Noisy and aggressive during courtship, they are silent and wary once the nest is being built. Display includes bowing, bill-touching and a 'Penguin walk' in which male drags wing-tips. Birds seen snapping twigs off the top canopy or pulling at soft roots of raspberry canes are probably gathering material, but it is not easy to follow them back to nest-site. They desert readily if disturbed when building and also during early stage of incubation.

**House Sparrow** *Passer domesticus.*

*Breeds* mainly April–August (occasionally March–September), nearly always close to houses or buildings, including densely populated cities. (In British Isles, Europe and Scandinavia.)

*Nest* usually in a hole or crevice at a height of 10 ft or more, often under eaves and in creepers against walls, sometimes in branches of trees and old nests of other species may be

**House Sparrow**

used; both sexes build a domed structure of dead grass and straw, lining consists mainly of feathers. Nests in lamp-posts, hedgerows and cliff caves have also been recorded. Nest-boxes are used.

*Eggs* 3–6, whitish with dark markings. Incubated by female for nearly 2 weeks; male covers the eggs but does not develop incubation patches.

*Nestlings* no down, pinkish-yellow inside mouth, pale yellow flanges. Fed by both parents. Leave nest after about 2 weeks.

*Adults* familiar 'small brown bird'; male has dark grey crown (not rich brown as in Tree Sparrow), black bib and chestnut nape; female is more drab and has no black bib. Different forms are present in Italy and parts of Spain.

*Fledglings* rather similar to adult female.

*Hints* nest-building can be seen at any time of the year and at least one of the pair is at the nest-hole during the day all the year round. Chirruping calls proclaim ownership of the site and are heard from September onwards when pairs are formed. Sexual activity reaches its height in January when noisy parties chase about and dive into cover. Fights between members of the same sex are often seen, the birds fluttering up with breasts touching, then tumbling down, holding on to each other. Display includes males strutting about near females, holding their wings stiffly and raising their tails, looking 'self-important'. Females adopt submissive attitudes, shivering their wings and uttering a soft 'tee tee tee'.

**Tree Sparrow** *Passer montanus.* Pl. **200**, *377*

*Breeds* late April–August, in old hedgerows with trees, gardens and orchards, including suburban areas, occasionally on cliffs. (In British Isles, Europe, S. Finland, Norway and S. Sweden.)

*Nest* usually in a hole, often in pollarded tree, thatch or wall crevice, but also in branches of bush or tree and recorded in nests of other species; similar construction to House Sparrow's nest, built by both sexes, material may be largely feathers. Nest-boxes used.

*Eggs* usually 4–6, smaller but otherwise similar to House Sparrow's. Incubated by both sexes for nearly 2 weeks.

*Nestlings* no down, pink inside mouth, sometimes with dark spot at top of tongue, pale yellow flanges. Fed by both parents. Leave nest after nearly 2 weeks.

*Adults* smaller and daintier than House Sparrow; sexes similar, rich brown crown, cheeks look very white and smudgy black mark at sides has the effect of giving a half-collar.

*Fledglings* resemble adult.

*Hints* they are more common in south and east of England and comparatively rare in Wales, Scotland and Ireland. Less quarrelsome than House Sparrow but metallic quality of call-notes attracts attention. The male's display is somewhat similar to House Sparrow and there is often a similar delay between nest construction and egg-laying. It is worth looking for holes in any area where they are seen perching regularly, giving a harsh 'chik' call or a double note 'chit-tchup'. Several pairs often nest in the same area.

**Starling** *Sturnus vulgaris*. Pl. **199**, 378

*Breeds* April–June (occasionally in autumn and winter), in built-up areas and countryside with woods.

(In British Isles, Europe and Scandinavia. Mostly absent Spain but has bred.)

*Nest* in a hole of any kind, height varying from ground-level up to about 25 ft, in trees, walls, thatch, crevices in cliffs, etc. Nest built by male, lined by female, material consists chiefly of straw and feathers. Nest-boxes are used and holes of boxes intended for smaller species are sometimes enlarged.

*Eggs* 4–6, pale blue. Incubated by both sexes for nearly 2 weeks.

*Nestlings* greyish down, bright yellow inside mouth, pale yellow flanges. Fed by both parents. Leave nest after about 3 weeks.

*Adults* sexes look similar at first sight, but female has broader feathers which give a more spotted appearance; blackish-bronze with purplish-green sheen; plump body with triangular flight silhouette of broad but pointed wings and short tail.

*Fledglings* brownish with white throat.

*Hints* a babble of gurgling and whistling notes can be heard throughout the year, but some individuals are remarkably good mimics and it is worth listening to the idiosyncrasies of individual Starlings in your neighbourhood. Males chase females in flight and sidle along branches. The wings are often drooped and fluttered during song. When carrying nesting material they are usually conspicuous as they tend to gather long wisps of straw, but if you miss the building stage, nests are often revealed by the incessant calls of the nestlings begging for food. When making a census of Starlings in stone wall country this can be a useful method for locating nests. A single egg is sometimes found on the ground.

**Golden Oriole** *Oriolus oriolus*. Pl. **201, 382**

*Breeds* late May–June, in orchards, gardens, parkland and plantations. (Throughout Europe and in S. Sweden. Has bred England.)

*Nest* often near water, attached to the underside of a forked branch; built chiefly by female out of bark fibres and grass, decorated with paper and flower-heads.

*Eggs* 3–5, white with dark markings. Incubated by both sexes for about 2 weeks.

*Nestlings* buffish-white down, bright pink inside mouth, whitish flanges. Fed by both parents. Leave nest after about 2 weeks.

*Adults* roughly Blackbird-size; male is golden-yellow with black wings; female is more drab with streaked under-parts, dark wings and tail. Frequently remain in dense foliage, moving from tree to tree and flying up to the top canopy before settling.

*Fledglings* resemble adult female.

*Hints* flute-like 'weela weeo' notes and a harsh scream, reminiscent of Jay, are usually the first indications of their presence. Courtship includes fast chase amongst trees, the male almost touching the female's tail. The nest is most likely to be under a horizontal bough where two branches meet at an angle. Nests have been reported from various counties in England and several breeding records come from Kent.

**Siberian Jay** *Perisoreus infaustus*. Pl. **203, 379**

*Breeds* March–April, in birch and conifer forests in N. Scandinavia.

*Nest* usually in fork of tree close to the trunk, height from 6 ft to 20 ft above ground; made of twigs, lichen, grass and feathers, lined with lichen and a little hair; probably built by both sexes.

*Eggs* 3–5, white or greenish-white with dark markings. Incubated by both sexes for about 2½ weeks.

*Nestlings* no description available. Fed by both parents. Leave nest after about 2½ weeks.

*Adults* smaller than Jay, *Garrulus glandarius*; sexes similar, rounded dark brown head, grey-brown back, orange-red patches on rump, wings and outer tail-feathers, pinkish-buff breast.

*Fledglings* paler and less colourful than adult.

*Hints* birch forests in Finland are the most likely breeding areas, but in Sweden they are usually in conifers. They are less wary than the British Jay and family parties of adults and fledglings are described as comparatively tame and confiding. Various calls include a soft 'pjip pjip' which ends in a falsetto warble. This species has not been recorded in Britain.

**Jay** *Garrulus glandarius*. Pl. **202, 380**

*Breeds* late April–June, chiefly in woodlands in the country but also in town parks and gardens with plenty of trees and bushes. (In British Isles, Europe and most of Scandinavia. Local in Scotland.)

*Nest* usually in a tree or bush, height varying from about 4 ft to 30 ft or more, but also recorded in heather. Sticks and twigs are interlaced to form a deep bowl, lined with rootlets and sometimes horsehair, built by both sexes. Unusual site recorded in hollow tree.

*Eggs* usually 5–6, greenish-brown with delicate markings. Incubated by both sexes for about 2 weeks.

*Nestlings* no down, pale pink inside mouth, pinkish flanges. Fed by both parents. Leave nest after about 3 weeks.

*Adults* slightly smaller than Wood

Pigeon; sexes similar, pinkish-brown body, black and white flecks on crown, bright blue and black patch on wing, black tail contrasts with white rump as it flies away from you. Continental Jay is paler and has greyer upper-parts. Hops along the ground as though bouncing on springs, flight rather laboured.

*Fledglings* similar to adult but reddish rather than pinkish hue.

*Hints* raucous screams betray its presence, but the Jay tends to keep in cover and the nest-site is hard to find. They do not flush easily when incubating, but having located a pair, it is worth looking at any tree with shoots sprouting from the side of the bole as the nest is often built in these. There are ceremonial gatherings, similar to Magpie, in which the birds are seen chasing each other, flapping their wings slowly.

## Magpie *Pica pica*. Pl. **207**, *381* ‹

*Breeds* late March–June, in open country with tall hedges, at edges of woods and moors, often near farms and towns. (In British Isles, Europe and Scandinavia. Local in Scotland.)

*Nest* usually in tall tree or thorn bush but height very variable, and sites include on bank (Isle of Man) and under eaves (Scandinavia); domed nest of sticks, lined with mud and fine roots, built by both sexes.

*Eggs* usually 5–8, greenish with dark markings. Incubated by female for about $2\frac{1}{2}$ weeks.

*Nestlings* no down, pink inside mouth with white spurs, pink flanges. Fed by both parents. Leave nest after about $3\frac{1}{2}$ weeks.

*Adults* roughly Jackdaw-size not counting the long tail; sexes similar with boldly contrasting black and white plumage. Tail streams out horizontally in flight, elevated at an angle when on the ground. Hops and sidles when excited.

*Fledglings* shorter tail than adult.

*Hints* in January and February numbers of Magpies take part in social displays, bouncing about and flying short distances in an excitable manner as though showing off the white areas of their plumage; crown feathers are erected and their tails are fanned and lifted up and down. Nesting sites are hard to locate unless you happen to see where the birds go with nesting material, but providing the leaves are not out, the actual nest is usually pretty obvious. One observer likened a nest to a clothes basket lodged in a straggly hedge.

## Nutcracker *Nucifraga caryocatactes*.

*Breeds* mid March–May, in conifer forests and mixed woodland in mountains of Central and SE. Europe and in S. Scandinavia.

*Nest* usually on bare branch of pine tree, at height varying from 10 ft to 30 ft; crow-like structure of twigs, lichen, moss and mud, felted with grass and lichen, built by both sexes.

*Eggs* 3–5, bluish-green with delicate markings. Incubated by both sexes for about $2\frac{1}{2}$ weeks.

*Nestlings* fed by both parents. Leave nest after 3–4 weeks.

*Adults* slightly smaller than Jay; sexes similar, dark brown plumage with white speckled appearance and

**Nutcracker**

long pointed bill; in flight, underside of short tail has white border when seen from below. Actions are reminiscent of Jay. Often seen diving, wings closed, from prominent perch in tall tree.

*Fledglings* paler than adult.

*Hints* the temperature may be as low as −17°C. when eggs are laid and the change-over at the nest does not take place until the partner is on the rim of the nest which is often powdered with snow. They are said to be comparatively silent and secretive during the breeding season. In Britain they are occasionally seen on passage, mainly in the south-east in the autumn.

## Chough *Pyrrhocorax pyrrhocorax*

*Breeds* April–June, chiefly on coastal cliffs but also inland. (Local in Cornwall, Wales, Isle of Man, Inner Hebrides and Ireland, NW. and SE. France; also in the Alps, S. Italy and Spain.)

*Nest* in a crevice or hole of cliff or quarry, sometimes in roof of sea-cave; bulky pile of sticks, heather, gorse, etc., built by female but male sometimes brings material lining; may include wool, hair, grass and feathers. *Eggs* 3–6, whitish to yellowish-green with dark markings. Incubated by female for about 2½ weeks.

*Nestlings* scanty greyish-brown

**Chough**

down, pink inside mouth with white spurs, yellow flanges. Fed by both parents. Leave nest after about 5 weeks.

*Adults* Jackdaw-like except for curved red bill and red legs; sexes similar, characteristic 'fingered' effect in flight, feathers separated and curving up at the wing-tips. Frequently seen soaring, wheeling and diving in flight. Alpine form has much paler wings, yellow bill and red legs.

*Fledglings* bill and legs more orange than red.

*Hints* aerobatic displays in which they roll over on their backs and dive with half-closed wings are accompanied by high-pitched 'tchuff' and 'kyaa' calls. Courtship feeding takes place, the female begging for food, quivering her wings. Choughs are now rare in Britain, but one place where one can be reasonably certain of seeing them is on Bardsey Island, 5 miles by sea from Aberdaron on the Caernarvonshire coast. Nesting sites are carefully protected by the Warden of the Bird and Field Observatory but visitors usually catch sight of these beautiful birds with their remarkably slender red bills. There are usually a number of pairs nesting in the same area.

## Jackdaw *Corvus monedula*. Pl. **205**, *383*

*Breeds* mid April–June, chiefly on agricultural land with mature trees, but also on coastal cliffs, in quarries and built-up areas. (In British Isles, Europe and S. Scandinavia.)

*Nest* usually in a hole or crevice, often in chimneys but also in trees and occasionally in burrows; varying amount of material carried by both sexes which may include large quantity of sticks as well as a pad of wool, hair and rubbish. Open-type nests in trees usually have lots of sticks and are sometimes built on foundation of old nest of other species.

*Eggs* 4–6, light blue with dark markings. Incubated by female for about 2½ weeks.

*Nestlings* scanty pale grey down, purplish-pink inside mouth, pale yellow flanges. Fed by both parents. Leave nest after 4–5 weeks.

*Adults* distinctly smaller and neater than Rook; sexes similar with pale grey nape and pale grey eye. Scandinavian form has paler collar and under-parts. Often seen in flocks, individuals chasing each other, twisting and turning in flight.

*Fledglings* browner than adult.

*Hints* they often roost in nesting sites throughout the year and noisy gatherings, inspecting holes, can be seen as early as January. High-pitched 'chacking' calls attract attention to these sites. Courtship display includes bowing and raising feathers on crown. When collecting nesting material they sometimes perch on farm animals and pull out tufts of hair, gathering a beakful before flying back to the nest-hole.

**Rook** *Corvus frugilegus.* Pl. **208**, *384*

*Breeds* March–April, chiefly on agricultural land with some trees, but also in built-up areas which are not too crowded with buildings. (In British Isles and most of Europe. Local in Spain and S. Scandinavia. Has bred Switzerland. Absent Italy.)

*Nest* many nests close together, usually in the top canopy of tall trees, occasionally in bushes and on buildings and exceptionally on ground. Same site often occupied for many years, old nest being repaired each year. Both sexes build a pile of sticks and mud, lining the nest with grass and leaves.

*Eggs* 4–6, similar to Carrion Crow,

but not as blue. Incubated by female for nearly 3 weeks.

*Nestlings* scanty dark grey down, pink inside mouth, yellowish-pink flanges. Fed by both parents. Leave nest after about 4 weeks.

*Adults* slightly smaller than Carrion Crow; sexes similar with distinctive greyish-white bare patch at base of bill. Loose feathers on thighs look like 'plus-fours'. Faster wing-beats than Carrion Crow and more often seen in flocks than singly or in pairs.

*Fledglings* similar to young Carrion Crow, but more slenderly built; bare face patch not acquired until first summer.

*Hints* a rookery can scarcely be missed as the birds wheel about and give repeated cawing notes when building their nests. They usually break twigs off trees rather than collect them from the ground and they frequently steal material from each other. Courtship display includes bowing and see-sawing up and down, sometimes with their bills engaged. Females are often seen begging for food, arching their wings and quivering their tails. During incubation a male sometimes lands on a female and is then mobbed by other males, causing a commotion.

**Carrion Crow** *Corvus corone.* Pl. **204**, *385*

*Breeds* late March–June, almost anywhere with trees, including built-up areas, also on coastal cliffs. (In Britain and most of Europe. Absent Ireland, Scandinavia and most of Denmark and Italy.)

*Nest* usually in fork of tree from 30 ft to 40 ft, occasionally on buildings and poles with crossbars; also on rock ledges of cliffs and recorded on the ground; bulky structure, built by both sexes, of twigs and mud, lined with wool, grass, etc.

*Eggs* 4–5, greenish-blue with dark markings. Incubated by female for nearly 3 weeks.

*Nestlings* scanty grey down, pink inside mouth, yellowish-pink flanges. Fed by both parents. Leave nest after 4–5 weeks.

*Adults* may be confused with Rook, which is roughly the same size and with Raven which is much larger; sexes similar, black feathers run right down to base of bill, no bare patch as in Rook; wings look more rounded than Raven's in flight and the tail is squared off rather than graduated. Often seen in pairs.

*Fledglings* browner than adult, similar to young Rook but plumage looks less glossy.

*Hints* nest is usually in a tree standing on its own in open part of woodland or at the edge, either against a stout fork or far out on a bough below the twig canopy. There is usually only one nest in the area, but sometimes a pair build in a rookery. Twigs in occupied nests look fresher than those in nests of previous year. Display includes bowing and standing in a hunchbacked attitude, either on the ground or in a tree. The most usual call-note is a hoarse 'kraa', repeated several times.

**Hooded Crow** *Corvus corone cornix.* Pl. **206**

*Breeds* late March–June in hilly country and along coastal cliffs of Scottish Highlands, Ireland and Isle of Man; also in Denmark, Germany, Italy and Scandinavia.

*Nest* similar to Carrion Crow, built by both sexes, in tree, bush or cliff crevice; locally amongst heather and has nested on telegraph-pole.

*Eggs* 4–6, similar to Carrion Crow.

*Nestlings* similar to Carrion Crow.

*Adults* similar to Carrion Crow except for distinctive grey back and under-parts which contrast with rest of black plumage.

*Fledglings* browner than adults.

*Hints* see Carrion Crow.

**Raven** *Corvus corax.* Pl. **209,** *386*

*Breeds* February–May, on coastal cliffs and rocky outcrops of moor and mountain, locally in tall trees. (In British Isles and most of Scandinavia. European range includes Italy, Spain and Switzerland; local in N. Europe.)

*Nest* on ledge or in crevice; both sexes build solid structure of sticks and twigs, stuck together with earth, grass, moss and leaves, lined with hair or wool, sometimes with grass. Nests in Sweden have no earth and are lined with lichens.

*Eggs* 3–6, greenish-blue with dark markings. Incubated by female for nearly 3 weeks.

*Nestlings* greyish-brown down, purplish-pink inside mouth, yellowish flanges. Fed by both parents. Leave nest after 5–6 weeks.

*Adults* larger than Carrion Crow; sexes similar, glossy black plumage, heavy bill. In flight, wings look longer than Carrion Crow's, neck more extended and tail more wedge-shaped.

*Fledglings* browner, less glossy than adult.

*Hints* you rarely see a Raven at close quarters, and deep croaking notes are usually the first indication that one is high in the sky. Spectacular acrobatic displays include steep dives, wings half-closed, turning right over and gliding upside-down. The nest should be somewhere along the cliff and the Raven may shoot out below you; try to mark this place and get a better view of it from a different angle. If you see any whitening at the site, there are probably nestlings as the twigs become fouled with droppings.

# SELECT BIBLIOGRAPHY

Austin, O. L. (1961) *Birds of the World*. London, Paul Hamlyn.

Bannerman, D. A., and Lodge, G. E. (1953–63) *The Birds of the British Isles*. Edinburgh, Oliver & Boyd.

Campbell, B. (1953) *Finding Nests*. London, Collins.

Campbell, B. (1964) *The Oxford Book of Birds*. Oxford University Press.

Davidson, A. (1954) *A Bird Watcher in Scandinavia*. London, Chapman & Hall.

Dresser, H. E. (1902) *A Manual of Palearctic Birds*. London: published by the author.

Fisher, J., and Peterson, R. T. (1964) *The World of Birds*. London, Macdonald.

Fitter, R. S., and Richardson, R. A. (1954) *Pocket Guide to Nests and Eggs*. London, Collins.

Géroudet, P. (trans. Barclay-Smith, P.) (1965) *Water Birds with Webbed Feet*. London, Blandford.

Gosnell, H. T. (1947) *The Science of Birdnesting*. Liverpool: printed for C. H. Gowland by W. Jones & Co. Ltd.

Hvass, H. (trans. Vevers, G.) (1963) *Birds of the World*. London, Methuen.

Peterson, R. T., Mountfort, G., and Hollom, P. A. D. (1954, revised 1966) *A Field Guide to the Birds of Britain and Europe*. London, Collins.

Thomson, A. L. (ed.) (1964) *A New Dictionary of Birds*. London, Nelson.

Vaurie, C. (1959–65) *The Birds of the Palearctic Fauna*. London, Witherby.

Voous, K. H. (1960) *Atlas of European Birds*. London, Nelson.

Welty, J. C. (1964) *The Life of Birds*. London, Constable.

Williamson, K. (1965) *Fair Isle and its Birds*. Edinburgh, Oliver & Boyd.

Witherby, H. F., Jourdain, F. C. R., Ticehurst, N. F., and Tucker, B. W. (1938, revised 1943) *The Handbook of British Birds*. London, Witherby.

## SOCIETIES AND JOURNALS

The British Ornithologists' Union, c/o Bird Room, British Museum (Natural History), London S.W.7. Quarterly publication *The Ibis*.

The British Trust for Ornithology, Beech Grove, Tring, Herts. Quarterly publication *Bird Study* (and others).

The Royal Society for the Protection of Birds, The Lodge, Sandy, Beds. Bi-monthly publication *Birds* (and others).

The Wildfowl Trust, Slimbridge, Glos. Annual Report (and others).

*British Birds*, a monthly journal published by H. F. and G. Witherby Ltd., 61 Watling Street, London, E.C.4.

# INDEX OF ENGLISH NAMES

# INDEX OF LATIN NAMES

273

274